CALIFORNIA DREAMING

SUZANNE M. WILSON

California Dreaming

REFORMING MATHEMATICS EDUCATION

YALE UNIVERSITY PRESS   NEW HAVEN AND LONDON

Designed by Rebecca Gibb. Set in Scala type by Integrated Publishing Solutions. Printed in the
United States of America by Vail-Ballou Press, Binghamton, New York.

Library of Congress Cataloging-in-Publication Data

Wilson, Suzanne M., 1955–
California Dreaming : reforming mathematics education / Suzanne M.
Wilson.
    p.   cm.
Includes bibliographical references and index.
ISBN 0-300-09432-9 (cloth : alk. paper)
1. Mathematics—Study and teaching—California—History—20th century.
2. Educational change—California—History—20th century. I. Title.
QA13.5.C2 W57 2003
510'.71'097940904—dc21
2002007031

10 9 8 7 6 5 4 3 2 1

To my mother, and her mother
Three little fishies and a mommy fishy, too

Preface

Cannery Row in Monterey in California is a poem, a stink, a grating noise, a quality of light, a tone, a habit, a nostalgia, a dream. Cannery Row is the gathered and scattered, tin and iron and rust and splintered wood, chipped pavement and weedy lots and junk heaps, sardine canneries or corrugated iron, honky tonks, restaurants and whore houses, and little crowded groceries, and laboratories and flophouses.
—John Steinbeck

The California of today differs drastically from Steinbeck's 1940s version: the sardine canneries have been converted to sushi bars, the honky-tonks into cafés. But some things remain the same: it is still a poem and a stink, a honky-tonk and laboratory. It is simultaneously beautiful and troubled, replete with rust and hope. The homeless are everywhere; a woman in San Francisco's Washington Square offered to sell me a child one day. When I lived there, I filled my pockets with ones every morning, for the insistent requests from the poor are ubiquitous. Forty-five minutes away, health conscious Silicon Valley executives run along the Bay's shoreline during their lunch breaks, rollerblade and windsurf on weekends. Four hours south, Mexicans legally and not enter the country, grabbing at the American dream, California-style. The waves of immigrants have slowly turned the sum of the minorities into California's majority.

Actually, there is no *one* California, for the state stretches 840 miles along the Pacific Ocean. Thirty million people live in one of many "Californias": the hills of Palo Alto are a round, sensuous, brilliant green in spring. The farms of the Central Valley stretch for miles, and cattle stand idly on mountains of dark earth. It takes an hour to inch one mile during rush hour traffic in L.A., while snow banks seven feet high can tower over you in Tahoe in May.

California's schools reflect this variety and, like Steinbeck's Cannery Row, are ripe with color, clash, clang. While some school boards move toward conservatism and tradition, others experiment with innovation. Some schools teem with children of farmers and ranchers. Others serve the children of scholars, researchers, and entrepreneurs. Across the state, somewhere between 20 and 30 percent of children entering school speak a language other than English. Large urban school districts regularly tally up to 80 languages in their student counts. In 2000, over 250,000 teachers taught nearly 6 million students.

As a teacher, it would be hard enough just to keep up with the changing demographics of one's students. But California teachers are asked to do much more. Reforms and mandates abound. The state has always considered itself ahead of the curve, especially where education is concerned. Between 1958 and 1975, fifty-two education reform initiatives were penned in Sacramento. In the mid-1980s, educators were directed to "teach for understanding," to use small groups and hands-on "manipulatives," and to move away from traditional "fill in the bubble" tests. In the 1990s, the messages changed: balance your curriculum, teach phonemic awareness, don't rely too heavily on calculators. Class size reduction, a reading initiative, and accountability indices were instituted in the late 1990s in attempts to raise the academic achievement levels of California's children. As the new century turned, teachers faced even more mandates: summer school and intensive instruction for failing students, pupil retention and promotion policies, comprehensive teacher education institutes, beginning teacher support, an academic performance index, high school exit exams, and the like.

Although I had lived in California while in graduate school, I did not become a student of California's educational system until 1986 when, as a faculty member at Michigan State University, I collaborated on a study of the state's efforts to reform mathematics education through state-level curricular policies. A group of educators created a new policy for mathematics education—the *Mathematics Framework for California Schools, K–12*—that advocated a less traditional, more progressive approach to mathematics education, moving away from rote memorization and the dominance of worksheets toward "teaching for understanding." Curious about efforts to reform mathematics teaching in elementary schools, my colleagues and I talked to teachers and policy makers, Department of Education staff and local district officials. We visited schools, observed professional development meetings, attended policy development conferences. We conducted a statewide survey, talked to people on the phone, corresponded with others through email and letters, and, in later years of the study, surfed the web. We wanted to know if, how, and when reforms took hold.

When I started this work, I had the idealism of many young faculty (others might experience this idealism alternatively as arrogance or naïveté), rooted in a faith that there were clear answers to big educational problems. As a former teacher, I "knew" that traditional mathematics teaching was simply too narrow, too mechanical, too prescriptive. I had met far too many people—children and adults alike—who feared mathematics and regularly displayed a negative knee-jerk reaction to anything resembling math. I was sure, as a fresh university faculty member, that mathematics education needed to be opened up, and children had to learn the wonders and power of mathematics through "authentic" problems, investigations, and the like.

Yet as I spoke and interacted with more people—many of whom I now count as lifelong colleagues and friends—I was alternatively surprised and sobered. The California mathematics reform story in its early years was relatively simple: A group of committed mathematics educators, inclined toward progressive educational views, aligned a set of state level curriculum policies to improve mathematics education for all California youth. While their efforts were sometimes momentarily thwarted by unexpected disruptions, things moved along in a promising sort of way: there was a curricular policy that supported their vision, new assessments were developed that would line up with that curriculum, and new textbooks and instructional materials began appearing nationwide. It was the heyday of systemic reform.

But around 1992, as our study drew to a close, the reform became the target of much criticism. I continued to follow the story (albeit from afar) as new reformers entered the scene, driven by their concerns about what they believed to be the impact of the earlier reform. This group advocated a more traditional (but not entirely) approach to mathematics teaching. My trusty informants told me their "horror stories" of encounters with the opposition. I read the headlines in California and national papers, many of them bitingly sarcastic about progressive mathematics educators. Yet, when I met or listened to the members of this new wave of reform, most of them seemed to be reasonable people who were trying to do the right thing. My original story—about a group of California educators and how they experienced, shaped, reacted to, and influenced educational policy aimed at the reform of mathematics education—became the story of what happened to their efforts when a new coalition of reformers—including parents, many more mathematicians, teachers, and the public—became involved.

E. D. Hirsch, in *The Schools We Deserve and Why We Don't Have Them*, argues that "both educational traditionalists and progressives have tended to be far too dogmatic, polemical, and theory-ridden to be reliable beacons for public policy. The pragmatist tries to avoid simplifications and facile oppositions."[1] Hirsch, though often misread by progressives and traditionalists alike, has aimed to position himself as just such a pragmatist. Taking seriously his charge to avoid facile generalizations, I tell this story neither to demonize one or another of the involved groups, nor to oversimplify the events.

Thus, the story that follows has no heroines or heroes, and I have worked hard to present each participant in a respectful light. I encountered few crazy people in the journey that led to this book, and I intentionally resist reducing the story to simple dichotomies of right and wrong, conservative or liberal, Republican or Democrat. Students of history know that there is never one cause of a war: World War I did not start because of the murder of Archduke Ferdinand, nor did the Civil War begin because of Lincoln's position on slavery. The causes of individual and social behavior are neither singular nor completely determinable.

In *Culture of Complaint: A Passionate Look at the Ailing Heart of America*, Robert Hughes argues that, while polarization might be addictive, it does not help us make progress in solving our social problems.[2] Here, then, I aim to avoid the polarization that characterizes much of the activity around mathematics education and its reform, both within California and nationally. Instead, I aim for a middle ground from which the reader might view and understand how and why Americans disagree about the education of our children.

I aim for a middle ground in another way as well. My story is told to multiple audiences: my sisters and brothers, concerned parents all; my doctor who helped me with a bone infection while I helped him understand the issues at play at his local school board meetings when interests groups argued about the adoption of a new mathematics curriculum; my friend Judy Grant, a longtime elementary school teacher who wants "good" curriculum; other parents, teachers, and professionals; and, of course, the educational establishment of which I am a member, albeit an ambivalent one right now. Readers interested in the more "academic" details—related scholarship, for example—will find such information in the notes. Other readers, I hope, will be able to understand the narrative—about why some people want to change schools, while others worry about those reforms and propose new reforms of their own, and the complex currents that run underneath and shape the debates about education in the United States—without these distractions.

Acknowledgments

As I put the finishing touches on this book, I realized that I have been immersed in this project for nearly my entire career at Michigan State University. This makes sense, for MSU is one of the only institutions I know where faculty, students, and teachers try to maintain a bifocal vision: with one eye firmly on the practical realities of schools and the other steadfastly on theory. David Cohen, Deborah Ball, Penelope Peterson, and I (as well as several others) wrote the original proposal July 4th weekend in 1988, after which we went to see fireworks in a quiet, pastoral Michigan town (little did we know the fireworks would become such a leitmotif of our study). One result of having been at this so long is that my debt to others who have helped along the way is extensive.

The work was conducted with the generous material and intellectual support of many institutions: The National Academy of Education and the Spencer Foundation supported the work early in my development as a scholar, and encouraged me to read and re-invent myself intellectually with a postdoctoral fellowship that supported my work for two years. Several large research grants made this work possible. From Congress to the Classroom (1996–2000) was a project sponsored through the Center for Policy Research in Education and funded by the Annie E. Casey Foundation and the Pew Charitable Trusts, as well as the Office of Educational Improvement (OERI). The Educational Policy and Practice Study was supported by a number of grants: State Instructional Policy, Teaching Practice, and

Learning in Elementary Schools (Center for Policy Research in Education, a proposal to the OERI), Teachers' Learning from Reform: The Case of Mathematics Instruction in California (a proposal to the National Science Foundation), Supporting State Efforts to Reform Teaching (a proposal to the Carnegie Corporation of New York and to the Pew Charitable Trusts), and The Effects of State Level Reform of Elementary School Mathematics Curriculum on Classroom Practice (a proposal to the Office of Educational Research and Improvement). Deans Judy Lanier and Carole Ames encouraged me to combine my love for teaching and research into a career in the College of Education at Michigan State. The Carnegie Foundation for the Advancement of Teaching, under the wise eye of President Lee Shulman, provided a balance of professional and personal sustenance as I tried to impose a narrative order on a chaotic, sprawling story.

Although most of the people I interviewed and visited for many years must remain unnamed in this story, I am grateful to them all. As a teacher, I was taught to think that policymakers were some cold and distant lot who knew little about teaching and its complexity. Meeting the policy folks of California forced me to re-evaluate my assumptions; I feel fortunate to have been given so much of their time, in days and months packed with meetings and crises. They opened their offices and busy lives to us, and unafraid, allowed us to watch as they learned and grew, made mistakes, changed their minds. They were models of thoughtful educators and learners. As were the teachers and teacher-leaders whom we visited year after year and who reminded us constantly that classrooms are chaotic places in which adults try to teach and care for children who come from vastly different backgrounds. Sometimes in the debates that ensued, things were so aswirl that it was hard to tell which end was up. The teachers and leaders were, always, a moral compass. As were the mathematicians whose insights I solicited near the end.

Thanks also to the over two dozen graduate students and faculty who worked on these projects over time: Peggy Aiken, Carol Barnes, Jennifer Borman, Dan Chazan, Tammi Chun, Angela Shojgreen Downer, Beth Herbel-Eisenmann, Pamela Geist, Margaret Goertz, S. G. Grant, Ruth Heaton, Nancy Jennings, Nancy Knapp, Jo Lesser, Sarah Theule Lubienski, Diane Massell, Steve Mattson, Sue Poppink, Richard Prawat, Jeremy Price, Ralph Putnam, Janine Remillard, James Spillane, Susan Wallace, and Karl Wheatley.

I've been fortunate to have generous readers along the way who understood what I was trying to accomplish and pushed me to go one step further, including Charles Abelman, Joan Akers, Max Angus, Susan Arnold, Dick Askey, G. Gretchen Bank, Hyman Bass, Jennifer Borman, Nicholas Branca, Marilyn Burns, Walter Denham, Joan Ferrini-Mundy, Geno Flores, Jodie Galosy, Amy Gerstein, Heather Hill, David Labaree, Magdalene Lampert, Judith Mumme, Connie Orr, Lynn W. Paine, Susan Florio Ruane, Michael Sedlak, Andrew Shouse, Elizabeth Stage, Lynn Steen, Gary Sykes, Chris Wheeler, Sam Wineburg, Lynn Winters, Hung-Hsi Wu. I have been working on this argument for years, and many other unmentioned readers have also helped with equal doses of keen insight and encouraging support. They have all been marvelously challenging readers. My editors at Yale University Press, first Susan Arellano and then Nancy Moore Brochin, made this a much better book. Nancy's gift for knowing what I wanted to say, and helping me say it, came at just the right time.

I was spoiled early on in my career, for Lee Shulman taught me that it was possible to have fun while working hard, and to learn best in the company of people who challenge you constantly. I have been blessed with a line of such collaborators, more than any one person deserves, including David Cohen (with his piercing capacity to find the one thing underdeveloped), Deborah Loewenberg Ball (a talented boundary crosser), and Robert Floden (a calming and pragmatic friend). They talked to me for 14 years about mathematics reform, in and out of California, and any insight I might demonstrate here is no doubt due to their good counsel and keen minds. Mistakes, of course, remain my own.

My parents—Don and Jules Wilson—and a clutch of six siblings supported me throughout this work, although no one could keep track of when I was in Michigan or California. The extended Cusick clan has always offered encouragement, over warm family meals at Thanksgiving and Christmas. My best reader and friend remains Philip Cusick, who read every word three times, saw things I never would have seen, and gave me a farm and a dozen gardens. Hunched over tomatoes and spinach, thinning cosmos and sunflowers, I told myself the story. In front of the fire in the field each night, he listened carefully and encouraged me to write it down.

1   Curriculum Wars

> The California Dream is the most outlying, the most distant, the
> most exotic, the most fashionable piece of the American Dream.
> California doesn't live in the shadow of the American Dream. It
> magnifies and improves it.
> —Richard White

We often think of U.S. schools as safe havens, sheltered environments designed to nurture and teach our children. Their walls deceive us into thinking that these places are escapes from the larger American society where
children can acquire knowledge and self-esteem, learn the rules of social
behavior and intellectual work, and find a place and identity of their own.
But schools, as part of the larger social fabric, cannot escape our large, complex, and contested social landscape. This point was poignantly brought
home to us repeatedly at the turn of the twenty-first century, as children
killed children and adults in Columbine and Paducah.

Of course, not all stories of our society's larger issues play themselves out
so violently in schools. Other incidents involve the swapping of barbs rather
than bullets. Nonetheless, these debates are heated, the participants' passions palpable. David Cohen and Barbara Neufeld once wrote, "The schools
are a great theater in which we play out these conflicts in the culture; they
are the stage for the long war over the character of [American] adult life."[1]
The language of "war" is not unique to Cohen and Neufeld, for it appears
repeatedly in accounts, both popular and academic, about modern society
and its schools: the culture wars, the reading wars, the math wars. Historian Lawrence Levine argues that "academic history in the United States,
then, has not been a long happy voyage in a stable vessel characterized by
blissful consensus about which subjects should form the indisputable cur-

riculum; it has been marked by a prolonged and often acrimonious struggle and debate."[2]

"War" may seem a bit extreme to an outsider—the elevation of minor ideological skirmishes to an undeserved status. But to insiders in such debates, there is drama, intrigue, fierce disappointment. Rumors abound: I heard several times about one incident in which two prominent mathematics educators came to fisticuffs. There were rumors of bribes to a prominent school board member's relative. Antagonists feel dismissed, disrespected, misunderstood, wronged. Fanning these inflamed discussions has been the media, which has often played a significant role in heightening that intensity, including local San Francisco columnists, national radio personalities like Rush Limbaugh, and prominent political and intellectual leaders like Lynne V. Cheney, former chairman of the National Endowment for the Humanities.[3]

My tale unfolds during the 1980s and 1990s, a period marked by sustained attempts by many organizations to establish educational standards— for teachers, students, curriculum, assessment, teacher education, beginning teachers. With those standards came fierce debates about their content. The language of war was omnipresent. Nicholas Lemann recounted "the reading wars," describing California's curriculum battle between phonics and whole language. Catherine Cornbleth and Dexter Waugh, as well as Gary Nash, Charlotte Crabtree, and Ross Dunn, documented the "culture wars" over history standards.[4]

During that same time, the language of war crept into many debates about mathematics education. The "math wars" made the *Wall Street Journal:* "New Math will *take its casualties,* especially among the poor, adding to the already mounting costs of the decline in national educational standards."[5] In an address to mathematicians in January 1998, Secretary of Education Richard Riley asked for a "cease-fire": "This is a very disturbing trend, and it is very wrong for anyone addressing education to be attacking another in ways that are neither constructive nor productive. . . . It is perfectly appropriate to disagree on teaching methodologies and curriculum content. But what we need is a civil and constructive discourse. I am hopeful that we can have a 'cease-fire' in this war—and instead harness the energies employed on these battles for a crusade for excellence in mathematics for every American student."[6]

Despite such calls for "civil and constructive discourse," little progress appears to have been made. In the winter of 2000, over 200 research mathematicians signed a critique of the U.S. Department of Education's endorsement of "exemplary" curricula in a *Washington Post* advertisement published in the form of an open letter to Riley. "It is not likely that the mainstream views of practicing mathematicians and scientists were shared by those who designed the criteria for selection of 'exemplary' . . . curricula," the authors wrote. They close the letter: "We further urge you to include well-respected mathematicians in any future evaluation of mathematics curricula conducted by the U.S. Department of Education."[7]

A flurry of letters in support of and opposition to the request followed, some sent to Riley, others emailed across the country among like-minded colleagues. For the signatories, the group responsible for assessing exemplary curricula needed to include higher-education-based research mathematicians. Why the comment about "well-respected mathematicians"? Some educators asked why research mathematicians—who know little of K–12 schools—should make curriculum decisions. Some signatories, who had originally signed out of allegiance to colleagues, later asked that their names be removed. Hyman Bass, then president-elect of the American Mathematical Society, observed: "What disturbs me about the open letter is that it throws an important discussion into an arena where nothing can be accomplished, and a lot of damage will be done."[8] Of course, some critics would argue that the damage to children's mathematical education that poor curricula and teaching can do is as important as damage to public discourse.

When new national standards for mathematics education were issued by the National Council of Teachers of Mathematics (NCTM), a similar flurry of activity erupted, with critics and supporters alike feeling attacked and misunderstood. Critics of the earlier NCTM *1989 Standards* proclaimed victory, asserting that the later *Principles and Standards for School Mathematics* (PSSM) (NCTM, 2000) retreated to the basics. Others saw the new standards not as a regression to previous educational orthodoxies and not as a victory for educational conservatives over educational progressives, but rather as a next iteration toward articulating a "balanced" curriculum.[9] Still others worried that the document contained mathematical errors. The roots of these disagreements are deep, and in the course of this book I explore some of the history of mathematics education reform, for those debates—past and present—are the backdrop for my story, which focuses on mathematics education reforms in California in the 1980s and 1990s.

California has always considered itself a political and intellectual leader among the states and, in the case of mathematics education reform, this has certainly been true. Starting in the 1980s, a modest effort to improve mathematics education in California slowly gained momentum and snowballed into something much larger (at least from a policy perspective). In the 1990s, interest and concern grew to and eventually reached near-noxious levels, with rumors flying and the emergence of websites. Several of these sites included hypercritical remarks that some participants felt stepped over the line of "civil" discourse, and all sites anticipated later national developments like the open letter to Riley.

There are those who will say that because this story takes place in California, it is not generalizable, California being an atypical state full of surfers and starlets, seashores and mountains. But mine is an American story of education, and the issues faced by Californians are those facing us all, in the past, present, and not-too-distant future. Mark Baldassare argues that Americans should pay attention to California for several reasons. Major events in California—like economic trends—are felt nationwide. Further, with fifty-two delegates in the U.S. Congress, and fifty-four Electoral College votes, the state is a major player on the national political scene. And California—with all its diversity—is a political, social, economic, and financial microcosm of the United States, as well as a social trendsetter for the country.[10] To paraphrase Richard White, the California Dream magnifies and illuminates the American Dream, whether that dream involves living in a diverse society or the content and character of mathematics education.[11] Indeed, the story of mathematics education in California was the trendsetter for the ensuing national debates.

But why would so many people become so ardent about mathematics? Well, for one, a common experience in mathematics class might be one of the only things that all Americans share, for there is a national script for teaching and learning math: class begins with a homework review, followed by a teacher demonstration of the algorithm-of-the-day. Ample time is usually left for practicing problems, and an audible collective sigh of relief is heard whenever word problems are not assigned. Although not everyone recalls these experiences fondly, they are part of a national school heritage, and undermining that heritage involves raising questions of who we are as a people. Some observers would argue that mathematics is a gatekeeper in our society and that those who know math have access to opportunities, status, and power that others do not have. Those social critics go on to argue that any effort to disturb the status quo of power and wealth—including empowering more Americans with more mathematical knowledge—is suspect.

For these reasons and others, traditional mathematics teaching has been a target of criticism and a cause for concern in America since at least the late nineteenth century. Thus, my story is in some ways the contemporary chorus of an age-old song, as educators in the 1980s and 1990s tried—again—to solve the problems of teaching mathematics. How they attempted to address the problem, and the ensuing public, political, and professional conversations that erupted, is the object of this inquiry. As a way of setting the stage for this story of California's attempts to reform mathematics education, I begin with a brief sojourn through the history of school mathematics and its critics.

2 "Ours Is Not to Reason Why. Just Invert and Multiply": School Mathematics and Its Critics

The Heart of Algebra
You are like-ly to find as you go through the course
And con-quer your task math-e-mat-ic,
That ev-'ry so of-ten you will be o-bliged
To com-pute the roots of a quad-rat-ic.
Suppose that it's giv-en in typ-i-cal form,
With a, b, and c in their pla-ces;
The fol-low-ing for-mu-la gives the re-sult
In all of the pos-si-ble ca-ses.
Write b with its sign changed and af-ter it put
The am-big-u-ous sign plus or mi-nus,
Then the square root of b squared less 4 times a c,
(There are no real roots when that's mi-nus.)
Then be-neath all you've writ-ten just draw a long line,
And un-der it write down 2a;
E-quate the whole quan-ti-ty to the un-known
And check in the u-su-al way.
—Norman Anning

Mathematics in School

School mathematics is not typically considered the stuff of high drama. It's predictable, familiar. You walk into class, take out your homework. The teacher goes over the answers, stopping to solve problems raised by students. In elementary school, students work out problems on the board; in secondary school, teachers talk through the answers, scribbling proofs when necessary. After the homework review, papers are passed forward to be checked by the teacher.

After reviewing homework, everyone opens their books to the next two-page spread about a new topic (in high school the topic might take up as many as five pages). The teacher introduces the topic, demonstrates a few applications, works some sample problems. Topics are often presented as processes for how to solve relevant problems, and these processes, in turn, get presented as "steps": Invert and multiply when dividing by a fraction. Multiply the height of a rectangle by its length to find the area, check "in the u-su-al way." One memorizes the quadratic formula, the Pythagorean theorem, the multiplication tables.

Classroom talk is highly predictable, tightly controlled. Students raise their hands, the teacher acknowledges the student and the question, directing the answer back to the questioning student. Students typically don't talk among themselves (unless they are misbehaving). The teacher and text are the center of attention. Midway through class, the teacher assigns homework problems (often the ones that don't have answers in the back of the book). Students sit quietly, scratching out answers. The teacher sits, also quietly, reviewing homework papers, helping students with specific problems. Mathematics in these classrooms is presented as a collection of facts and procedures; learning mathematics is a process of practice and memorization. *The Teaching Gap,* by James Stigler and James Hiebert, is the most recent description of this thoroughly American script of teaching that emphasizes terms and procedures—the skill dimensions of math—and that often excludes exploration of the mathematical ideas related to those skills.[1]

Throughout my schooling, I loved classroom math for these very features. Because it was predictable, straightforward, and clear, I knew what to expect and how to get the right answers. A shy student, I found math class a relief: I could do really well by mastering procedures. I did not have to talk to get As; I could just read the book and do my homework. I was occasionally discouraged by the stick-to-the-rule-edness of some teachers. I eventually solved this problem in fourth grade, by always giving teachers the answer I knew they wanted, and then sometimes scribbling questions about the validity of alternative solutions in the margins of my worksheets. Similarly, knowing that my teachers wanted me to "show my work," I always wrote out the steps they expected to see, even if I had taken another, more efficient route to the answer.

In graduate school, less shy, I still found the problem sets of mathematics and statistics classes extremely satisfying. Unlike writing essays, there was one right answer and I knew when I'd gotten it. Doing homework, I felt like I was exercising my brain in a different way, a step-aerobics class for my mind.

Others have very different memories: threatening piles of problems, undoable, impossible to understand. For every one of us who enjoyed math, there are probably three or four who hated it. I am reminded most often at the grocery store, when the clerk at the checkout looks panicked as he tries to calculate a 10 percent discount on my wine. These students were not just neutral on the subject, but frightened, sometimes hostile. As it turns out, many are females and minorities. For example, the National Center for Education Statistics reports that women, non-Asian minorities, and the poor take fewer high-level mathematics courses. National assessments show Asian-Pacific Islanders and whites outscoring all other groups, including Native American, African American, and Hispanic students.[2] Math can seem really hard because answers can be wrong. These students learn that mathematics is sometimes hard (which it is). But students also learn that it is scary and impossible to do if you don't have a "number head" (it is not). Thinking of mathematics ability as a capacity that is inborn, not learned, these students quickly shut down when they decide they can't learn mathematics. For some, as my friend Philip recalls, mathematics was used as punishment: if he misbehaved during school, the nuns would keep him after everyone else went home and make him do long division problems. Browsing bookstore shelves, one can find a virtual treasure trove of math self-help books written for the casualties: *Fear of Math: How to Get Over It and Get on with Your Life; Defeating Math Anxiety; Math: Facing an American Phobia; Math Without Fear: A Guide for Preventing Math Anxiety in Children; Math Panic; Overcoming Math Anxiety.* There are other books, usually in the children's sections of bookstores, that present mathematics in engaging and wondrous ways, like Mitsumasa Anno's math books. But many adults are so sure they have dyscalculia that they never even try to read them.

Even those of us who loved math can become discouraged. In college, my teachers dismissed my questions and observations, suggesting that they were "trivial" and "obvious." Little did I know that these words have technical meaning for mathematicians. An outsider to this discourse community, I found the labeling of my comments as "obvious" embarrassing, rude. The flames of my discouragement were fanned by the fact that my teachers were international students who had trouble communicating across language and culture. Not only was the discourse one of dismissing students' questions, but the English was hard to understand. Mathematics is difficult, especially as one creeps up the curricular ladder. It became impossible (even though I had loved it) in the face of bad teaching. I left the mathematics department for history, where the introductory courses were taught by professors who seemed willing to entertain questions, to help me learn.

My experience was not unique. The Committee on the Mathematical Sciences in the Year 2000 noted that women drop mathematics as a major at alarming rates, that most of the teaching is done through lectures, and that the use of teaching assistants (often nonresident foreigners) is deeply ingrained as a structural feature in mathematics departments that helps units work within their budgets.[3] While neither lectures nor international teaching assistants are inherently problematic, serious questions have been raised about the commitment to a quality education in undergraduate mathematics courses.

The Critics

> By the old system the learner was presented with a rule, which told him
> how to perform certain operations on figures, and when they were done
> he would have the proper result. But no reason was given for a single
> step. . . . And when [the learner] had got through and obtained the re-
> sult, he understood neither what it was nor the use of it. Neither did he
> know that it was the proper result, but was obliged to rely wholly on
> the book, or more frequently on the teacher. As he began in the dark, so
> he continued; and the results of his calculation seemed to be obtained
> by some magical operation rather than by the inductions of reason.[4]

Made in 1830, this commentary is perhaps most troubling in how much it still applies to contemporary mathematics education in many K–12 classrooms. Indeed, the themes of our contemporary dissatisfactions with mathematics education resonate throughout the history of education. In 1893, the National Education Association's panel—the Committee of Ten—recommended the removal of some arithmetic from the curriculum, especially arithmetic that seemed designed "solely . . . to exhaust and perplex the pupil."[5] It also advocated the teaching of algebraic symbols and simple equations, the introduction of geometry training as early as possible, and the systematic teaching of geometry by age 10.

In 1902, Eliakim Hastings Moore addressed the American Mathematical Society, arguing that mathematicians must attend to issues of K–12 schooling, that pure mathematics could be woven together with applied mathematics, that the secondary school curriculum ought to be reconceptualized in ways that integrated the theoretical and practical aspects of algebra, geometry, and physics, and that students ought to have a chance to experience the research aspects of mathematics as well as master algorithmic knowledge: "This program of reform calls for the development of a thoroughgoing laboratory system of instruction in mathematics and physics, a principal purpose being as far as possible to develop on the part of every student the true spirit of research, and an appreciation, practical as well as theoretic, of the fundamental methods of science."[6]

In 1911, Alfred North Whitehead described the school mathematics problem:

> The reason for this failure of [mathematics] to live up to its reputation is that its fundamental ideas are not explained to the student disentangled from the technical procedure which has been invented to facilitate their exact presentation in particular instances. Accordingly, the unfortunate learner finds himself struggling to acquire a knowledge of a mass of details which are not illuminated by any general conception. Without a doubt, technical facility is a first requisite for valuable mental activity: we shall fail to appreciate the rhythm of Milton, or the passion of Shelley, so long as we find it necessary to spell the words and are not quite certain of the forms of the individual letters. In this sense, there is no royal road to learning. But it is equally an error to confine attention to technical processes, excluding consideration of general ideas. Here lies the road to pedantry.[7]

In 1923, the National Committee on Mathematical Requirements issued a report suggesting that three major goals of mathematics instruction should include: (1) helping students gain insight into and control over their environments; (2) helping students appreciate the progress of civilization; and (3) developing habits of mind that would improve students' powers of understanding and analysis. In part, this report was fueled by concerns about the poor quality of mathematics teaching: "The excessive emphasis now commonly placed on manipulation is one of the many obstacles to intelligent progress. On the side of algebra, the ability to understand its language and to use it intelligently, the ability to analyze a problem, to formulate it mathematically, and to interpret the result must be dominant aims. Drill in algebraic manipulation should be limited to those processes. . . . It must be conceived throughout as a means to an end, not as an end in itself."[8]

In 1934, the preeminence of drill, coupled with a lack of emphasis on meaning, remained a target for criticism. Frank McMurry commented: "What arithmetic suffers from is a lack of rich content. The process should never be the main material; for children can manipulate them for a month at a time without gaining a single idea interesting enough to talk about. The heart of arithmetic must be found in its problems; these should deal with vital subjects, and their answers should tell a story. When these facets are recognized, attempts to enrich the curriculum in arithmetic will become fashionable, and that subject will then become progressive. It is progressive in a few schools today, where tool phases are subordinated to purposes."[9]

In 1941, military officials complained loudly about the lack of mathematical skills and knowledge of young men entering the armed forces. The Commission on Post-War Plans recommended in 1944 that the teaching of arithmetic be improved, that drill in mathematics teaching be used more wisely, and that teachers receive better mathematical educations. Thus, even as these reformers argued for a return to basics, they cautioned educators not to return to Whitehead's instructional pedantry.

New Math

The concerns continued. In the late 1950s, mathematicians—in both the United States and Europe—expressed concerns about the number of students who were not advancing on to high school and college mathematics. In 1950, UNESCO and the International Bureau of Education sponsored a conference and survey of forty-six countries that examined primary school mathematics. Six years later, sixty-two countries were surveyed, and UNESCO examined education at the secondary level. *The Saturday Review* ran an article entitled, "Why Johnny Can't Add" in 1956. The launching of *Sputnik* and the subsequent public debate about the state of American and European technology and innovation spurred the effort on, and in 1959, American and European mathematicians met at a conference in Royamount, France, to discuss the future of mathematics education.[10]

Their concerns were many. Some mathematicians argued that the content of mathematics had to change, for the field was expanding rapidly and the "new" mathematics was more important for technological advancement. One famous address was entitled, "Euclid Must Go." The mathematicians were also quite concerned about the low numbers of students going on to take college mathematics courses. Mathematicians and mathematics teachers alike were concerned with teaching. Their criticisms echoed those of earlier generations: too much emphasis on rote memorization and drill, too little emphasis on authentic problem solving and thinking.

Similar conversations were being held among scientists who were equally concerned with the state of education. Jerome Bruner's essay *The Process of Education* was the result of a conference at Woods Hole, Massachusetts, in September 1959, where preeminent scholars from across the disciplines gathered to discuss the state of public education in the United States.[11] In part, these efforts were a response to a tidal wave of criticism aimed at progressive educators: "What was needed was rigor and discipline, the critics said. To them, student interest had little relevance when national security was at issue. The organized subjects could provide the needed discipline, both in their content and in their methods. Students would act like scientists in the laboratory and would master the complex relationships of concepts and principles."[12]

It was a heady time for many scholars, who were confident they could change U.S. education and were willing to devote considerable intellectual energies to doing so.[13]

In mathematics, the criticisms led to a wave of innovative curricula collectively known as New Math ("New Maths" across the Atlantic). But just as there is no *one* California, there was no one New Math. Projects sprang up nationwide, each directed by a group of passionate mathematicians and educators who were sure they could help schools. Prior to the launch of *Sputnik,* Max Beberman had met with faculty from colleges of education, liberal arts and sciences, and engineering. They collectively formed the University of Illinois Committee on School Mathematics. Beberman (who was not a mathematician) described the project as an attempt "to bring to the mind of the adolescent some of the ideas and modes of thinking which are basic in the work of the contemporary mathematician."[14] At Yale University, Ed Begle directed the School Mathematics Study Group (SMSG) (one of the best-known versions of New Math in the United States), sponsored by the American Mathematical Society (AMS), the Mathematical Association of America (MAA), and the National Council of Teachers of Mathematics. That project moved to Stanford in 1961. Merrill Shanks, Charles

Brumfeld, and Robert Eicholz established the Ball State Teachers College Experimental Program. Patrick Suppes had a project at Stanford University; David Page, a project at the University of Illinois. Similar projects sprang up in Europe, including the Nuffield Projects in Great Britain, Alef in West Germany, Wiskobas in the Netherlands, and Analogue in France.

Despite their variety, New Math programs shared a set of common commitments. Ed Begle, at SMSG, announced five guiding assumptions:

1. No one can predict the mathematical skills that will be most important in the future.
2. No one can predict the career path of an individual student.
3. Teaching that "emphasizes understanding *without neglecting the basic skills* is best for all students," regardless of their future careers.[15]
4. Understanding mathematics is an essential feature of intelligent citizenship.
5. Any normal human being can appreciate some of the beauty and power of mathematics.[16]

Two streams of change ran throughout all versions of New Math. There were changes in content, as some vocal mathematicians argued that contemporary advances in mathematics required similar advances in school mathematics. New Math curricula introduced new ideas into high school, including set theory, vector spaces, and matrices. In large part, this aspect of the reform was motivated by the sense that school math was out of step with mathematics in the university, and "it needed a complete overhaul. The language of sets, relations, and functions would provide not only a more coherent discourse in the mathematics classroom but also a more meaningful structure for learning. Students would be drawn to mathematics by seeing how it fit together and, in particular, how the great ideas of modern mathematics brought order into the chaotic curriculum of literal numbers that were not really numbers at all, a notation for angles that did not distinguish between an angle and its measure, and operations on numbers that included turning them over, bringing them down, canceling them, and moving their decimal points around."[17]

At the same time, there was a shift in teaching strategies (based on changing assumptions about how students best learn). More emphasis was placed on inquiry and the research side of mathematics, less on memorization and lecture. While some scholars have argued that the change in content was the reform's most noteworthy aspect (it was, after all, called "teaching the *new math*" not "the *new teaching* of mathematics"), there has always been confusion about what people mean when they speak of New Math: Do they mean the new content that appeared, or are they referring to "discovery"-oriented teaching?[18]

For about ten years, the programs flourished: new curricula were written and purchased, teachers attended workshops, funding from private and federal agencies (including the National Science Foundation) rolled in. But enthusiasm eventually waned and no curricula found long-term success. In the end, New Math left a disastrous legacy, for there were rumbles of concern all along, some of which were summarily dismissed by New Math advocates. Some concerns were voiced by mathematicians. They worried about the content, arguing that the mathematics was much too formal and inappropriate for K–12 schools. They worried about the mathematical knowledge of some New Math leaders: not everyone was a mathematician, and some of the mathematicians who participated were not highly respected. Finally, they worried about the portrait of traditional mathematics teaching. As one mathematician told me, "I was never told to memorize proofs, I often had to do problems that were nonroutine. One of the best teachers I ever had lectured for about five minutes in any given class. The rest of the time, we solved problems."

Some concern came from parents and the public. My younger sister Katie came home with homework that baffled my father the physicist: set theory, vector space, matrix algebra. She always seemed to be drawing Venn diagrams. I'd never seen such things. Ten-year-old Katie was frustrated; our parents, knowing only "old" math, could not help her. While her older sisters were doing traditional algebra and trigonometry, she was talking about sets. Other parents had similar experiences, as Tom Lehrer's famous song portrays. At one performance, Lehrer explained:

> Some of you who have small children may have perhaps been put in the embarrassing position of being unable to do your child's arithmetic homework because of the current revolution in mathematics teaching known as the New Math. So as a public service here tonight I thought I would offer a brief lesson in the New Math. Tonight we're going to cover subtraction.
>
> This is the first room I've worked for a while that didn't have a blackboard so we will have to make due with more primitive visual aids, as they say in the ed biz. Consider the following subtraction problem,

which I will put up here: 342−173. Now remember how we used to do that. 3 from 2 is 9 carry the 1 and if you're under 35 or went to a private school you say 7 from 3 is 6, but if you're over 35 and went to a public school you say 8 from 4 is 6, carry the 1 so we have 169, but in the new approach, as you know, the important thing is to understand what you're doing rather than to get the right answer.[19]

Although several thoughtful analyses were written after that fact, large-scale, thorough, longitudinal empirical studies of how teaching changed (if at all) during the implementation of New Math and the relationship between those changes and what students learned (or did not learn) were never done. A report by the National Advisory Committee on Mathematical Education (NACOME) in 1975 argued that New Math had never even existed (given its weak implementation in schools). The lack of data leaves New Math vulnerable to claims based on personal experience, rumor, and myth.[20]

And such myths and personal experiences abound. Understanding why New Math failed, and the major concerns and criticisms aimed at it, is important background for the California mathematics education reforms of the 1980s and 1990s. I had always heard New Math failed because the reforms did not include the necessary sustained professional development. This turns out to be not so true, for many New Math projects involved a serious commitment to the ongoing education of teachers. Jeremy Kilpatrick, however, notes that most of these efforts were, "college mathematics courses retooled for teachers. They provided new content but did not address the pedagogical problems of teaching that new content. Moreover, almost no attempt was made to deal with the conditions under which teachers work that inhibit their ability to change their teaching. . . . Curriculum reform efforts in the new math era tended to concentrate on out-of-class product rather than in-class process."[21]

Other scholars suggest that the New Math reform failed because it was led by mathematicians, not mathematics teachers, who were therefore unenlightened about the realities of schooling. Many teachers complained that they could not teach the new curricula because they did not know the mathematics. Having never learned about vectors, they found one- or two-week summer workshops insufficient preparation for teaching an entirely new curriculum. Nonetheless, the reforms were characterized by close partnerships between scholars and teachers. John Goodlad argues that it was the disintegration of these partnerships that eventually led to the reform's demise.[22]

Historians of reform would argue other causes: Larry Cuban, David Tyack, and others would likely argue that New Math—like all reforms that intrude into classrooms—didn't stick because it tried to tamper with teaching. And such reforms have never stuck.[23] Some mathematicians would argue that the mathematics was inappropriate or that the wrong mathematicians were involved.

Whatever the reasons (and they were probably multiple), the backlash was considerable. Tom Lehrer, the satirist and university mathematics teacher, wrote a song ridiculing it. Morris Kline published the scathing *Why Johnny Can't Add: The Failure of the New Maths,* and mathematicians and journalists wrote about the demise of "hard subjects," the "obsession with new methods," and the "math nightmares."[24] Hans Freudenthal, a German mathematician living in the Netherlands, wrote:

> At the end of the 1950s, the *Sputnik* shock stirred up distrust of the factual teaching of mathematics and science, which spread from the United States over most of the world. In Europe, the OEEC (later OECD) caught and passed on the message that mathematics taught at school were lagging a century behind the present state of mathematics. Conferences at Royamount (1959) and Dubrovnik (1960) set the pace: trying to catch up for a lag of a century, proposing mountains of new subject matter and translating it into new textbooks called new maths— a fierce competition between experts and charlatans with, in general, distressing results. Those who could not catch up were the poor people in the classroom who were expected to learn new maths, which most often was rather new nonsense—unteachable, unbearable, unmathematical.[25]

Eventually, the pendulum swung back toward the recognizable "basics." The tide turned, based on "common sense," public opinion, and personal experience. The "new nonsense" and "unmathematical" aspects of New Math lodged in our collective memory—a powerful legacy that played a significant role in the late twentieth-century California reforms—for the specter of New Math was invoked regularly by critics of the reforms we were following. These critics recalled New Math as yet another attempt by "fuzzy-headed" "educationists" to drum content out of the curriculum and replace it with process. That some vocal enthusiasts were mathematicians was forgotten. It was also forgotten that more students did end up entering university mathematics departments.

At no time has anyone pointed to research on New Math and its impact as a basis for these critiques. As Donald Freeman and his colleagues noted, "In the folklore of education, popular claims often survive with little or no empirical verification."[26] And so it is with the contemporary folk wisdom that surrounds New Math, for the vehemence of the negative reactions to the reform presumed that the reform had actually taken root in American classrooms (and done considerable damage). There exists no evidence to support this view or, for the most part, the opposite perspective (assuming that New Math did improve student learning). Indeed, research on mathematics teaching and learning suggests that mathematics teaching remains much like was in the mid-1800s—which might be the most troubling thing about New Math. Changes need to be made, and the resources, public will, and enthusiasm were present to do just that. That missed opportunity still haunts some mathematicians and mathematics educators.

So What Is Everyone Complaining About?

Clearly, this is only a cursory overview of the history of debates in mathematics education. Nonetheless, it is hard to decide which is more striking: the consistent, insistent calls for reform decade upon decade or the failure of any reform to actually stick. Furthermore, it is hard to determine just *what* the reformers of a given time period were most worried about.

In part, this is because *who* the reformers are (educational progressives or educational conservatives) shifts over time. Throughout the book, I aim to *not* use inaccurate and inflammatory labels to signify various groups. This will lead to some confusion, no doubt, for, as Maureen Dowd has pointed out, the use of stereotypes and caricatures is easy because they erase complexity.[27] For the purposes of my analysis, I borrow a distinction drawn by E. D. Hirsch and Diane Ravitch, who both make the important point that one's position on education can differ from one's political position.[28] I use "educational conservatives" as the name for advocates of an education that includes more traditional than progressive features and tilts toward traditional. This includes more teacher-dominated instruction, more focus on skills and mastery of the basics, and more emphasis on a "canon" of legitimate knowledge. I use "educational progressives" to refer to advocates of an educational posture that is based on a Dewey-ian conception of the child and curriculum as two sides of the same coin. This position places emphasis on process as well as content, on the child as well as the curriculum. It also places emphasis on students and teachers working together, and on teaching "higher-order thinking" or "conceptual understanding" as well as the basics.

Unfortunately, the politics of education has led professionals and the public alike to see conservatives and progressives as warring factions. The disagreements have been fanned by three significant forces. One is the media, which often searches for a "story" by looking for or creating drama. This is a popular trend in our society, as Deborah Tannen has pointed out, in which a tidal pull creates heated debates rather than dialogue, the former being much more compelling and interesting than the latter. "No fight, no story."[29] The other source of conflict originates in misguided attempts at implementation, in which a good idea is misrepresented through poorly conceptualized and planned execution. Poor implementation happens in both traditional and progressive education. Much traditional education is delivered weakly, leading to caricatures of teachers who speak in monotones and hand out worksheets. So, too, has progressive education been delivered poorly, leading to other caricatures of teachers teaching only process, and no content. A third force are the extremists who align themselves with a view (traditional vs. progressive education) but then present an idiosyncratic and extreme case of that view. These extremists are dangerous elements, for the "opposing camp" will often point to one and say, "See, that is what all progressives are like" or, "That is how crazy all mathematicians are." The media, poor implementation, and extremists complicate the conversation about mathematics education, introducing extremes that serve to heighten both passions and righteousness.

This is an unfortunate consequence, for in their "pure" forms—when not politicized or caricatured—these positions have much in common, which we shall also see in this story. Both educational conservatives and progressives want children to master basics. That is, they want them to know the fundamentals of mathematics. Both groups agree with Whitehead that it is "equally an error to confine attention to technical processes, excluding consideration of general ideas."[30] But these similarities are obscured when extreme cases are mistakenly used as representative ones, when comments are wrenched from their contexts, when passions flare, and when rumors run wild.

Points of Difference

That said, there are significant points of difference among the various actors who participate in discussions of mathematics education. Discussion of the range of issues over which reformers and their critics disagree can provide important background information for understanding this story, so a brief accounting of several major points of difference is in order here.

Concerns about Mathematics

Sometimes the rhetoric is that of a changing *mathematics*. The argument goes something like this: as knowledge "explodes" and mathematics changes—in its contents, foci, relevance, and applications—the content of school mathematics must change. The New Math of the 1960s, in fact, was a reform of content—the introduction of set theory, for example—as much as it was a reform of method (how students learned). This concern focuses on the issue of what to do with K–12 mathematics as the discipline of mathematics expands and develops. The focus here is on the question: What substantive mathematical ideas should children learn?

Yet, there is another way to think about the *content*. Every subject matter consists of both "stuff"—ideas, concepts, products—and "ways of knowing"—methods of problem setting, problem solving, and publicly testing and proving knowledge claims. These skills of inquiry, interpretation, critical analysis, and proof are fundamental to scholarship. From this perspective, "content" is about both substantive mathematical ideas and mathematical ways of knowing.

Some critics argue that the problem with traditional school mathematics is that it robs the lay public of an understanding of what mathematics really is. If children learn early on that mathematics is intriguing, these critics argue, they will be motivated to learn more. They point out that, as a form of intellectual work, mathematics is much messier than the boring memorization rites of school. Georg Polya makes a distinction between the "two faces" of mathematics: the rigorous science of Euclid, which is systematic and deductive, versus "mathematics in the making," which is experimental and inductive.[31] In *A Mathematician's Apology*, G. H. Hardy calls mathematics "the most curious [subject] of all—there is none in which truth plays such odd pranks." Mathematics is not so much about rules as it is about patterns. "A mathematician," Hardy claimed, "like a painter or a poet, is a maker of patterns."[32] Mathematics involves creativity. Reuben Hersh calls this the "social-cultural-historic" or "humanist" view of mathematics, the view that highlights mathematics as "a *human* activity, a *social* phenomenon, part of human culture, historically evolved, and intelligible only in a social context."[33] School mathematics is seldom experienced as human or social.

Although this is not the image of school mathematics one most often encounters, it is the view of mathematics one finds in books written for the general public. Consider the books about Paul Erdos—*The Man Who Loved Only Numbers* and *My Brain Is Open*—or those about or by other mathematicians, including *A Beautiful Mind* (which has been adapted as a major motion picture), *Prisoner's Dilemma: John Von Neumann, Game Theory and the Puzzle of the Bomb, Fermat's Enigma* (a very successful BBC series), or *Archimedes' Revenge*. The public seems hungry for such stories of mathematics, even while a math phobia courses through American society.

Critics argue that in schools, mathematics is stripped of these aspects of its character, reduced to the algorithmic and technical. School mathematics is not the math of Gauss, who claimed that mathematics was "non notationes, sed notiones" (not notations, but notions). Students do not learn, for example, that mathematics is work that entails conjectures and concepts; they seldom discover why definitions, examples, theorems, proofs are so important, or interesting. They know little of the loosely coupled community of scholars who investigate problems and offer their proofs for public critique. Instead, they learn that mathematics is about rules and rigid steps.

Concerns about Children
Critics also raise questions about the children. Some have worried about the changing American student population, raising questions about how teachers will reach *all* students, especially students with backgrounds and experiences quite unlike their own. Often, these critics argue that the traditional teaching of mathematics has left many poor and minority children behind. Yes, these critics concede, traditional mathematics teaching seems to work for some children. But many other children—those who live in urban, impoverished settings, non-Asian minorities, and sometimes females—don't survive the traditional curriculum, dropping out at high rates. The "damn the torpedoes, full speed ahead" approach to mathematics teaching—a tradition that faults the student for not working hard enough, not reading the book or doing her homework, or not being motivated enough—these critics argue, must go. This, of course, is a complex argument. On the one hand, one wants to hold high standards for all children. On the other hand,

it is not clear whose responsibility it is to respond when children do not meet those high standards. In college, if you fail one class, you simply cannot enroll in the next one. In elementary school, if you don't learn your third grade math, no matter what teachers do, then the school is left to decide whether you ought to go on to fourth grade without third grade mathematical competency. Does one hold a student back indefinitely? If students without enough knowledge are promoted, won't the problem simply snowball?

Other critics raise a different sort of question about students, urging us to rethink our assumptions about what children are capable of learning. School tradition and practices often treat young children as if they are incapable of complex thought. Basics first, some argue. Only after the basics are mastered can students begin to explore interesting mathematical problems. Some mathematicians and reformers have questioned this assumption (which, like many assumptions about mathematics education, is based on "common sense," "intuition," or personal experience), arguing that even young children are capable of understanding significant mathematical concepts. Very little research has informed this debate, although careful documentation of what children can and do learn in mathematics classrooms has begun to accumulate. International comparisons, in particular, offer us much insight into how much children can learn when the curriculum is focused and rigorous.

Concerns about Teaching and Learning

Since 1830, critics have also worried about pedagogy: how mathematics is actually taught. Critics note the predominance of drill and worksheets, of teachers talking and students memorizing. Some believe that teachers ought to be free to select their own methods of instruction based on their personal preferences and "teaching style."

Others disagree, arguing that instructional methods are not simply a matter of psychological preference. Rather, these educators assume that *how* we teach affects *what* we teach. As Joseph Schwab wrote: "We also have the task of learning to live with a far more complex problem—that of realizing that we will no longer be free to choose teaching methods, textbook organization, and classroom structuring on the basis of psychological and social considerations alone. Rather, we will need to face the fact that methods are rarely if ever neutral. On the contrary, the means we use color and modify the ends we actually achieve through them. *How* we teach will determine *what* our students learn."[34]

Echoing Marshall McLuhan's "the medium is the message," this concern about the impact of pedagogy on the content actually learned was a theme that ran throughout the reforms of the 1960s.[35] Scientists and mathematicians were concerned that students needed to learn both the substance *and* the methods of a discipline.

Often these worries are intertwined with assumptions about how students learn. Learning theories abound: one learns through practice, through random reward, through punishment, discovery, manipulating physical objects, experience, and the like. Individual differences also factor in: some students prefer lectures (short or long), others prefer to do hands-on activities.

Throughout the history of debates concerning mathematics education, parents and educators have raised concerns about how students best learn. Some argue that one learns mathematics through practice. Just as athletes go through drills in order to teach their bodies to respond automatically, so students can train their minds through drill and practice. Others argue that mathematics must be "discovered," that students will not remember something they have learned or be able to apply their knowledge to novel settings without "experiencing" the mathematics: modeling problems, representing fractions, manipulating objects. Some educators argue for "hands-on" activities in school partly from the belief that these kinds of activities will engage and motivate students who find the manipulation of abstract formulas offputting.

Assumptions about how students learn are often linked to theories of how one should teach. If students learn through absorption, then teachers telling them what to know makes sense. If students learn through "mucking around," then opportunities to investigate and to use hands-on materials seem more appropriate. Hence, some critics argue for traditional teaching, with teachers and texts as the dominant authorities, while others argue for more progressive visions that allow more room for students, their questions, their investigations.

The passions fueling these debates often have a reductive effect, turning a complicated discussion into a battle fought by two caricature discussants: traditionalists (who, after all, care only about a strict diet of regimented drill and practice) versus progressives (who obviously care only about process and have no interest in rigorous content). Neither caricature is fair, and both impede curricular reform. Lost is the fact that almost everyone thinks basics are important, as well as a conceptual grasp of mathematics. Lost is the complexity, the web of tangled assumptions (and disagreements) about how children learn, which children have the right to access what kind of knowledge, and how instructional models and strategies influence what is learned.

Part of the complexity is due to the interaction of these issues of learning theory, pedagogy, politics, and epistemology. This can be seen in the language of "basics," for basics to some are the 3 Rs—reading, 'riting, 'rithmetic—with no frills. To others, the "basics" include procedural and conceptual knowledge (both the algorithm for long division and the mathematics of long division); to still others, they also include learning about how mathematicians think, reason, and discuss ideas.

Finally, also largely ignored is the fact that these arguments about curriculum and teaching are only partially about mathematics. Running beneath the surface of these disagreements are concerns for equity, differences in assumptions concerning the goals of public education in the United States, and the kind of schooling parents want for their children. These would all become important issues in the California story.

Mathematics Education Reform, 1980s Style

A debate is staged for him, contrasting the merits of traditional education with those of the new discipline of Socratic argument. The spokesman for the Old Education is a tough old soldier. He favors a highly disciplined patriotic regime, with lots of memorization and not much room for questioning. He loves to recall a time that may never have existed—a time when young people obeyed their parents and wanted nothing more than to die for their country. . . . Study with me, he booms, and you will look like a real man—broad chest, small tongue, firm buttocks, small genitals (a plus in those days, symbolic of manly control).

His opponent is an arguer, a seductive man of words—Socrates seen through the distorting lens of Aristophanes' conservatism. He promises the youth that he will learn to think critically about the social origins of apparently timeless moral norms, the distinction between convention and nature. He will learn to construct arguments on his own, heedless of authority. He won't do much marching. Study with me, he concludes, and you will look like a philosopher: you will have a big tongue, a sunken, narrow chest, soft buttocks, and big genitals (a minus in those days, symbolic of lack of self-restraint). . . . The message? The New Education will subvert manly self-control, turn young people into sex-obsessed rebels, and destroy the city. The son soon goes home and produces a relativist argument that he should beat his father. The same angry father then takes a torch and burns down the Think-Academy.[36]

Martha Nussbaum argues that Socrates is still on trial. In the case of K–12 mathematics education, this appears to be true. In the 1980s and 1990s, we witnessed yet another resurgence of the war between the Old Education and the New, accompanied by the familiar calls for reform. Reports of the sorry state of mathematics education in the United States began to appear, as did urgent calls for a new kind of work force. Research demonstrated that textbooks and "skill-and-drill" continued to dominate contemporary classrooms, that mathematics was seen as fixed, abstract, and immutable, that students spent the majority of their time memorizing rules they did not understand.[37]

The most recent example of these calls was the response to the Third International Mathematics and Science Study (TIMSS). Multiple press releases about the poor performance of American children in international comparisons appeared throughout 1997 and 1998. Perhaps most compelling were the results of the Stigler and Hiebert analyses of videotapes, which document clearly the predictable and anti-intellectual script enacted in mathematics classrooms in the United States, and this country's poor showing when compared to the rich discussions of mathematical content in other countries. Articles appeared in the *Wall Street Journal* and the *New York Times;* international comparisons were discussed in *The Economist.*[38]

But well before TIMSS, missives claiming the downfall of the American education system began to accumulate in the 1980s. The 1983 report *A Nation at Risk* is often pointed to as a watershed publication. One group that responded to these calls was the National Council of Teachers of Mathematics (NCTM), a professional organization of teachers, teacher educators, curriculum specialists, and educational researchers that was founded in 1920. Membership runs to 110,000 members, with 260 affiliated groups in the United States and Canada. The organization publishes four journals, sponsors national, state, and local annual meetings, issues a news bulletin, and updates teachers on the web about developments in the practices and politics of mathematics education.

In the mid-1980s, the NCTM began convening a series of panels and committees to draft a set of standards for K–12 mathematics curricula. In 1989, the organization published its *Curriculum and Evaluation Standards for School Mathematics,* which made recommendations for improving and updating the mathematics curriculum and the evaluation of students' achievement. Two years later, *Professional Standards for Teaching Mathematics* offered recommendations for how mathematics teachers could create and manage "successful learning environments" for every student, as well as continue their own professional development. And, in 1995, *Assessment Standards for School Mathematics* described a comprehensive program delineating criteria for judging high-quality assessment.[39]

Consensus documents written by committees, these policies were meant to inspire and support change, including a radical overhaul of K–12 school mathematics, teacher preparation, and assessment. They advocated the development of an "inquiry" approach to school mathematics, with a heavy emphasis on problem setting and solving, on conjecture and hypothesis, on exploration and inquiry. Students were to debate and discuss ideas, become mathematical authorities alongside teachers and textbooks, and justify their answers with reasons and logic instead of mastery of rote processes. In fact, the first four curriculum standards (strategically placed at the beginning of the list) don't sound like the mathematics that I found so comforting as a child: mathematics as problem solving, mathematics as communication, mathematics as reasoning, and mathematical connections. Instead, they sound like the mathematics that progressive reformers advocated for the better part of the twentieth century: a mathematics of practicality and poetry, of relevance and relationships. The NCTM *1989 Standards* were not simply lists of things children should learn.[40] The documents were annotated with vignettes from classrooms—narrative "snapshots" intended to bring to life a different image of teaching.

In the wake of these publications, there was much ado. Organizations dealing with other subject matter drafted their own standards: English and language arts, history and social science, science, geography, and the arts among them. Diane Ravitch reported that the federal government used the NCTM *1989 Standards* as a model for how to shepherd other academic subjects through the process of developing standards.[41] And an avalanche of reforms continued to accumulate throughout the late 1980s and 1990s: Goals 2000, New Standards, systemic reform initiatives. At the heart of each was the rhetoric of *A Nation at Risk,* which called for higher, more rigorous standards for all American children.

In addition to a trend that appeared to endorse the NCTM *1989 Standards,* there was considerable concern. Critics of the standards—including teachers, mathematicians, and parents—spoke of the lack of attention paid to the basics and argued that the standards should list what students are to know, not how teachers are to teach. After all, teachers are professionals who might choose to teach in any number of ways. Instructional methods were not the concern of curricular mandates; rather, agreement about what students should learn was critical. Other critics pointed out the mathematical errors in the document, concerned that a *national professional* organization of educators did not get the mathematics right. Over time, as the world wide web began to flourish, websites proliferated with links to papers, presentations, newspaper editorials, and the like concerning the weaknesses of the NCTM *1989 Standards.*

But I'm getting ahead of myself. In 1985, four years before the NCTM published its standards, the California Department of Education (CDE) had issued a "curricular framework" for mathematics. Although not as elaborate as the NCTM *1989 Standards,* the *1985 Framework* nevertheless drew on the same research, commitments, and ideas: "teaching for understanding" and "mathematical power" were to replace memorizing rules and "drill-and-kill." Teachers were to guide more, talk less. Students were to explore more, cooperate on problems they themselves had identified. Foreshadowing the NCTM *1989 Standards,* California's *1985 Framework* painted a different portrait of school mathematics. This picture would more closely resemble the work of mathematicians: children would learn abstractions, but in the service of dealing with more vaguely defined, messier problems. They would have a voice, and they would be invited to offer explanations of their reasoning in public settings where their ideas would be debated, tested, and critiqued. Correct answers would take a back seat to reasoning, and community activity would displace solitary work on photocopied worksheets. Riding the curl of the reform wave, California's curriculum framework seemed a document ahead of its time. It was this document that first drew us to California.[42]

As I have mentioned, the debate to come would be contentious, and when we began the study we were sympathetic to the progressive reforms (we were not "believers," but we were sympathetic). Although I aim for a balanced account here, no story comes value-free, and who I am as a teacher will necessarily affect the story I tell. Therefore, I have used two rhetorical mechanisms to allow readers to make their own decisions about the actors and the debate I describe in the chapters that follow. First, I have woven aspects of my autobiography throughout (providing some hints as to why I might interpret a particular situation in the way I did).[43] Second, I have offered many—sometimes long—quotations and descriptions. A. S. Byatt writes, "My quotations are like the slides in an art history lecture—they are the Thing Itself, which is in danger of being crushed under the weight of commentary."[44] Mine is a story in which many actors leapt quickly to gross generalizations and facile commentary, forgetting first to actually see and hear what people were doing and saying. I offer thick descriptions first.

3   Capturing Professional Consensus: The California State Department, 1983–1990

> It was part of the strategy . . . first, decide what you want and then go after all the leverage points in the system that determine whether you get it.
> —Bill Honig

> The Legislature hereby recognizes that, because of the common needs and interest of the citizens of this state and the nation, there is a need to establish a common state curriculum for the public schools, but that because of economic, geographic, physical, political, and social diversity, there is a need for the development of educational programs at the local level, with the guidance of competent experienced educators and citizens. Therefore, it is the intent of the Legislature to set broad minimum standards and guidelines for educational programs, and to encourage local districts to develop programs that will best fit the needs and interests of the pupils, pursuant to stated philosophy, goals, and objectives.
> —California Education Code

Louis "Bill" Honig is a tall, wiry, athletic man. He's opinionated, electric, energetic, not shy. Charismatic and peripatetic, he is respected both for his intelligence and energy. He is known as an avid reader, and his colleagues are in awe of his memory.[1] Honig was born into a wealthy California family and—after a short stint as an attorney—started his career as a teacher. Attending San Francisco State in the 1960s, Honig had been taught to teach mathematics with a problem solving orientation:

I was taught by a guy . . . who had joint appointments by the math department and the education department. And he taught us the way it
was supposed to be. We knew the math. We knew how kids screw it up.
We knew how to use the manipulatives.[2] We knew examples of how to
do it. We got educated in math. It was a great program and I couldn't
have taught without it. My kids had the highest math scores in the city.
This was the ghetto group from Hunter's Point. And I don't think that
I'm that great a teacher and I didn't go that far in math. I never took
trigonometry, I never took other things. But I like math, I like numbers,
I'm comfortable with it. My goal was to give kids number sense. We had
reinforcement. We did it every day and I wouldn't let some kids go out
to recess until they got it. We did oral math. We broke them up into
groups. We did whole group stuff. It was everything. We had games, we
did geometry. These kids came up from knowing nothing to being four
or five years above grade level. But they knew math and they were interested. It was a good class.[3]

Honig was on California's State Board of Education in the 1970s. While
a board member, he was active—aggressively so. According to some insiders, Honig ran for state superintendent because he was frustrated with the
lack of responsiveness of earlier superintendents to his ideas. Elected in
1982 as state superintendent, he took office in January 1983; his tenure
lasted ten years. Throughout his stint as state superintendent, his relations
with both Republican governors—Deukmejian and Wilson—were fiery.
Little time was spent on either side being conciliatory, and their tempestu-
ous, ongoing battles were high profile and provided much grist for the journalists' mill.[4] Budget policies were the center of Honig's debates with the
governors; control over school policy was the center of his long-lasting and
bitter battle with Joseph Carrabino, chair of the state board.

Before Honig's administration, the California Department of Education
(CDE) had been working on programs in early childhood, school finance,
and school improvement. Little had been done systemwide about curriculum
direction and organization. Historically, the state had issued "frameworks"
intended to describe, in broad strokes, the goals of K–12 curriculum in all
the subject matters. But Honig and his colleagues had bigger plans: they
wanted to change testing, curriculum, teacher education, school organization, parent and community involvement—across all grade levels, across
all subjects. A Nation at Risk—a national report calling for higher, better

standards—appeared five months after Honig took office.[5] Our students need to learn how to think critically, the authors claimed, and moving the American educational system forward would involve sweeping reforms of professional development, curriculum, testing, and school organization.

Honig placed California in the lead of states willing to rise to the challenges put forth in A Nation at Risk. But Honig's sweeping school reforms went further, for they were conceptualized as a coherent package that tied assessment to curriculum to school organization to teacher education. All state policy levers would carry the same message: higher standards for all children. Accountability for all educators. Harmony would characterize the policies of his superintendency, not the typical incoherency (almost cacophony) that pervaded most state policy environments.[6]

This attempt to change the educational "system" became, shortly afterward, a driving force on the national education scene. In part, this was due to a series of studies conducted by researchers in the Consortium for Policy Research in Education (CPRE), who found that the 1980s U.S. state education reforms lacked coherence and were not based on challenging standards.[7] Moreover, scholars like David Cohen and James Spillane pointed out that teachers received multiple, often conflicting, messages about how and what to teach: teacher education programs taught one thing, student textbooks another, statewide tests another. Other research demonstrated that this was particularly true in elementary mathematics. In an analysis of fourth grade mathematics textbooks and tests, Donald Freeman and his colleagues found that only a limited number of topics were emphasized in all the textbooks used by Michigan teachers. More troubling was that matched textbooks and tests failed to provide a "congruent message of what ought to be taught."[8]

In the words of Cohen and Spillane, it was a "great carnival of instructional guidance": "In such a carnival, students and teachers can make up their own minds about many matters. Though many are aware of different sorts of advice, few are keenly aware of most of it; for few voices can cut clearly through the din of the multitude. But many educators know that most guidance is either weakly supported or contradicted by other advice. That much they can learn from experience. Most also know that much instructional guidance can safely be ignored. The din of diverse, often inconsistent, and generally weak guidance offers considerable latitude to those who work within it."[9]

In an important essay that influenced both the national discourse about education and state policy making, Marshall Smith, then dean and professor of education at Stanford University and later undersecretary of education in the Clinton administration, wrote about this reform strategy with his colleague Jennifer O'Day. In that essay, they coined the phrase "systemic reform," which involved "increasing coherence in the system through centralized coordination and increasing professional discretion at the school site. Thus while schools have the ultimate responsibility to educate thoughtful, competent, and responsible citizens, the state—representing the public—has the responsibility to define what 'thoughtful, competent and responsible citizens' will mean in the coming decade and century."[10]

In the late 1980s, systemic reform became a highly touted solution to many education problems. However, as with any idea, "systemic reform" took on different meanings for different people in different contexts. Most versions shared two features: an emphasis on comprehensive change (using a broad array of levers) *and* policy coordination around a collection of clear and explicit outcomes. The National Science Foundation offered grants to states attempting such efforts in mathematics and science. The National Governors' Association, the Business Roundtable, and the Education Commission of the States also enthusiastically supported the idea.

Honig and Smith were in conversation at this time, and Honig probably both influenced and was influenced by the discussions of systemic reform. Honig earmarked California's curriculum frameworks as his starting point, for his strategy began with the need to "define a cooperative vision and establish a curriculum."[11] Frameworks have a thirty-year history in California. The first one for mathematics—*Strands of Mathematics*—was published in 1963. Although these frameworks did not dictate the content of curriculum in California, they played an important role in the state's attempts to have a rational educational system that drew on professional expertise and enabled consensus.

California Curricular Policy Making

California has a bicameral legislature, consisting of a Senate and an Assembly. The governor appoints the State School Board of Education (SBE), with all the appointments approved by the senate. Authorized in 1921, the SBE was initially given limited constitutional authority, mainly to adopt instructional materials in grades 1 through 8. However, over time, the State Board's sphere of influence progressively expanded. It currently has extensive power, overseeing most of the education activity in the state, approving emergency teaching credentials and waivers, hearing cases concerning exceptions to state laws, approving curricular frameworks and textbook adoptions.

There is also a state (in this case, California) Department of Education (CDE), headed by an elected (allegedly nonpartisan) state superintendent of instruction. Both the structure and ranks of the CDE change frequently; each new superintendent typically reorganizes the department at least once during his or her tenure. Officially, the CDE cannot mandate what is taught or learned in schools. Instead, this department typically assists school districts, providing resources and ideas as well as monitoring schools' adherence to state policy. The relationship between the State Board and the Department of Education (with its elected state superintendent) historically has been "murky." According to long-time observers, the relationship has been affected more by personalities than by politics: some state superintendents have gotten along very well with the board, others have not.

To make things still more confusing, there exists a Curriculum Development and Supplemental Materials Commission (commonly known as the Curriculum Commission, or CC) to assist the SBE with its curricular responsibilities (see Figure 3.1).[12] The CC has eighteen members, thirteen of whom are appointed by the State Board. Other members are appointed by the governor (one), the speaker of the assembly (one), and the Senate Rules Committee (one). One senator and one assemblyperson also serve as CC members. Competition for positions is announced statewide. Teachers, administrators, teacher educators, and those involved in higher education are invited—sometimes actively recruited—to apply. Commissioners serve four-year terms and represent a range of K–12 grade levels and subject matters. The commission oversees, orchestrates, and manages several critical curricular processes, including writing and revising the frameworks and textbook reviews and adoptions. The CC is assisted by the CDE, and one or two CDE staff members manage the nomination, development, review, and adoption processes.

Frameworks are the state's curricular vision, providing guidance for curriculum development in every subject area. The California State Education Code officially enumerates nine purposes for the frameworks:

1. Establishing guidelines and providing direction to aid districts in revising curricula, evaluating programs, assessing personnel, and developing strategies to best serve the needs of all students

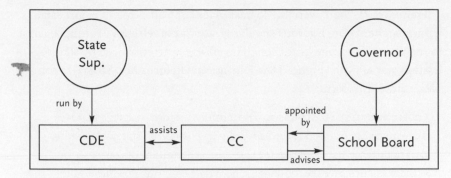

Figure 3.1. Curriculum Decision Making in California

2. Providing the basis for the education of teachers and administrators
3. Serving as a resource for state and district personnel responsible for in-service education
4. Providing direction for textbook and instructional materials development
5. Furnishing guidance at the state, county, and local levels to individuals responsible for developing curriculum
6. Serving as a basis for the development and revision of state and local testing programs
7. Providing the basis for the development of criteria for selecting instructional materials
8. Providing information on the curriculum to parents and the public
9. Providing guidance for the review of secondary (grades 9–12) materials

Although the Curriculum Commission orchestrates framework development and textbook adoption, the relationship between the CC and the SBE is strictly advisory, and the State Board is under no obligation to heed the recommendations of the CC. Historically, however, the board—often composed of noneducators—had respected most of the commission's recommendations. While there had often been discussions about aspects of frameworks (and subsequent textbook adoptions), the board had most often gone along with the recommendations of the heavily educator-weighted CC. The policy traditions in California, in fact, had been remarkable in their attention to and respect for teachers' professional experience and practical knowledge.

Frameworks, then, were the logical place for California to begin establishing higher, more rigorous standards. And upon election, Honig began to mobilize forces to rewrite them. His efforts were enhanced by state legislation, namely the Hughes-Hart Educational Reform Act (SB 813), a complex, unwieldy reform:

> California's 1983 SB 813 was an $800 million reform package that was extraordinarily complex. It included the imposition of statewide graduation requirements; provision for state board definition of competency standards; incentives for a longer school day; continuing education requirements for teacher certification; a mentor teacher program of annual stipends for teachers who help new teachers or develop curriculum; increased beginning salaries; an alternate route for high school teachers; reforms in personnel management that made it easier to dismiss and transfer teachers; and expanded authority for expulsion and suspension of problem students, amid dozens of other provisions.[13]

Within this web of mandates, we were following the life and effects of California's curricular vision, which Honig and his staff saw as the driver for all the other reforms. Traditionally, frameworks were to be examined on seven-year cycles to see if they were in need of tinkering, elaboration, or major overhaul. Science was the first up for review in 1984 (although its revision was started prior to Honig's push for systemwide reform). Mathematics was scheduled for review in 1985; English/Language Arts would follow in 1987. One of Honig's deputy superintendents explained the strategy:

> We have a general strategy and there are variants on the theme for each of the subject areas. Basically, the overall strategy for reform in California is curriculum-driven. We start with the idea that you have to define what is a high quality mathematics program, high quality science program, and so forth. And the way we did that—and I think it's notably different than the way that it's done in a lot of other states and the way we used to do it in this state—is that we try to capture a professional consensus of what is a high quality program. We don't make it up in the state department. And we don't try to get a version that makes everybody happy. We try to get a professional consensus from the leadership of the profession. We bring together the leadership, the people that we think

are the most influential and who have thought about it and who are most likely to give us a clear point of view.

Then what we strive for is a clear point of view. It's not whether you can do a little of this, a little of that. We try to be very clear. Now frameworks are a little tricky to develop because they are a leadership document. They are a statement of policy and philosophy. They need to be sufficiently clear and explicit and concrete that one can look at them, compare a program and say, "Yes, we're doing it or not doing it." On the other hand, they can't be so prescriptive that you would end up with a state curriculum that would say, "On December 14th, every kid in the state is on page 127 in a certain textbook."

The framework development process is the same for every subject matter area: because the Curriculum Commission is small and covers all grade levels (K–12) and subject matters (from language arts to health to music to science to mathematics to history to physical education), there is not sufficient expertise on the commission to write any one framework. Hence, the CC splits into Subject Matter Committees (SMCs), with the SMC for each subject matter overseeing the development of the framework and its field review. The relevant SMC then appoints a Curriculum Framework and Criteria Committee (CFCC). The SMC members survey school districts and key informants for the names of individuals who might be CFCC members. They compile a list of thirty or forty teachers, teacher educators, curriculum directors, and specialists with expertise in the subject matter as candidate members. Each CFCC consists of between nine and fifteen members, "selected by the SMC, appointed by the CC, and approved by the SB."[14]

Although they are the primary tool for curriculum guidance, the California frameworks had traditionally been viewed as "vague" and "watered-down" documents that tried to satisfy diverse constituencies, groups with differing views about curricular content and the purposes of schooling.[15] But Honig and his staff wanted to change that by identifying a cadre of experienced teachers who would write a version of high standards: neither watered down nor compromised, neither vague nor too prescriptive. Following policy, the CDE staff assisted the mathematics SMC and collected nominations of highly regarded teachers, as well as state and national experts in mathematics education. The SMC put together a slate of nominations, which was forwarded to and then approved by the CC.

All meetings of the CFCCs are open to the public, and the CFCC chairs are required to spend time at each meeting in an open forum, allowing any and all attendees to express their views. After the framework is drafted, the SMC conducts a field review of the document. Instructional Materials Display Centers are scattered throughout the state. Each receives copies of a draft framework. Relevant parties—professional organizations of educators and administrators—also receive copies. National experts are asked to review them as well. The public usually has between forty-five and sixty days to comment and react, and the SMC is then charged with editing the document before submitting the next draft to the full CC. After the CC approves the draft framework, it is forwarded to the SBE for discussion and approval.

Drafting the 1985 Mathematics Framework

Writing the *1985 Mathematics Framework* was an arduous task. The committee was composed of teachers, teacher educators, and curriculum specialists. Disagreements in stance, tone, message, and organization erupted regularly, something that anyone who has written by committee comes to expect. Several people on the committee had a long history of teaching mathematics in more inquiry-oriented ways. Joan Akers, for instance, started out as a third-grade teacher in San Diego in the early 1960s, and had been participating in professional development opportunities for teachers for twenty years at that time. While on the framework committee, she was also a member of the state's Curriculum Commission, and went on to work in the CDE for many years. She was a member of the NCTM board of directors.

Akers recalled many arguments in the monthly meetings of the CFCC in 1984 when working on the *1985 Framework:* "We'd hold our meetings about once a month. You get into subgroups [elementary, middle, high school] and you talk things over in the open meeting. Then you go off and do some writing and everyone pulls it together. You critique it, and you argue a lot."

Walter Denham, then director of the CDE's mathematics office, assisted the group. Denham had been an applied mathematician for fifteen years before arriving at the steps of the State Department of Education in Sacramento. For ten years after his arrival, he described himself as a bureaucrat, working on school program planning and evaluation before moving into mathematics education. Like many people, he found himself in mathematics education because he was good with numbers, not because he had had extensive experience in teaching mathematics—at any level: "I have no experience in K–12 classrooms except for one semester when I taught an Algebra II class. So, in 1983 I got a job in mathematics education because Mr. Honig wanted curriculum to be the center of things. It had been way out on the edge during the previous twelve years, and we wanted it to be right at the center."

Like Honig, Denham believed that people had it right thirty years ago— that we have known for a while that traditional mathematics instruction that emphasizes only the basics is not productive. Although present at the CFCC meetings, Denham could play only a supporting role (albeit a very active one), for CDE staff could not officially control the content of the frameworks; that was the job of the committee. However, given his job as CDE mathematics head, he would later become an advocate for the 1985 *Framework* and a critical player in the events that followed.

When the draft was sent to the State Board, sparks started flying. Henry Alder, a University of California, Davis professor who was on the SBE, wanted, as one informant put it, " to ditch it entirely . . . it was overwritten and vague, imprecise." Alder was irate at the "wishy-washy" language. He tried to get the State Board to throw it out, but the CC took "a strong stand," insisting that the State Board could not take over the process of framework writing from the professional educators. The SB and the CC compromised, adding several new members to the CFCC to help with revisions. Among them was Elizabeth Stage, who later stepped in and edited the final draft. She recalled: "The commission let Henry Alder add three people to the committee, which he added from the Mathematics Diagnostic Testing Project,[16] and the commission added three people, which they added from the California Mathematics Council, and then they added two other people from the California Mathematics Project: me and Judy Kysh. Judy was the facilitator and I was editor. . . . So we went and we had this meeting, and the big deal was if we could come up with a good definition of problem solving, we'd be home. Then I'd just edit it."

Some members of this newly augmented committee thought of themselves as enemies; the enhancement of the committee by selecting three people from two "sides" added to this. The MDTP folks were caricatured as "traditionalists"—educators and mathematicians who believed in "traditional" views of mathematics teaching (memorization, decontextualized problems, a heavy emphasis on drill), while the California Mathematics Council people were identified—again, perhaps caricatured—as "progressives," concerned more with process than with content.

John Dewey fought against the tendency of educators to dichotomize their thinking in these ways, for the dichotomies neither accurately represent the complexity of instructional issues nor promote helpful discussion about educational means and ends. Unfortunately, Amy Gutmann notes, his efforts were often to no avail, for all too frequently educators think in terms of either/or: content or process, basics or higher-order thinking skills, cognitive or affective.[17] In discussions educational, people are quickly pigeonholed: if someone mentions the need for practice, she's a traditionalist; if someone mentions the need to consider the child's interests, he's a progressive. Things were no different on this committee, and discussions were interpreted as a battle of the traditionalists versus the progressives.[18]

When the members of the augmented CFCC met, however, several participants reported that the discussions went remarkably well. The mathematicians didn't like the imprecision of the definition of problem solving, so they discussed how to better describe it. They started with a phrase from one of the "traditionalists": "applying one's knowledge and skills to new and unexpected situations." A more "progressive" committee member then suggested the group edit the statement, adding "experience": "Applying one's knowledge, skills, and experience to new and unexpected situations." Everyone agreed, and some people—who had assumed they didn't like one another—became friends.

Stage then went on to smooth out and edit the final document. Armed with a doctorate from Harvard in science education, Stage is smart, pragmatic, and politically astute. After gaining state prominence for her role in this process, Stage went on to serve in several critical roles. She was vice president (1985–86) and then president (1987–88) of the California Mathematics Council board, a member of the Curriculum Commission starting in 1987 (which she then chaired in 1989–90). She started the California Science Project in 1989, and later went on to participate in national endeavors, including stints with the National Research Council and the New Standards project.

Published in 1985, the *1985 Framework* received a lot of press. The introductory remarks by the State Board quietly imply that the process was complicated, thanking Alder for "providing direction at critical points in the writing process. . . . We join Dr. Alder," the State Board notes, "in the hope that this framework will help students in this state appreciate the 'power and beauty of mathematics.'" Alder is the only committee member mentioned in the foreword: singling him out for thanks was an eerie harbinger of the maelstrom to come.

A lean document, the *1985 Framework* had some familiar elements, and some new ones. Because our research team was interested in understanding the relationship between California curricular policies and teachers' practices, I focus almost exclusively on aspects of this document (and others) that related to elementary school teaching.[19] Like previous frameworks dating back to 1963, the *1985 Framework* organized the content of the curriculum around "strands," in this case: number (develop facility with a variety of methods of computation), measurement (using nonstandard units of measure at first and then standard units, recognizing that standard units are needed for communication and simplified notation), geometry, patterns and functions, statistics and probability, logic, and algebra. Within those seven strands, sixty-one major mathematical concepts are listed.

But the *Framework* committee knew what traditionally happened to such lists: they became checklists of isolated items to be noted in curricula and classrooms. The committee members did not want this framework to be reduced to an arid, detached list. They took pains to emphasize a conceptual orientation to mathematics, as the introduction suggests: "The inherent beauty and fascination of mathematics commends it as a subject that can be appreciated and enjoyed by all learners. The study of mathematics helps students to develop thinking skills, order their thoughts, develop logical arguments, and make valid inferences." The committee continued: "The goal is for all students to be able to use mathematics with confidence; therefore, every student must be instructed in the fundamental concepts of each strand of mathematics, and no student should be limited to the computational aspects of the number strand."[20]

Overall, the *1985 Framework* described a "constructivist" version of mathematics teaching and learning (although the language of constructivism was not yet part of common educational parlance and does not appear in the document). Constructivism is a theory of learning that was gaining popularity (some would say a popularity that resembled religious fervor) in the mid-1980s. According to constructivist thought, learning is best thought of as a process of constructing knowledge. Instead of assuming that students learn like sponges, absorbing information that teachers spout, constructivist theorists emphasize the fact that students come with experience and beliefs—sometimes helpful, sometimes not—and that their prior experiences and beliefs influence what and how they learn.

All versions of constructivism place the student in a role of active constructor of knowledge rather than passive absorber. But beyond that shared assumption, there is considerable variation among theorists, with some emphasizing the role of the individual in constructing knowledge and others emphasizing the role of communities developing shared knowledge. As Denis Phillips explains, the faces of constructivism are many: some radical, some less so; some individual, others social. In addition to theoretical variation, there is considerable variation in how well developed an individual's understanding of constructivist learning theory is. As George Bernard Shaw is reputed to have said, a good idea is not responsible for the people who believe in it. And so it has been with constructivism. To paraphrase Phillips, good, bad, and ugly versions of the theory abound.[21]

The variation—while sometimes healthy—has also led to a great deal of confusion, for people might use the same language but mean entirely different things. Some critics, unfortunately, are quick to lump together all versions. Someone hears a radical constructivist—as I once did—argue that to tell students *anything* is to "rape" their minds, and then suddenly everyone who believes in some version of constructivism becomes tarnished by association. The extremists get treated as representative.

Constructivism also is often confused with "discovery learning," an instructional strategy that became popular in the 1960s, especially in New Math curricula. Max Beberman, for example, designed "guided discoveries" as part of the New Math materials developed for the University of Illinois Committee on School Mathematics. Jeremy Kilpatrick explains: "Students would be led to see patterns in mathematical expressions and thus to arrive at generalizations that would not need to be made explicit in the materials (until a later lesson). The materials apparently worked well when restricted to teachers who had been trained in their use. When they were later published in the form of commercial textbooks, however, the guided discovery feature was greatly attenuated in order to capture a larger market."[22]

Like all innovations, discovery learning was used by teachers who did not have sufficient knowledge or skill to implement it with a high degree of fidelity. And like all innovations, it was sometimes embraced too wholeheartedly, with teachers throwing the baby of direct instruction out with the bathwater of conventional mathematics teaching. And as happens in our contemporary culture, critics quickly confound these examples of poor or questionable implementation with the definition and goals of discovery learning. Constructivism, suffering from similar woes—superficial understanding, overuse, and association with progressive educational ideas—soon became a red flag for many concerned parents, educators, and scholars. Thus, discovery learning and constructivism have been seen alternately as both the darling of the educational establishment and the bête noire of the establishment's critics.

One consistent mistake has been to assume that a constructivist theory of learning has simple and direct implications for a theory of teaching. When constructivism (the learning theory) is used interchangeably with "constructivist teaching," this is a faulty linguistic and pedagogical turn. For it is possible for a teacher to believe that constructivist learning theories have some merit, and to also believe that more behavioral theories of learning—theories that emphasize training and repetition—also have merit. Of course, "true believers" would disagree with me here, arguing for a more singular and dogmatic use of the theory. As a teacher, I tend to be more ecumenical. If scientists can, as Ellen Gilchrist wrote, see light as "both wave and particle," so teachers should be able to be both constructivists and behaviorists.[23] Alba Thompson put it this way: teachers' "conceptions of teaching and learning tend to be eclectic collections of beliefs."[24]

That said, constructivist theories of learning do have implications for one's teaching practice. Teachers who believe that students' experiences, knowledge, and thinking influence—in part—what they understand in class spend time learning about what students know and how they are making sense of a new idea. They ask questions about what students mean. Teachers who believe constructivist learning theories also sometimes put students in more active roles as learners: working in small groups, building models of their understandings (sometimes using manipulatives), and explaining their reasoning. Teachers who hold to constructivist theories of learning tend to have classrooms that are noisier, classrooms in which students share center stage with the teacher and the text, and where questions about authority and the location of truth are central.

This emphasis on talking—often called "discourse"—acknowledges the centrality of concepts, culture, and language to the development of understanding, an idea not foreign to mathematicians. As the mathematician Reuben Hersh has written:

Why can we converse about polynomials? We've been trained to, by a training evolved for that purpose . . . polynomial is a shared notion. . . . And polynomials are objective: They have certain properties, whether we know them or not. These are implicit in our common notion, "polynomial."

To unravel in detail how we attain this common, objective notion is a deep problem, comparable to the problem of language acquisition. No one understands clearly how children acquire rules of English or Navajo, which they follow without being able to state them. These implicit rules don't grow spontaneously in the brain. They come from the shared language-use of the community of speakers. The properties of mathematical objects, like the properties of English sentences, are properties of shared ideas.[25]

In addition to discourse, the 1985 *Framework* authors emphasized something they call "mathematical power": "the ability to discern mathematical relationships, reason logically, and use mathematical techniques effectively."[26] Mathematically powerful students "find key mathematical elements of problem situations; explore mathematical relationships and formulate hypotheses; demonstrate and explain their unique resolution of the problem through diagrams, graphs, charts, and other methods and extend their mathematical thinking to related problems or situations; and communicate their findings effectively to an audience."[27]

Some critics of education might be tempted to call the language of "mathematical power" another instance of educationese, the use of jargon that obfuscates rather than clarifies communication. But it turns out that the phrase has historical roots, for reformers in the 1930s—including mathematicians—were concerned about an overemphasis on drill and a concomitant lack of understanding. "Manipulation as an end is to be eliminated," one report argued. "Mechanical work can be justified only when necessary for understanding and using fundamental principles. The chief objective of the course is power, not skill."[28] By "power," the authors of this report meant the capacity to "solve problems, which arrive in [students'] everyday experiences. These problems require not only the skills and concepts previously mentioned, but also ability in thinking, analyzing, and reasoning. Pupils do their best thinking when they are confronted with a challenging, thought-provoking problem situation. Growth in power to reason results from success in reasoning in a variety of situations."[29]

Similarly, the *1985 Framework* portrayed students with mathematical power as curious inquirers who probe, experiment, persevere, conjecture. They use mathematical procedures—subtraction, addition, multiplication and the like—with facility and accuracy. They collect, analyze, display, and process data. They use representational systems and calculators. They ask good questions, know how to pursue them, and can judge the validity of various answers. The framework emphasized problem solving and deemphasized computation. It supported the use of calculators, and the development of the skills of estimation and mental arithmetic in *all* students. Later documents—including the NCTM *1989 Standards*—carried similar messages. Students were no longer to exclusively spend mathematics time in school filling out worksheets, taking timed fact tests, memorizing algorithms. Instead, they were to become problem solvers: seeing mathematics in the real world, using mathematical processes to explore and investigate, inventing methods while solving problems.

This view of problem solving was quite different from the one I experienced as a child, or even the one I had when I became an emergency-credentialed mathematics teacher. Traditionally, mathematics class includes "word problems," the bane of many a student's existence. Those problems typically took the form of a vignette: "Two trains are approaching one another. They are 150 miles apart. One train is going 50 miles an hour, the other is going 30 miles an hour. Where will they pass each other?" Or "Susie and Beth both have cookies for their classmates. Susie has 6 more cookies than Beth does. Between them, they have 100 cookies. How many cookies does Susie have?" Although these "problems" were supposed to teach students to flexibly use the algorithm they had most recently learned—applying a newly learned rule to "real world" situations—learning to solve such problems was a study in the reduction of the real world to rigidly used recipes. "If Beth has c cookies, how many does Susie have?" I would prompt students, peering into the sea of vacant faces (some students simply tune out as soon as you mention "word problems" because they are sure they won't understand them). "If Beth has c cookies and Susie has $c + 6$ cookies, what equation could you write to describe the problem?" Eventually we would get a formula on the board:

"Beth has c cookies," I would prompt. Silence.

"So Susie has 6 more cookies." Silence. "More means plus, so Susie must have c plus 6 cookies, right?"

"All together . . . that means plus . . . so they must have $c + (c + 6) = 100$."

"If we add the c's, we get: $2c + 6 = 100$. What do we do next?"

One of the more confident students might then remember a rule: "Subtract 6 from both sides: $2c + 6 - 6 = 100 - 6$."

I'd subtract on the board:

$2c = 100 - 6$

$2c = 94$

"Now what can we do?"

Another student might remember a similar rule: "Divide each side by 2 . . ."

$2c = 100 - 6$

$2c = 94$

$2c/2 = 94/2$

"So c must be equal to 47," I would say, feeling like I'd been pulling teeth.

This experience is typical in mathematics classrooms. Some students aren't naturally curious about puzzles and problems; classroom teachers know this. Some were never curious. Others, once curious, lost their interest somewhere along the way, perhaps owing to poorly taught or poorly conceptualized mathematics curricula. Teachers have to deal with the twin curses of school math—fear and ennui—every day. They dread the moment when students' eyes glaze over, when one feels like one is all alone in a room full of at best passive, at worst, hostile adolescents who have learned to see math as mumbo-jumbo. Carl Sandburg captures their experience in "Arithmetic":

> Arithmetic is where numbers fly like pigeons in and out of your head.
> Arithmetic tells you how many you lose or win if you know how many
>   you had before you lost or won.
> Arithmetic is seven eleven all good children go to heaven—or five six
>   bundle of sticks.
> Arithmetic is numbers you squeeze from your head to your hand to
>   your pencil to your paper till you get the answer.
> Arithmetic is where the answer is right and everything is nice and you
>   can look out of the window and see the blue sky—or the answer is
>   wrong and you have to start all over and try again and see how it
>   comes out this time.
> If you take a number and double it and double it again and then double
>   it a few more times, the number gets bigger and bigger and goes

higher and higher and only arithmetic can tell you what the number
is when you decide to quit doubling.
Arithmetic is where you have to multiply—and you carry the
multiplication table in your head and hope you won't lose it.
If you have two animal crackers, one good and one bad, and you eat one
and a striped zebra with streaks all over him eats the other, how many
animal crackers will you have if somebody offers you five six seven
and you say No no no and you say Nay nay nay and you say Nix
nix nix?
If you ask your mother for one fried egg for breakfast and she gives you
two fried eggs and you eat both of them, who is better in arithmetic,
you or your mother?[30]

Students—the more confident ones—march through the requisite
steps; they remember that you can subtract 6 from both sides, or divide
both sides by 2. But it was always clear how much *no* one was thinking—
really thinking—when most students stopped there, answering the question with 47, not realizing that the question asked for how many cookies
Susie had ($c + 6$), not how many cookies Beth had (c). To people who
haven't spent time in math classrooms, this might seem ridiculous, a trick
question at best. But for teachers who are trying to help children learn to
reason, it is an uphill battle to convince them that mathematics requires
thinking, not a simple mechanical progression through a number of predetermined steps. Historically, this has been the form of "problem solving"
experienced in schools, and this is what the members of the 1985 *Framework* committee were trying hard to counteract.

Problem solving in the 1985 *Framework* took almost two pages to describe. "In problem solving the teacher should serve as a group facilitator
rather than as a directive group leader," the document reads. Teachers need
to encourage students to "consider a variety of alternative and even un-
promising approaches." They need to create classrooms in which students
can take risks, manage their own perplexity, explain their thinking.

This kind of problem solving also had steps, but steps quite different
from "do the same thing to both sides" problem solving. First, students had
to formulate problems (verbalize questions, identify mathematics in those
questions, formulate reasonable hypotheses, identify missing or extrane-
ous information). Second, students had to analyze problems and select
strategies (make models, draw pictures, organize information in tables,

identify similar problems, act out the situation, restate the problem, search for patterns, guess and check, work backward). Third, they had to find solutions, followed by a verification stage (Is this answer reasonable? Was there a better way to solve it? Can my solution be improved?). This problem solving is quite different from those word problems we all solved—and taught. This problem solving is messy, less readily reduced to the script I read when solving the cookies problem with my students.

This portrayal of mathematical problem solving in the 1985 *Framework* illustrates several problems the writing committee faced. Central was the problem of how to discuss the content of mathematics. In the framework, the mathematics content included both process (mathematical reasoning and discourse) and substance (mathematical concepts and facts). This led to confusing descriptions, however, as was the case with descriptions of problem solving. Readers could not differentiate between descriptions of mathematics content and those of mathematics pedagogy. Frameworks were not intended to dictate pedagogy, only content. But since the content of the curriculum, for the committee, included both learning substance and learning process, the descriptions of learning and thinking mathematically sometimes were misinterpreted as descriptions of how teachers should teach mathematics. Later critics of many of the 1980s and 1990s standards documents (including the NCTM's) would observe as much—rightfully so. Teachers who had been trying to improve mathematics teaching for a long time—including the teachers who were part of the framework writing committee—believed that, to paraphrase Marshall McLuhan, the medium historically had been part of the message in mathematics classrooms. Traditional teaching of mathematics marched students lockstep through all sorts of algorithms, even on word problem days. Students learned that mathematics is facts and rules, procedures. And the experienced teachers worried that many students—too many students, to paraphrase Colburn's earlier comments—started in the dark and ended in the dark, with no sense of what they were doing.

The reformers wanted students to learn to *think,* to exercise judgment, to use mathematics powerfully, to solve problems in the light of day, with eyes wide open, and maybe even with interest. Their conception of mathematics content embraced both conceptual knowledge and mathematical reasoning. Their hunch was that the *way* mathematics was taught—without much intellectual engagement on the part of the students—was as problematic as *what* was being taught. Later critics would note—legitimately—that there are several ways to teach something well, and the confounding of descriptions of instruction with those of content troubled many people. "We have an obligation to list what ought to be taught; teachers should be left to use their professional discretion with how to teach those things," they argued. But even Aristophanes' description confuses how something is taught with what is learned: the Old Education involved memorization, obedience, and little questioning; the New Education involved constructing arguments and questioning authority. As I mentioned earlier, this confounding of method and content is a point of controversy—yet to be resolved—among many participants in debates concerning mathematics education.

The *1985 Framework* committee also knew that the weight of tradition is strong, and that the default would be teaching that emphasized routine and memory rather than thought and judgment. So they erred on the side of the unusual and wrote almost exclusively about reasoning rather than paying equal attention to basic skills and problem solving. The *1985 Framework* was written within an intellectual and historical context that shaped what was said—and not said. Everyone assumed readers understood teaching the basics; "drill-and-kill"-dominated teaching was the historical context. Hence, basic skills and algorithms were deemphasized in this particular text, while other, less familiar ideas like problem solving were discussed extensively. Early on, this relative lack of attention to traditional teaching was the cause for some confusion; later, for considerable criticism.

When we first interviewed him in 1987, Bill Honig understood that there was some concern about the role of algorithms: "We're not going to get rid of algorithms. We're going to do it more efficiently but that should only be a small portion of what [students] do day-to-day." He also sensed that there was some worry that California's 1980s version of a mathematics curriculum was a new version of the 1960s New Math: "We're carrying the baggage of New Math. Is this all going to be conceptual? Not really. It is solving problems and understanding what you are doing and thinking about what you are doing."

While the *1985 Framework* appeared to present a united front and consensus, in fact, it cloaked considerable internal debate and difference. Honig had a clear sense of what he wanted, based in part on his experiences learning to teach. Others disagreed with him, for they had something much more radical in mind. For example, both within California and nationwide, there were wildly different interpretations of the implications of constructivist learning theory for teaching practice. Some scholars believed that constructivist theory leads directly to the conclusion that teachers should *never* tell students anything. Others took a more balanced approach, suggesting that there is a time and a place for a range of instructional strategies, including the traditional lecture.[31] The standards documents—those issued by the NCTM, as well as the 1985 *Framework*—masked these differences. Written to satisfy multiple communities, the documents said everything and nothing. The twin problems of a lack of specificity and the watering down that can occur when groups aim for consensus would become important issues later on. As Marilyn Burns, another leader in the mathematics education community, would later say, "I think of the *Standards* as a document that's a consensus document and therefore can't have *a* particular point of view. It has to represent a spectrum of points of view. And it can't say, 'This is harmful and not harmful.' So you could essentially prove any point you want. I can quote it and get validation for any point I want."

Much of the cloaked disagreement was among the most central characters. Honig, for example, saw some of the mathematics educators as "zealots." He worried that "they don't want any basic skills, they don't want any answers. They're going to go . . . too far. . . . The problem with some of the people who are working on the math stuff is that they get so trapped in the ideology. . . . They get the Holy Grail. They get . . . trapped in the purity of what they are trying to sell."

One person who risked being seen as such a zealot was Walter Denham, who was fond of saying things like, "Live by the sword, die by the sword." In one interview, he explained his position: "This is the big lie in mathematics, in describing mathematics in the past, is that there are a set of skills that everybody has to have and there are 300 of them and we all have to go through all 300 before we can do anything else. That's a big lie. There are almost *no* skills in the traditional sense that people have to have." Denham continued:

> There is no place in the curriculum of the future for even thinking
> about them in isolation. Now—of course—there are lots of concepts,
> lots of skills that are relevant and useful and interesting and important
> in different ways. But none of the isolated concepts and skills is crucially
> important in and of itself. Big ideas—like uncertainty—are things that

everybody needs to engage in in some way. But there aren't [sic] a subset of topics that we need every kid to have studied in some depth. Now that's a radical position. It is not a majority view, but it is the prevailing view in math ed leadership. The math ed leadership nationally is cohesive.

Denham overstated the position of the mathematics education community in California at the time, for many teachers and teacher-leaders wanted a balanced position. Elizabeth Stage recalled rewriting parts of the 1985 Framework to assuage Honig's worries: "There was a tendency on the part of some of the authors who were working at the draft stage to project the image that you're going to be excommunicated if you don't have the right beliefs. . . . So when I cleaned up the draft, I got rid of the arrogance and the pompous language and the 'It is imperative that. . . .' You know, the wording that suggested that you will go to hell immediately without passing go if you don't teach in a certain way."

There were, indeed, zealots, and on more than one occasion I was struck by the religious metaphors used in talk of the reform. "He's seen the vision," "She was born again," "This is the way." The press even called California's governor a "born-again advocate of educational progress."[32]

On some occasions, the progressive proselytizing was suffocating. As a participant-observer in one professional development seminar, when asked to solve a math problem, I used the quadratic formula. When asked to present my results, I did, surprised to discover the hostility that erupted among my colleagues: "You *can't* use formulas. You have to *think*." No one asked me if I had thought, or whether I understood the formula I had used (which I did). I was perplexed by being marginalized because I knew something. I was sympathetic, understanding that there were multiple ways to solve the problem and that the algorithm might alienate some of the less mathematically comfortable participants. Yet I did not understand why, in an effort to open the floor to multiple solutions, standard practices were dismissed.

Perhaps the extremes that some people went to were a by-product of living in California. As Peter Schrag writes, "California does little of consequence without excess."[33] Unfortunately, other people—teachers, parents, school board members, and the like—had experiences similar to mine. And these extremists planted seeds early on for a later assault by critics who too would recall stories of marginalization and zealotry. The passionate commitment to a new view of teaching that was more empowering

for children was commendable; the fact that—in more than a few instances—the passion turned into its own constraining and inflexible
dogma would become a problem.

In addition to masked, internal disagreements about what should be
taught, when, and how in mathematics, much of the 1985 *Framework* was
based on a mathematics teaching that few of us had experienced—either as
teachers or students. How many of us have witnessed mathematics classrooms in which students debate the pros and cons of alternative solutions?
How many of us have seen classrooms with diverse populations like those
in California—with Vietnamese, Hispanics, African Americans, Samoans,
Filipinos, to mention just a few of the eighty-or-so ethnic, racial, and cultural groups that flood California classrooms (many of whom do not speak
English as their primary language)—engage in deep and extended thinking about mathematical problems? What do we really know about what
children learn from such activities and in such settings? Do they learn what
they need to? As the authors themselves note, the 1985 *Framework* is "a vision of elementary and high school mathematics programs [based] not on
expanded research but on expanded commitment."[34]

Granted, there was a growing body of carefully documented research that
examined mathematics learning and teaching. However, this research was
part of a wave of education scholarship that moved beyond the boundaries
of traditional experimental and quasi-experimental psychological research
into methods more qualitative and ethnographic. While such research
(when done well) is necessary (shedding important light on issues that only
up-close analyses can), much of it was done poorly and little large-scale research was available. The uneven quality of this research, too, would become a subject of criticism, as would the tendency of many mathematics
education researchers to conduct *only* qualitative, small-sample inquiries.

The 1985 *Framework* was distributed to every school district in the state,
yet individual teachers encountered it erratically. We interviewed and observed over two dozen teachers across the state. Some reported that they
had seen it waved in front of them in a faculty meeting; others never saw
it. Some assumed that new textbooks that arrived years later were the
framework. A smaller number of teachers we met had their own well-
thumbed copies, and often they were teachers who were part of the draft
review process or were the designated mathematics specialists for their
school or district.

The 1986 Textbook Adoption

According to state policy, after a framework is issued, the Curriculum Commission then oversees a process of textbook adoption. This process takes about eighteen months, for textbooks and other instructional materials are distributed throughout the state for teachers, administrators, and parents to review. Once the state issues a list of approved texts, school districts also have a year for review. Typically, school districts create committees of educators and parents who review the approved texts and agree to a plan for pilot testing one or several of those approved texts throughout the district. After the pilot year, the district then decides which textbook it will purchase. In the 1980s, districts were allowed to adopt nonapproved textbooks, but only 25 percent of state funds could be used for such purchase. Given the state review and adoption process, and local pilot testing, teachers often do not receive newly purchased textbooks (intended to align with the framework) for close to three years after the framework has been issued.

Textbook adoption begins with two events. First, the State Department of Education drafts an "invitation for submit"on behalf of the State Board. The invitation is supplied to all interested publishers in the country and contains detailed information about the adoption process and its timeline, information concerning the legal requirements for participation in an adoption, guidelines for social content, and subject area criteria and evaluation instruments. At the same time, Instructional Materials Evaluation Panels (IMEPs) are formed through a process similar to the one used to constitute the CFCCs. At least 51 percent of each IMEP has to be practicing schoolteachers (see Figure 3.2).

On a date specified by the State Board, publishers must submit to the CDE a list of all basic instructional materials to be submitted for review and evaluation. This list allows the department and IMEPs to plan their work schedules. Then, on a later date, copies of the materials for review are submitted. Because 30 IMDCs are located across the state, publishers commonly have to submit up to 150 copies of materials for review—for each display center, each curriculum commissioner, each member of the IMEP, and every State Board member who cares to review the submissions.

The SMC appoints the IMEP. Appointments traditionally have been weighted in favor of teachers and subject matter specialists (who know the content and use the materials). The size of the panel depends on the volume of submissions. Members are nominated by the SMC, reviewed and approved by the full CC, and then reviewed and approved by the State Board. Each panel serves for one year. In 1986, the IMEP group received several days of training designed and delivered by Joan Akers and Marilyn Burns.

Throughout the process, textbook publishers were provided with copies of the *1985 Framework,* abridged versions of training materials, as well as the criteria for the review. Publishers were also allowed to make presentations to the IMEP to explain and present their materials. They were forbidden to contact any IMEP member outside of that meeting.

The IMEPs evaluate each submission and meet, reviewing their evaluations and summarizing the results. If publications are seen as lacking, publishers can make presentations to the panel. After these hearings, the chair of the IMEP prepares a list of the submissions, indicating recommendations for adoption or rejection, and summarizing each text's strengths and weaknesses.

The members of the Subject Matter Committee then review the IMEP report, revising and editing it as they see fit before submitting its final recommendations to the CC. Upon receipt of the SMC report, the CC goes through a similar process before they submit the official Curriculum Commission's recommendations for textbook adoptions to the SBE. Throughout the process, all curriculum commissioners and State Board members have access to the materials and reports. No matter what their subject matter or school experience, it is the prerogative of any commissioner and board member to vote on the materials under review. The SMC must provide a rationale for any and all rejections on the list. Traditionally, most of the responsibility for recommendations has rested on the shoulders of the IMEPs. After all, these are the committees (of practitioners) that read each textbook carefully (members of the CC, remember, come from all grade levels and all subject matters and feel less than confident in evaluating textbooks outside their area of expertise). As of 1985, the Curriculum Commission had never radically changed the recommendations made by an IMEP, nor had the State Board typically changed the CC's recommendations. The full formal process includes other steps as well, as illustrated in Figure 3.2.

The process culminates in a State Board meeting. The board holds at least one public hearing about the nominations, discusses the list, and edits it according to its evaluations of the adequacy of the submitted materials.

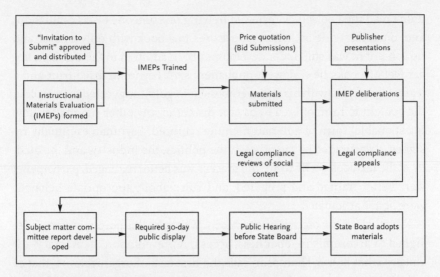

Figure 3.2. Textbook Adoption Process in California

According to State Board policy, then, its approval constitutes a "binding agreement" or contract between the publishers and the SBE.

Teachers who have participated in various textbook adoption processes, as well as CDE staff, report that the process is both cumbersome and vulnerable to political pressures. Publishing houses have a lot at stake. At that time, the state spent about $27 per pupil (recall the more than 5 million students in K–12 schools in California) on textbooks in one round of adoptions for a single subject matter. The result is that about $135 million is at stake for the adoption of K–12 mathematics textbooks, for example. As one state department insider explained, "The State Board is free to do anything they want. They usually take the advice of the Curriculum Commission. Some boards are highly susceptible to lobbying, and, of course, the publishers all know that, and so they are lobbied heavily. So the State Board can rarely make up its mind in less than three or four meetings. The process drags on and on."

In the past, lobbying had been the name of the textbook game. Richard Feynman, the Nobel Prize–winning physicist, was invited to be an IMEP member in the 1960s. He was appalled both by the content of the mathematics and science texts that he reviewed *and* by the process. The books were, in his words, "false," "hurried," "UNIVERSALLY LOUSY!" The panelists didn't read the books they reviewed (relying on someone else's evaluation) and, on at least one occasion, gave scores to a book with only a cover and no content (it was still under development). In addition to the eighteen linear feet of books he reviewed, publishers sent Feynman dried fruit and a leather briefcase (with his name embossed in gold), suggested they explain the content to him, offered to pay for dinner or any other (no matter how questionable) form of entertainment he required. Feynman eventually resigned, discouraged by the process, the politics, the industry, and the quality of the textbooks.[35] By 1986, the process was better managed, participants were better trained and prepared, and rules about appropriate behavior were better articulated.

Nonetheless, the process was tortuous. Whatever this porous system is designed to accomplish—openness, access, representation, democracy—it violates what James Thompson calls the first task of organizations, that of reducing uncertainty in its environment.[36] Most organizations, as Thompson explains, try to close off—or at the very least control—environmental uncertainty. Not this system. Even assuming that the men and women working on these overlapping assignments are of good will and intent, this system does not limit uncertainty. Quite the opposite happens, actually, for it fosters uncertainty by opening itself up at several points to those with possibly different views, and giving them a forum in which to express those views. State Board members, parents, teachers, mathematicians, teacher educators, textbook publishers, legislators, everyone had their day in court. This is not a system designed to make decisions.

Perhaps this is why the textbook companies did not anticipate having to actually respond to the *1985 Framework*. Throughout the drafting of the framework, all meetings—of the SMC, the CFCC, the CC—were open. There were no secrets, no surprises. Textbook companies knew that California was headed toward higher standards and inquiry-oriented instruction. Yet the publishers did little to change their textbooks. Insiders claimed that only one textbook series—published by a company called Open Court—was noticeably different. The IMEP used twenty-eight standards that had been developed to scrutinize the submissions: "Lessons for every student, below as well as above average, include the major concepts for every strand. No student is excluded from studying some areas of mathematics because of difficulty in other areas."[37]

Early reviews suggested that all the textbooks were seen as inadequate. Despite heavy lobbying, in November 1986 the State Board of Education rejected all the textbooks submitted for consideration. This was a landmark decision for the Curriculum Commission that sent shock waves through the industry. Textbook companies had counted on cornering the California and Texas markets. The fact that no company had its textbook series accepted had serious financial consequences for these publishing houses.

Bill Honig explained:

> It was part of the strategy . . . first, decide what you want and then go after all the leverage points within the system that determine whether you get it. One of those leverage points is textbooks. We had the framework; we had the criteria. . . .
>
> We met with the publishers; we went over the framework and said, "Here's where we are now: we repeat large chunks of material each year, and that's not very efficient. There's too much emphasis on skills and not enough on meaningful application." But the publishers didn't believe we were serious. They said, "We've got 15 million dollars invested in these books, and we're not going to make different ones just for California." Even in the second round when they knew we meant business, they changed only about 15 to 20 percent of their books for us. The math and science books are still not really as good as they have to be.[38]

Beginning in January 1987, the process was officially extended. For a year, both Joan Akers and Walter Denham—working with a committee of six technical advisers—spent hours coaching the publishers in how to revise the texts. Eventually, seven publishers—Silver Burdett; Houghton Mifflin; Open Court; D. C. Heath; Holt, Rinehart and Winston; Scott Foresman; and Addison-Wesley—submitted revised textbooks that were accepted, although the CDE staff were discouraged about most of the changes. Every publisher left the pagination unchanged (except for the kindergarten book published by Open Court). The revisions generally consisted of completely replaced lessons inserted in an otherwise traditional textbook. These were not reconceptualized curricula that took mathematics or the 1985 *Framework* seriously. CDE staff estimated that 90 percent of the texts had remained essentially the same.[39]

The 1987 K–8 Model Curriculum Guide

Meanwhile, Bill Honig searched for additional leverage points, for he wanted school districts to receive clear and steady guidance that insisted on higher standards. His aim was clear and consistent instructional guidance, rather than the instructional and curricular carnival typically found in schools in the United States. Model curriculum guides seemed a logical lever, for they were intended to translate the frameworks into guidelines for elementary and middle schoolteachers. And the Hughes-Hart legislation had stipulated that local school districts needed to compare their curricula to state-issued model curriculum standards every three years. The model curriculum guides were seen as "the strongest possible professional consensus about the content that every student should be exposed to."[40] One insider explained, "The framework is a political document. It gets approved by the State Board of Education. . . . The curriculum guide, on the other hand, was the result of department action. . . . I believe it was Honig's idea that we develop a K–8 model curriculum in each subject area. It did not have to go through the approval process by the Curriculum Commission or the State Board. I think it's much more exciting to read than the Framework."

A group of teachers and mathematics educators from around the state were invited to be members of the committee to draft the *K–8 Model Curriculum Guide*.[41] Members of the committee were people well known in the mathematics education community like Joan Akers, Judy Kysh, Karen Morelli, Elaine Rosenfield, Carol Langbort, Kathy Richardson, Ed Silver, Elizabeth Stage, and Jean Stenmark. The group consisted of math specialists, resource teachers, curriculum coordinators, teachers, teacher-leaders, and education professionals. Many of them were leaders in organizations like the California Mathematics Project and the California Mathematics Council.

These were the experienced practitioners the CDE staff member alluded to when describing the department's strategy, "the people that we think are the most influential and who have thought about it and who are most likely to give us a clear point of view." They were committed to an inquiry-oriented mathematics teaching that engaged students in solving problems, not memorizing rules. They believed that learning is not linear, but spiraling and layered. They wanted teachers to "lead discussions, frame questions, and design activities that contain multiple levels of learning."[42] Most of them had experience teaching in these ways; many had experience helping other teachers learn to do the same. Of like mind, this committee spent little time negotiating consensus and more time spinning out scenarios.

They did, however, have many discussions about the purpose of the guide and its audience. "Who was the intended audience?" Akers recalls asking,

"Administrators? Classroom teachers? Resource people? Parents?" The group decided that it was "all of the above" and that the guide should aim to clarify the 1985 *Framework*, "flesh it out . . . without giving a recipe of what the *Framework* might look like in action."

The *K–8 Guide* had several parts, including discussions of why mathematics teaching needed to change, the guiding principles of teaching for understanding, and descriptions of the essential understandings of numbers, geometry, patterns, functions, logic, and probability that K–8 students need to develop. It concluded with "elaborated classroom experiences," tales of teaching that are meant to bring to life the principles and practices described in visions. These scenarios consisted of descriptions of teaching and learning (including conversations between teachers and students) accompanied by annotations.

Subsequent standards documents, including the NCTM 1989 *Standards,* have popularized this two-column format of description and annotation as a way of representing and communicating reformers' visions. In part, this genre arose in answer to the problem of the power of traditional images of mathematics teaching. The reformers wanted teachers to break out of those traditional boxes and envision mathematics classrooms that "broke the mold." Vignettes, taken from actual classrooms and experiences of these teachers and others, were drafted to help with that re-envisioning.

Like the 1985 *Framework,* the *Model Curriculum Guide* was sent to every school district. Honig's hope was that the guides would help districts sift through instructional materials during the textbook adoption process (recall that districts have their own review process once the state has adopted a short list of possibilities). And although it was purported to support the message of the 1985 *Framework,* in actuality it was a document drafted by a group with much less internal disagreement. These teachers had been working together for years on various projects. While not mindless clones of one another, they did have a shared set of commitments and experiences. The 1985 *Framework* committee, on the other hand, shared much less by way of commitment, purpose, and values.

Rewriting the Tests

Tests were also seen as a significant lever in systemic reform schemes. Grant Wiggins, a popular education consultant and speaker who advocated the use of alternative assessments, has often said that the tests are "the Trojan horse of school reform." So it is not surprising that Honig and his staff were also mobilizing resources in the State Department to reconsider the content of the state examination system, aligning it more with the *1985 Framework* and the *K–8 Model Curriculum Guide*.

Statewide testing had a checkered history in California. In 1961, the state legislature had passed a bill requiring local districts to administer achievement tests; statewide testing began in 1962. And from 1962 through 1972, the state selected several standardized tests to be administered across various grade levels. But the tests were not designed to match the state's curriculum frameworks, and they often took up to four hours to administer. In 1972, then, the CDE decided to develop its own tests and the legislature enacted the California Assessment Program (CAP). CAP provided achievement data (in reading, mathematics, and writing) on schools and districts for grades 3, 6, and 12. From 1972 to 1983, the CAP program staff worked on the refinement of their matrix sampling and the application of item response theory so as to maximize the reliability of group scores. Scores on these tests were reported for schools and districts, never for individual students. All the tests emphasized the assessment of basic skills and knowledge.

In 1976, the legislature had also passed the California Pupil Proficiency Law (PPL), requiring districts to evaluate students in grades 7, 9, and 11. The law mandated the use of criterion-referenced tests, but districts were allowed to pick or develop their own. Within three years, the law was recognized as a failure. An early evaluation showed that only 8 percent of students did not graduate and 1 percent of students were denied a diploma as a result of a district's proficiency test. In 1980, researchers found that 80 percent of the school districts were using locally developed tests, which meant that there was considerable variation in quality and content of testing programs statewide. Further, there was no possibility of cross-district comparisons. Concerned with a lack of comparability and the considerable variation in quality, the state published a set of guidelines for helping districts improve their testing procedures.

By the time Honig took office, then, statewide testing was a muddle. Students in grades 3 (CAP), 6 (CAP), 7(PPL), 9 (PPL), 11 (PPL), and 12 (CAP) were tested, but the scores were not comparable, and the quality of tests varied widely. The tests were not aligned with the curriculum, and most of the time tested only "the basics." When test scores came out, it was hard to use them wisely.

In 1983, the California legislature passed the Hughes-Hart Education Act, the most comprehensive school reform package in the state's history. As noted above, the act granted $800 million in new funds for over eighty public education reforms to increase the length of the school day, refocusing the curriculum on the teaching of thinking rather than solely on the teaching of basic skills, and a mentor teacher program, among others. A critical piece involved putting more substance and coherence into the state assessment system. It expanded the scope of CAP, requiring that "all pupils in grades 3, 8 and 10, in addition to those in grades 6 and 12, be tested for achievement." The CDE staff busily got to work. They developed and implemented the new eighth-grade test, direct writing assessments that were to be used in grades 8 and 12, as well as the development of new portions of the grade 12 test. In 1987, in part to support the spirit of the *1985 Framework,* open-ended questions were piloted in the twelfth-grade version of CAP. The goal of these additions was to introduce more performance-based assessment into the testing system. Problems were designed to elicit multiple solutions, and students were required to explain their reasoning. One such item displayed two geometric figures: an isosceles triangle and a hexagon with a chunk missing. The question asked students to write a set of instructions for how another student could reproduce the drawings without ever seeing the actual figures. Flyers informing educators about the changes included the following sample problem:

> A friend of yours just moved to the United States and must ride the bus to and from school each day. The problem is that your friend does not know how to count American money.
>
> Help your friend find the right coins to give the bus driver. A bus ride costs 50 cents. Exact change is needed, and only nickels, dimes, and quarters may be used.
>
> Draw and write something on an 8 ½ × 11" sheet of paper that will show and explain to your friend what coins may be used for the bus ride.[43]

By December 1989, items like these became a regular fixture on the twelfth-grade CAP, along with the more familiar multiple choice test items. Responses were formally scored by a group of fifty educators, mainly teachers, who met for four days of intensive training and scoring.

Gradually, the move toward rewriting the tests gained momentum. The Department of Education conducted conferences around the state, proclaiming the need to move "Beyond the Bubble." In 1990, Walter Denham explained:

> For the public, administrators, and teachers alike, assessment that is used to measure school success in mathematics—most especially the assessment that is used for accountability purposes—is high stakes. It unavoidably drives curriculum: "What you test is what you get." It is futile to object to "teaching for the test." Given this inevitability, the only assessment strategy that can succeed is to have tests that we *want* taught to. This requires the development and implementation of assessment that measures students' productivity, their performance on tasks that require mathematical thinking in pursuit of a result that has meaning to the student. As these tasks will have essentially the same character as instructional tasks matching *Framework* specifications, their use will support new instructional as well as assessment purposes.

Denham's words are important here. He says "test," but he talks about "performance" and "assessment." Language—and its use—became very important in the reform of mathematics teaching, for words carry meanings and histories. "Tests," for example, conjured up multiple choice, true and false, and closed-answer tests of basic skills—tests easily passed if a student had developed some test taking skills and knew the basics. Indeed, a minor industry exists to help schools prepare students for standardized tests; districts often purchase special series designed to teach test taking skills (*Zap the Cap!* was one booklet we found in many California schools we visited). Experienced teachers have always worried about how these exercises detract from their curriculum, displacing time that might be used for teaching ideas rather than for test taking strategies. Granted, spending time learning to take tests well can be beneficial for anyone, but when such exercises elbow out time spent on ideas, teachers become concerned.

Teachers' concerns about assessment began gaining attention in the mid-1980s; by this time—both in California and nationally—there was a growing dissatisfaction with traditional tests. In addition to the time they soaked up, teachers complained that standardized tests seldom measured important knowledge and skill. Because of the overly technical language associated with testing and measurement, historically there had been a chasm between teachers and test developers. As Eva Baker points out, tacit bargains ensued where testing experts operated virtually independently of educators. In the late 1980s and early 1990s, there was a push toward de-mystifying testing. Questions were raised about the misleading impact of standardized tests, which led to serious questions about the norms that had been established and used repeatedly. Moreover, with the concomitant interest in international comparisons, American tests were inadequate; other countries regularly used essays and other indicants of student achievement. Much less concerned about validity, reliability, and general-izability, other countries were more flexible and inventive about their ac-countability systems. The United States, if it wanted to participate in viable international comparisons, would have to open up its testing repertoire, na-tionally and locally.[44]

Talk shifted from "testing" to "assessment," a linguistic turn meant to hold much meaning. Assessment was meant to invoke new conceptions of testing, methods that moved beyond the multiple choice measurement of superficial understandings to knowledge and skill that was considered more "authentic." Researchers began exploring alternative assessment methods—often drawing on work that had been done in other fields like medicine, law, and architecture—for ideas. Subsequently, talk of perform-ance and authentic assessment—which required students to perform a task (conduct a laboratory assignment, for example, or explain how they rea-soned through a mathematics problem), as well as talk of portfolios (com-pilations of student work that demonstrated growth over time using a variety of artifacts)—became de rigueur. Vermont experimented with a statewide portfolio system in mathematics and writing. The Educational Testing Service collaborated with a number of school districts in the devel-opment of "alternative assessments."

The underlying logic across these efforts went something like this: teachers teach to the test. When the test is bad, this means a "dumbing down" of curriculum. Therefore, if we change the tests, make them more challenging and more authentic, it will be okay for teachers to teach to the test. As Wiggins explained, "Rather than seeing tests as only after-the-fact devices for checking up on what students have learned, tests should be seen as instructional, the central vehicle for clarifying and setting intellectual standards. The recital, debate, play, or game . . . the 'performance' is not the check-up, it is the heart of the matter."[45]

By 1991, the CDE had issued *A Sampler of Mathematics Assessment*, which described four types of assessment being pilot-tested for the CAP: open-ended problems, enhanced multiple choice, "investigations," and portfolios.[46] Teachers were invited to reinvent their assessments and use a broad array of alternative methods for testing what students knew.

Moving Toward Alignment

New curriculum frameworks, new guidance (along with the new genre of illustrative vignettes), new textbooks, new tests. Every time we visited the Department of Education between 1987 and 1990, the place was abuzz with innovation and activity. State department staff were busy calling meetings of committees of educators—most often teachers. Everyone was excited, encouraged by the possibilities, committed to the work. The activity extended even further than this sample of activities, for other professional organizations and networks were also abuzz. (I will explain some of this related activity shortly.)

It was an extraordinarily rational view of education: line up the levers, make sure they were in agreement, provide a clear and consistent message about mathematics teaching. Teaching will change, learning will increase. It was also an extraordinarily hopeful view.

Underlying all these efforts was a vision of mathematics that was different from the one I experienced as a child. Although there was some internal variation in how "radical" the vision was, everyone agreed on some basic principles, and many of the teachers had been using their classrooms as laboratories for finding better instructional methods. There was remarkable agreement within the educational establishment that participated in this early stage of the reforms.

How was this possible? The vision certainly wasn't Bill Honig's, for he worried about the zealous views of some participants, and his specialty was language arts. Besides, multiple committees wrote these policies. And it was not the same cast of characters every time. So how was it possible that so many different people—the authors of the 1985 *Framework* and the 1987 *K–8 Model Curriculum Guide,* the teachers who helped write the new test items—had developed some collective sense about teaching mathematics differently?

4   Earlier Reforms and Their Legacies

Our history is a history of optimism dashed and optimism revived.
—James G. March

Joseph Featherstone once called us the United States of Amnesia, for we often forget or conveniently remember the past.[1] Yet understanding California's past efforts in education sheds important light on how the *1985 Framework* arose, where the teacher-leaders came from, and who inspired them. Understanding that past will also help us see why the subsequent backlash was so virulent. Before continuing with a description of the very busy State Department of Education and its systemic reform activities, then, we'll briefly consider here some of the historical roots of this 1980s math reform.

A Glance at Past Frameworks

That there was consensus about a vision of mathematics education— albeit achieved along a bumpy road with some disagreements—was quite remarkable. Such visions don't arise in vacuums, and the re-envisioning of mathematics classrooms by the mathematics educators who came to work on the *1985 Framework: Model Curriculum Guide,* and tests was no different. These new policies were products of a professional conversation that had been under way for years, in California and elsewhere. Echoes of those professional conversations can be heard between the lines of my earlier brief history of criticism aimed at mathematics education: decrease emphasis on drill, increase children's motivation and interest, highlight problem solving. And traces of these discussions had left a trail in California curriculum documents, starting in the early 1960s.

Before 1968, there were no frameworks in the state. However, the Cali-

63

fornia Department of Education did issue advisories intended to guide the content of mathematics instruction in the state. For example, in 1962, the CDE issued the *Strands Report,* the official report of the Advisory Committee on Mathematics to the Curriculum Commission. The advisory committee—composed of mathematicians, mathematics educators, teachers, and school personnel—worked for two years on the report. The presentation began with an introduction that sounds eerily familiar:

> Cultural changes occurring in our time have significant implications for the curriculum as a whole and for mathematics in particular. The technological revolution which is now taking place makes it imperative that every citizen have some understanding of mathematical reasoning and that, at every level of proficiency, a much larger group have an understanding of mathematical method. In addition to the traditional uses of mathematics in commerce and the physical sciences we now have mathematical models in the behavioral sciences, computers of a speed and complexity to challenge the most creative programmer, new problems in decision making, probabilistic mathematics in all areas from business to medical research to quantum mechanics, and a vast host of new applications of mathematics both old and new.[2]

The report's authors proposed a set of curricular "strands": numbers and operations, geometry, measurement, application of mathematics, functions and graphs, sets, logic, and mathematical sentences. They discussed each strand, noting "Since the current curriculum is well understood, more space is given in this report to the newer concepts. The space devoted here to a concept, therefore, is not to be construed as a measure of its importance." The authors stressed that they wished students to develop facility in computation, that a "reasonable amount of practice is required," and that "it is doubtful that either sound knowledge of principles or mastery of computation can stand well alone."[3]

The 1962 *Strands Report* paints a "dynamic" picture of good teaching: "Good mathematical instruction has a dynamic character. Pupils should be encouraged to make conjectures and guesses, to experiment and to formulate hypotheses and to understand. The applications of mathematics provide a wealth of possibilities for this kind of mathematical activity. And for many students such involvement is an important source of motivation." The authors also noted the importance of practice:

Perhaps it is sufficient to say that we urge achievement of a degree of mastery of facts and algorithms, which enables pupils to think through mathematical situations without being cluttered mentally by errors. A reasonable amount of practice is required to attain this goal. Practice should elicit thoughtful responses, establish relationships, and develop understanding. The amounts and types of practice should be adjusted to the individual needs of pupils. It is doubtful that either sound knowledge of principles or mastery of computation can stand well alone or need to stand-alone. One enhances the other not only in its usefulness but also in its attainment. . . . Knowledge gained in the absence of understanding is soon forgotten and not readily transferable to different situations.[4]

The report concluded with a list of available supplementary materials that teachers might find helpful. The list included materials published by many of the National Science Foundation–sponsored New Math projects: the Greater Cleveland Mathematics Program, the Madison Project of Webster College and Syracuse University, the San Diego Metropolitan Education Study Council, the School Mathematics Study Group, the Stanford Projects, the University of Illinois Arithmetic Project, and the University of Maryland Mathematics Project.

Five years later, the *1967–1968 Strands Report* was issued by the Statewide Mathematics Advisory Committee, which again consisted of mathematics professors (this time from UC—Berkeley, Fresno State, and the California Institute of Technology), five mathematics specialists from school districts across the state, one chair of a high school mathematics department, and an assistant to the superintendent of Fresno city schools. This report had two parts. The first briefly laid out the goals of K–8 mathematics instruction and curricula. The authors began with a description of "the climate of the classroom":

Perhaps the most significant feature of scholarly endeavor, be it mathematics, science, or the humanities[,] is its spirit of free and open investigation. There should be an infusion of this spirit into the classroom for it has important implications for good pedagogy, especially for mathematics. . . .

The most striking feature of the best presentations of mathematics is the establishment of a classroom climate under the direction of the teacher, which is pupil oriented, self-directed, and non-authoritarian in concept. In this climate, the teacher drops the role of an authoritative figure who passes judgment on what is right and wrong. Instead, he assumes the role of a guide who follows the leads of his pupils into uncharted regions. Following these leads, a teacher should frame questions which excite curiosity and encourage the pupils to exploit what they know and feel about the problem.[5]

Part two of the *1967–1968 Strands Report* was a detailed description of the content of each of this report's nine strands (a ninth strand, "problem solving," had been added to the original eight) which, the authors argued, fell into two distinct groups:

> The strands which we have selected for special emphasis split naturally into two categories. The first category includes the Strands of Number and Operation, Geometry, Measurement, and Probability and Statistics. These strands are the basic cognitive subdivisions of the mathematics curriculum itself. The other category includes the Strands of Applications, Sets, Functions, Logical Thinking, and Problem Solving. These strands are catalysts, or processes, which are present to some degree in every mathematical enterprise to facilitate mathematical analysis. No single Strand can stand by itself; together they constitute a strong viable program. To slight one Strand is to significantly weaken this program. It would be equally unfortunate to give undue emphasis to one particular Strand. A satisfactory curriculum will display and use these interdependent strengths in its development.[6]

An ad hoc committee was appointed in October 1973 to write another set of guidelines that were published as the *1974 Framework*. The authors urged teachers to place less emphasis on numeration systems and computation of fractions, and more emphasis on the improvement of attitudes, computational skills, problem solving, decimals, and the use of the metric system.

This report began by announcing the fact that the 1962 report was "far ahead of its time in many ways. This farsightedness created many problems, two of which were crucial: there was no textbook series containing the entire mathematical content recommended in the report, and teachers had not had the opportunity to develop an adequate background for teaching a program in mathematics based on the recommendations." It is clear that the authors of this document were influenced by discovery learning theorists:

> The ideal classroom climate fosters the spirit of "discovery." It also provides a variety of ways for pupils to direct their own learning under the mature, patient guidance of an experienced, curiosity-encouraging teacher. Self-directed learning requires pupil involvement in creative learning experiences that are both pupil-motivated and teacher-motivated. These experiences are seldom accomplished by "Now, here's how it goes" lectures. Instead, the teacher encourages originality, recognizing that there is more than one way to solve a problem and accepting solutions in many different forms. In the ideal classroom, credit is given to learners for their own productive thinking even when it differs from the pattern anticipated by the teacher.

Traces of other ideas that appear in later frameworks were also visible. Mention was made of the importance of manipulatives and of mathematically purposeful games (although neither was discussed in detail). It was noted that learning is "a group experience. Group behavior affects the learning process, as pupils do learn from one another. Mathematics becomes a vibrant, vital subject when points of view are argued, and for this reason interaction among students should be encouraged."

Subsequent frameworks and state curriculum documents have the same flavor. The view of mathematics education one sees through these documents suggests that progressive ideas—about both the content to be taught and the instructional strategies to be used—have long held a prominent place in state-level discourse about mathematics education. The teachers who came to the table to write the 1985 *Framework* and other documents had been part of a professional community imbued with those ideas and commitments—ideas and commitments that had roots in previous state and national mathematics education reforms. They had learned to think and talk this way in teacher preparation, professional development, research projects, and curriculum development efforts. They had—as longtime practicing teachers—also learned that this stance toward teaching mathematics worked, and that it helped more children gain confidence in and access to challenging mathematics. If these ideas had not panned out in their classrooms, these teachers—like most of their colleagues—would have abandoned the ideas and materials, replacing them with more effective ones. Of course, since research was not done on whether these reforms led to increased student achievement, this process—remarkable for the respect it afforded teachers, but limited in its empirical grounding—left open the possibility that the reforms were not adequately preparing students for the mathematics they would encounter in high school and college classrooms.

As we interviewed the teachers and leaders of mathematics reform, they referred to many professional development opportunities that had helped shape their understanding. Among the most often mentioned were Miller Math and workshops offered by Marilyn Burns Associates.

Miller Math

When we started our research, we presumed, naïvely, that the 1985 *Framework* would be the beginning of our story and that our job, as researchers, was to then trace its implementation and impact. Hindsight suggests another beginning, thirty years earlier—1956—and 2,631 miles away in Syracuse, New York. Clutching a brand new Ph.D. from MIT, Bob Davis joined the faculty of Syracuse University as a functional analyst with strong interests in classical analysis and mathematical physics. Someone suggested he hang out at Madison Junior High School in Syracuse and watch mathematics classes. Observing classes, primarily ones that served students who came from lower socioeconomic backgrounds, Davis was appalled at what he found. It appeared that these children had never had an intellectually challenging and engaging experience with mathematics. Never one to sit still, Davis decided to teach these students himself. The school was happy, the students seemed happy, Davis was happy. The Madison Project began.

It was an age of curricular reform, and Bob Davis became heavily invested in it. He continued teaching schoolchildren. Based on those experiences, both at Madison Junior High and in other settings, he began developing curriculum. Davis had very particular ideas about how to create experiences in which students could explore mathematical ideas, and his former staff members recall heated arguments about the mathematics of alternative approaches to the representation of some ideas.[7]

Davis's activities multiplied, private and public foundations expressed interest, funding rolled in, and eventually the Madison Project grew to be an umbrella organization for many interrelated activities involving both curriculum and professional development. In the early 1960s, Davis left Syracuse for Webster College in Webster Groves, Missouri. In 1966, the National Science Foundation funded a large piece of the Madison Project called "Big Cities." Davis hired around 30 people he had met in his travels. Some were professors of mathematics education, others were curriculum specialists in large school districts, still others were teachers. Everyone was enthusiastic about teaching mathematics in meaningful ways, and ready to work with teachers. At the same time, Davis canvassed large urban areas—Philadelphia, New York, Los Angeles, Chicago—locating hundreds of teachers willing to participate in two-week summer workshops. During these summer experiences, teachers would do mathematics and learn how to teach the kinds of lessons Davis had designed and tested. The Madison Project's reach was wide: over 20,000 New York teachers participated, and nearly 18,000 in Chicago.

California had been part of Davis's Big Cities Project, with sites in both Los Angeles and San Diego. In 1967, George Miller, a state legislator, sponsored the largest professional development bill for teachers that any state had ever envisioned. Called Miller Math by participants (officially the Mathematics Improvement Program Act, which was later amended in 1970), its roots were deep in Davis's Madison and Big Cities projects. The program had several components, including three experimental programs: the Specialized Teacher Program, the Mathematics Specialists Program, and the Accelerated Instruction Program. It also required the development of an achievement test in mathematics for grades 3, 6, and 8. This would enable the state to evaluate the student performance within the experimental programs, as well as statewide. Two-week summer workshops were offered to teachers in the Specialized Teachers Program. Applications ran to more than four times the number of teachers who could be accommodated. Their tuition was paid for and they received $100 of free materials. Many teachers who had participated in the Madison Project staffed these workshops.

Another component of Miller Math involved the development of "mathematics specialists." Building on the work of Project SEED (Special Elementary Education for the Disadvantaged, a program that enticed candidates for advanced degrees in mathematics to teach abstract mathematical concepts to disadvantaged children in Berkeley), this part of the program brought mathematicians into schools to teach kids, much like Davis had done. Because she had taken so many mathematics courses, Joan Akers—the teacher who later went on to be a member of both the Curriculum Commission and the 1985 *Framework* writing committee—qualified to become one such math specialist.

Some participants recall Miller Math fondly. For many of the elementary school teachers who participated, it was the first time they had had an invigorating and positive experience with mathematics. Evaluations of the experimental programs found that student achievement was significantly higher in the classrooms of teacher-participants. Students performed significantly better on measures of both comprehension and computation than did pupils whose teachers had not attended the summer workshops. Evaluation results found the Mathematics Specialists Program particularly effective in improving the mathematical achievement of students from disadvantaged areas.[8]

But like all legislatively supported endeavors, the program was subject to political winds, and funding was revoked in 1971. Summer workshops ended, teachers got other placements in their school districts, mathematicians withdrew behind the safe walls of higher education. Davis moved to the University of Illinois, Champaign-Urbana, where he headed a project that developed computer-delivered mathematics lessons to students in grades 3 through 7. This curriculum was based largely on his earlier experiences in the Madison, Big Cities, and Miller Math projects.

Meanwhile, although the projects were defunded in California, the Madison Project and Miller Math lived on. Bob Wirtz, a retired engineer who lived in Carmel, was very concerned about students' mathematical thinking and, using his considerable fortune, funded the Center for the Improvement of Mathematics Education, a not-for-profit organization committed to professional development of mathematics teachers K–12. He also started his own publishing company so that innovative materials would continue to be available to teachers.

The work also lived on in the lives of many of the early participants, including a cadre of teachers—many of them women—who came of age in the 1960s. Perhaps the most prominent of these teachers-turned-leaders was Marilyn Burns.

Marilyn Burns

The name "Marilyn Burns" popped up repeatedly early on in our investigations in California. When asked where they had gotten their ideas on how to teach mathematics, teachers and state department folks alike used Burns as an example. As Walter Denham told us, "Marilyn Burns . . . has maybe some of the clearest vision about what the mathematics should look like at the elementary level, and if I had to send people to one person to know what it's all about, I'd send them to Marilyn Burns."

Burns was an undergraduate at Syracuse University when she first met Bob Davis. I first met her at the ferry dock in Sausalito, home base for her company, Marilyn Burns Education Associates. She was dressed casually in linen and khaki, elegant shades of beige and green. Raised back east, Burns has that New York direct, guileless gaze. She says what she thinks. And she wants to know what you think. She told me immediately of her impatience with academics (including, perhaps, me); they're often too far removed from the front lines. Their language and jargon is off-putting, their sense of schools and children stale, outdated, uninformed, at times, arrogant. Educational researchers—in her book—are mostly for the birds. Burns is not a theoretician, but—as one teacher interviewed put it—a "marvelous pragmatist."

Upon graduation from Syracuse, Burns began teaching school, and several years later she began working for the Madison Project and Miller Math as a workshop leader. She stopped full-time teaching in 1970, supporting herself by giving summer workshops for teachers. She also wrote and published a series of children's books for Little, Brown, and Company, beginning with *The I Hate Mathematics! Book* in 1975. But around 1978, she started running out of money. When her car broke down, she took a job with the Learning Institute, an offshoot of *Learning* magazine, teaching summer workshops for elementary school teachers. The pay was good, the work manageable. *Learning* asked her to continue by developing a workshop that focused entirely on mathematics teaching, and Marilyn started putting together crews of people to do the work. But the Learning Institute was a high-profile "inservice" (educationese for professional development programs): they would fly in big names—George Plimpton, Studs Terkel—to visit with huge groups of teachers. Burns and her schoolteacher colleagues were not celebrities and the lack of regard they were shown (compared to the celebrities) grated on her nerves. She also doubted the value of "kamikaze" visits from talking heads. Wouldn't teachers be better served with seminars focused on the real work of teaching?

Burns thought her options were limited. With nothing but a B.A. degree, she doubted her ability to get grants. So, with a little prodding from a friend, she incorporated herself, becoming her "own grantor and own grantee." She acquired stationery and desks. She'd already developed a

course book through the work of the Learning Institute summer workshops. Book in hand, she offered—along with her friends—five or six summer workshops. Then, and now, her goals have remained the same: "The
overall goal is to make the world better for children. Math is a handy vehicle because adults don't understand it and they're fearful of it. They all think
they can read and write, but teaching math is something else. You can't
teach it if you don't understand. So the goal is to make the world better for
children in schools through mathematics. That's what it has to be about. . . .
That's how I got going."

Her original staff met in her living room, slept at her house, brain-
stormed strategies. Many of her workshop leaders were people she had met
through Miller Math. All were committed to changing mathematics teaching and learning in schools. All were struggling with "what was wrong," un-
able to articulate—at that time—what was not working. Burns chose them
because they respected teachers, cared about students, and were open to
learning new things.

Teachers themselves, Burns and her colleagues understood that the most
pressing need of teachers was materials and ideas: "make-and-take" workshops, as they were often called. But the group wanted to move it further;
they wanted to engage teachers in discussions about practice. They assumed
that activities alone wouldn't lead to good teaching. The best activities in
the world fall flat—or worse, become terribly distorted into superficial and
content-less games—in the hands of well-intentioned, good-hearted teachers who do not possess the knowledge and skill necessary to implement
them well. Burns and her colleagues wanted to create professional development materials and programs designed to respect teachers, give them what
they wanted (materials), and provide opportunities for them to acquire what
they needed (a knowledge of mathematics, a commitment to questioning
their own choices, the skills necessary to teach using a variety of methods).

The organization must have done something right, for since 1984, Burns
has offered summer workshops every year to growing numbers of teachers at over thirty-one locations in more than seventeen states. By the fall
of 1995, nearly 5,500 teachers had attended Math Solutions workshops
that year. Most (over 80 percent) were first-time attendees, participating in
Math Solutions I. This workshop became so popular that many teachers
wanted to return in subsequent summers, so Burns has developed advanced seminars—Math Solutions II and III—for alumni.

During two summers of our research, we spent several days visiting Math Solutions workshops. As staff set up for a week's work, they haul large, colorful plastic crates brimming with manipulatives and materials: Cuisenaire® rods, pattern blocks, color tiles; bags and boxes of brightly colored materials that have been designed to help students and teachers represent numerical and geometric relationships. When I was a kid, we used tongue depressors and Popsicle® sticks, bundling and unbundling groups of ten. But today, teachers can display geometric shapes on overhead projectors with transparent green triangles and red rectangles. Students can compare fractions by placing a two-thirds bar next to a one-half bar. They can stretch rubber bands across grids of pins to explore changes in shape, area, and circumference.

The Math Solutions staff are experienced teachers who know how to use these materials well in the service of developing students' mathematical knowledge. Most teach during the school year. All have years of experience listening to children. They feel valued, for Burns has handpicked them for their knowledge, skill, and character.

Throughout the workshops, participants work in small groups on mathematics problems, learn about new technologies, talk about their teaching. Energy is high, as is enthusiasm. The staff are respectful and satisfied, and humor abounds as teachers laugh at themselves and with others while solving problems. Something happens in these settings. Teachers, feeling safe and respected, often let their guard down and tackle the serious business of learning more mathematics, and pedagogy.

When she is available, Burns gives a talk, always to a standing-room-only crowd. She inevitably brings the house down. She is smart, well-educated, pragmatic. She knows it is hard to learn—math or anything else of substance. She knows that schoolteachers are underprepared, and that they need a lot of help. Burns revels in the challenges inherent in continually trying to be a better mathematics teacher. In her workshops she is as straight-up with the teachers as she was with me at the ferry dock: "Look, math is hard," she tells them, "and you need to know more to teach it well." Burns thinks the same is true for herself, and she's always questioning what she does and trying to learn from her experiences. Her talks are not canned, for she is a work in progress.

Carrying on the tradition of her mentor, Davis, Burns also teaches regularly, volunteering at a local elementary school where she can keep herself firmly grounded in the realities of practice and try out new lessons, new ideas. She collects students' work, reflects on her experiences, makes presentations to teachers and administrators. Early on, she started writing memos to herself, using her thoughts to work out ideas. Those memos became fodder for a Math Solutions newsletter. She's constantly testing her ideas, many of which eventually take the form of publications: new children's books, videotapes for teachers and parents, resource guides for educators. Encouraging other teachers to do the same, her organization has sponsored the publication of a growing number of books by practicing teachers. Burns writes "activity" books for teachers; books for children— *Math for Smarty Pants, The Book of Think, The Greedy Triangle, Spaghetti and Meatballs for All;* and books for parents—*Math: Facing an American Phobia.* Every year, she expands her reach—to parents and students and teachers and administrators.[9]

While these publications are written in the same spirit of the state and national policy documents, they are much more pragmatic and extensive. Instead of vignettes, Burns and her teacher-authors take teachers step by step through lessons, often illustrating their points with extensive samples of student work. These images of what Lee Shulman has called "the possible" are full of detail and complexity that one finds only in real classrooms. And, as David Cohen has suggested, such materials are essential to reform efforts: "Teachers would also need to examine vivid, extended examples of how other teachers helped students produce sophisticated work, along with examples of teaching that did not work. Good judgment thrives on comparisons—indeed, it cannot be cultivated without them. But few American teachers have any way to make such comparisons. A corpus of such examples would be an important proof that sophisticated teaching can be done in various circumstances, but it could also be a critical part of a curriculum from which teachers and others could learn and improve."[10]

Through her own efforts to disseminate and document her thinking about mathematics teaching and learning—as well as those of other teachers—Marilyn Burns became a beacon in the reform movement, often unwillingly, for she does not align herself with a particular ideology. When asked about her role in reform, she says: "I think of myself as a standard bearer because I set very high standards for myself. I'm always pushing myself. What I've accomplished by having my own organization is that my voice is larger. And I've made the choice to make myself more public. . . . But by choosing to write and make videotapes . . . my responsibility is then higher. So you make a standard as high as possible. And that means do only what makes sense to me—which is what I want people to have kids do—and question everything I do. And keep questioning and questioning. And keep getting better at my practice. So that everything is tied back to the children in some direct way."

Burns has not been a lone beacon, although, as she notes, her organization makes her voice more prominent. Other teachers—some of them who teach in her summer workshops or were collaborators in Miller Math—are committed to the same work, trying to improve their teaching practice, questioning everything they do. Burns's staff retreats are counted among teacher-leaders as treasured professional development experiences. Often, everyone gathers around a large seminar table and does mathematics. Bob Davis led the work at times. For teachers, these opportunities to delve into mathematics in meaningful ways satisfies a craving long felt. No teacher education or masters courses (offered by mathematics or education departments) has provided an opportunity to dive into the mathematics of elementary school in meaningful, rigorous, and thoughtful ways. Burns, with her dual commitment to teachers and to mathematics, has managed to create a satisfying marriage of the two.

Philip Cusick argues that the education "system" is much larger than the formal bureaucracy. The system consists of parents who support the swim team, others who have children with learning disabilities; local school boards, PTAs, teachers unions; the school band and the supporters of the football team; Future Farmers of America and the math club. It consists of parents and special interest groups, coalitions of people who wrap themselves around students and issues. Using Talcott Parsons's theoretical framework, Cusick argues that the educational system is "open, circular, and elastic," comprising loosely coupled collectivities—formal and not.[11]

Consistent with the logic of other systemic reformers, Bill Honig and his staff targeted levers in the formal bureaucracy. But the system within which that work went on was much larger than the tests and textbooks, the frameworks and curriculum guides. The system included other coalitions, such as the network of teachers who met with and worked for Marilyn Burns. But Burns's enterprise was only one subculture within this huge, often invisible system. Others existed, sometimes overlapping or intersecting with Burns's circle, most often independent of her organization.

The existence of these coalitions—these other parts of the enterprise of American education—turned out to be essential to Honig's efforts within the formal bureaucracy. It was teachers from these coalitions committed to the improvement of mathematics teaching and learning who staffed the policy writing committees, the Instructional Materials Evaluation Panel, the Curriculum Commission, the Curriculum Framework and Criteria Committee. In addition to Marilyn Burns Education Associates, two of the most prominent coalitions were the California Mathematics Project and the California Mathematics Council. These organizations were professional homes for the teachers who were quietly leading the reform.

5 Networks and Their Leaders: Broadcasting and Shaping Reform

Looking at learning as a demand-driven, identity forming, social act, it's possible to see how learning binds people together. People with similar practices and similar resources develop similar identities— the identity of a technician, a chemist, a lepidopterist, a train spotter, an enologist, an archivist, a parking-lot attendant, a business historian, a model bus enthusiast, a real estate developer, or a cancer sufferer. These practices in common (for hobbies and illnesses are practices too) allow people to form social networks along which knowledge about the practice can both travel rapidly and be assimilated readily.
—John Seely Brown and Paul Duguid

The ecology-of-games metaphor weans one away from images of a single, omniscient "policy maker." It suggests that there is not someone out there who could make things better if he only wanted to or if she "would only listen to me." Instead, it highlights the messiness and discontinuities in the policy process, the variety of games played by different people for different reasons and the loose linkages between those separate games. "Policy" as a chain of decisions stretching from the statehouse to the classroom is a by- product of all those games and relationships; no one is responsible for the whole thing.
—William A. Firestone

William Firestone argues for a view of the educational system that runs counter to our larger society's hopeful or naïve belief that policy—once mandated—makes a beeline for schools. Instead, he argues, the education system consists of loosely linked games: a state department game, a legislature game, a classroom game, a school district game. This view pushes on the rational idea of the formal education system, and asks us to consider a wider array of participants and communities who might have some say in education policy.

When I was in college, I played volleyball. I found out quickly that, in addition to "formal" institutions like Brown's volleyball team, there were extensive volleyball networks. One could play (as I did) for the United States Volleyball Association. You could play B, A, AA, or masters volleyball. You could also play for an American Turners club team (which I also did). Each network came with its own acronyms, its own local, state, and national tournaments. Our activities were serious. We paid dues so that we could rent the Turner hall for practices and pay the way of our volunteer coach to tournaments. We practiced two or three nights a week for three-hour stretches. We did push-ups and drills, we practiced blocking and setting. We occasionally got to scrimmage. For the most part, we voluntarily spent our free nights developing skills and knowledge through practice. We weren't extraordinary players, just ordinary people who were serious, committed, and enthusiastic about volleyball. And, although volleyball was our focus, we also became lifelong friends.

As it turns out, similar networks exist for mathematics education enthusiasts, networks that sponsor summer and weekend events. Teachers pay dues, work hard, find friends. Because these networks are not part of the "formal" education system that we set out to study, we had not planned to research them. But it became quickly clear that there was, as one informant said in a joking and kind way, a "math mafia," an extensive, sometimes invisible, underground of mathematics education organizations. Moreover, it also became clear that this subterranean world played an important role in reform: these networks were the source for many of the teachers and educators who were appointed to such California Department of Education committees as the Subject Matter Committee and the Curriculum Framework and Criteria Committee. The networks also broadcast the reforms: columns appearing in association organs were often devoted to updates of new policy developments, sometimes written by CDE staff. Later, when things became contentious, the term "mafia" would take on a more sinister meaning, for critics of the earlier reform saw these groups as impenetrable blocs of progressive educators.

Two networks were especially prominent in the talk of mathematics educators (although many more existed): the California Mathematics Project and the California Mathematics Council.

The California Mathematics Project

Given the nature of teachers' work, the existence of professional havens where one can discuss practice, trade ideas, discuss alternative theories is unusual. Schools are not built for collaboration, and teachers' schedules are not organized to support professional discourse. Professional development sponsored by school districts is often unappealing to teachers: it tends to come in the form of an outside expert, dropping in for a day, with little or no recent experience as K–12 teachers, spouting off a packaged—usually irrelevant—answer to some instructional problem. As a teacher, I always sat near the back of the room on "inservice" days, ready to sneak out at the first available minute, or surreptitiously grade papers or do the daily crossword.[1]

Despite the widespread teacher disdain for traditional inservice, many educators are hungry for help and ideas, for professional discussions with colleagues who have valuable and relevant expertise and experience. Good teachers, like Marilyn Burns, realize that the work of becoming a better teacher is never done. These teachers search out opportunities to learn, often paying for their professional development out of their own pockets. And in California, there is a virtual smorgasbord of options. For teachers interested in mathematics, one might attend a summer workshop for EQUALS, or Family Math, programs based at the Lawrence Hall of Science and devoted to providing equal access to mathematics to all racial, cultural, and ethnic groups.[2] One might sign up for Marilyn Burns's Math Solutions I, II, or III. Alternatively, one might take mathematics or education courses at a local state university. Most of the teachers we met in our travels had spent time in one or more of these programs. Many of them also had participated in a California Mathematics Project, another part of California's educational system.

The roots of the California Mathematics Project (CMP) can be traced back to the Bay Area Writing Project (BAWP), a professional development project for teachers of writing. Established in 1974 by James Gray at the University of California—Berkeley, the BAWP was based on a set of relatively simple assumptions about the kinds of experiences teachers need, want, and will learn from. Teachers are best taught by teachers (not outside consultants), the project staff assumed, for "top-down" models of professional development do not have a lasting impact on teachers' practices. The staff also assumed that teachers of writing must be writers themselves, that change takes time, and that teachers need places where they can talk about their teaching. Currently, over 4,000 teachers participate in the BAWP every year.[3]

The Bay Area Writing Project was a huge success. In 1979, the California legislature provided funding to extend the model statewide, creating the California Writing Project. Between 1982 and 1989, persuaded that this form of professional development might have implications for teachers of all subjects, the California legislature allocated funds for the development of similar subject matter projects in other disciplines, including mathematics in 1982.[4]

Historically, the state had invested in teachers' professional development through multiple, more often than not unrelated and disjointed programs. In 1987, the legislature was curious about the costs and benefits of the state's various investments in professional development. A policy study commissioned by the California Postsecondary Education Commission found that many staff development projects tended to be content-free, developed and implemented by outside "experts" who had little credibility with teachers. Teachers reported that this led to declining levels of morale and engagement.[5]

The researchers also concluded that the characteristics of effective professional development include: (1) staff development that is discipline- and grade-level-specific; (2) professional development that is organized by the central premise of teachers-teaching-teachers with a commitment to respecting teachers rather than assuming they need to be "fixed"; (3) a focus on knowledge and authority rooted in teaching that produces high levels of student achievement; and (4) long-term and explicit goals that are "clearly and consistently linked to student learning."[6]

Shortly after this report, in 1989, the California legislature wrote a professional development program that extended the structure of the California Writing Projects and embraced these four recommendations. The enterprise, entitled the California Subject Matter Project (CSMP), was a statewide professional development consortium of nine projects (covering the subject matters) and approximately one hundred regional sites. The CSMP network was administered through the Office of the President of the University of California in Berkeley, although it was a joint enterprise of the University of California and state university systems.[7] A "concurrence committee"—composed of representatives from the University of California, the CDE, CSU, the California Postsecondary Education Committee, the California community colleges, the Association of Independent California Colleges and Universities, and the Office of the Superintendent of Schools for Alameda County—oversaw the work, approved budgets, made recommendations, and contracted evaluations.

While there was some variation both in funding and structure, the projects were comparable during the initial phase of development. One CMP director explained described the process as:

> Basically bringing teachers in the summer.... Bring everybody in, discuss the big issues together, do some mathematics together. Then break off into grade level groups: high school, middle school, elementary, maybe even primary and do some specific stuff with teachers that was appropriate for their grade level.
>
> The plan was that we would teach. Put the participants in a learning situation and model for them the type of things you want them to do. And then we would have them feel that they could go back in their classroom and try some of these things out. We'd visit. We'd have them come back and talk about it. And if they could find colleagues, that would be nice.

The principles that guided the CMP were rooted in the experiences of the earlier writing projects. The CSMPs were discipline-specific, supported the development of teacher-leadership, placed a priority on serving the increasingly diverse student population in California, and involved K–16 collaboration among participants.[8] Teachers were respected. Time was made to "do" subject matter (to write, to do mathematics problems, to read).

The California Mathematics Project was one branch of the CSMP. Led by an executive director and an advisory board (comprising teachers and college faculty), the projects offered summer workshops and yearlong follow-up (each site also had a site director). Sites averaged about $100,000 per year to support their activities from the state; proactive sites then leveraged other funding through grants, with the average CSMP operating on a budget of about $187,000 each year in the late 1980s. Teacher-participants received stipends. Some sites offered monthlong summer institutes; others opted for more intensive two-week workshops. Most followed the same pattern, as described by one informant: "The typical Math Project was a four-week summer institute with a few follow-ups on Saturdays the next year." A typical calendar from the early 1990s is shown in Figure 5.1.

The learning curve was steep in the early years. Staff learned that it helped to have at least two people representing each school so that teachers would have built-in support when they returned to their buildings. The earlier you signed on administrators, the better. Staff members also learned that if you combined elementary and secondary school teachers, good things might happen. One executive director recalled a lesson from the early days: "Elementary school teachers—a lot of them—have real fears about math. Low self-esteem about math. We learned to consciously try to address that, giving them positive experiences. One of the things that I always did when I brought the K–12 people together and did math was to always try to pick some activities that I knew the high school teachers would sort of attack using formulas or something. And the elementary teachers would do it very differently. And what normally happened was they would impress the hell out of the high school teachers." Combining elementary and secondary teachers was not without its problems though, for the mathematical knowledge and skill of the participants varied widely.

The CSMP staff also learned how critical it is to create communities in which people can talk honestly, as well as how hard that is to do so. The leaders strove to help teachers overcome negative beliefs about students: "There is the notion that . . . different classes of people learn differently. Or we believe that some classes don't learn. People really believe that. They have these ongoing beliefs, and they may not even be aware of them until they've had to confront them."

In 1987, the site directors were able to convince the advisory board to approve projects for three-year cycles. Conceived as a way to alleviate the incessant writing and reporting that directors found themselves doing—and a way to give the directors and the CMP staff more time to work with teachers—the three-year idea eventually led to creative thinking about alternative CMP structures. Directors knew that teachers brought diverse interests. For some, a short-term, one-summer experience gave them what they wanted: exposure to new ideas, access to alternative materials. For others, one year whetted an insatiable appetite. Those teachers found themselves returning summer after summer (like those who returned to Math

Monday	Tuesday	Wednesday	Thursday
Opener: "Introductions" 9–11 am Rest of day spent in grade-level groups K–5 6–8 9–12	Opener: Site Director, "Introduction to Math Project and the 1992 CA Math Framework" Rest of day spent in grade-level groups K–5 6–8 9–12	Opener: "Issues of Equity and Access in Mathematics Education" Rest of day spent in grade-level groups K–5 6–8 9–12 1:45 "Survey & Graph" whole group	Opener: "An Introduction to IMP" (Interactive Mathematics Program) Rest of day spent in grade-level groups K–3 K–5 6–8 9–12 (leader from IMP)
Opener: The "Biological Basis of Thinking and Learning" 9–12 noon Rest of day spent in grade-level groups K–3 4–5 6–8 9–12	Opener: Family Math: Past, Present, Future" Rest of day spent in grade-level groups K–5 (leader from Family Math) 6–8 9–12	Opener: "Mathematical Insight Through Writing" Rest of day spent in grade-level groups K–5 6–8 9–12	Opener: "Broadening the Trail into Mathematics at All Levels" Rest of day spent in grade-level groups K–5 6–8 9–12 "Paper folding and Number Theory" All—1:45 "Tessellations"
Opener: "Assessment: Who's Doing the Learning?" Rest of day spent in grade-level groups K–5 6–8 Curriculum Units 9–12	Opener: "Mathematics in the Concrete" Rest of day spent in grade-level groups K–5 6–8 9–12	Opener: "Teaching Mathematics in a Language-Diverse Classroom" Rest of day spent in grade-level groups K–5 6–8 Implementation strategies 9–12	Opener: "The Eighth Strand: What Is Discrete Math?" Rest of day spent in grade-level groups K–5 6–8 (math case studies) 9–12 (morning presenter)
Opener: "Mathematical Card Tricks" 9–11 am Rest of day spent in grade-level groups K–5 6–8 9–12 Focus on Implementation Issues (3–12th)	Opener: "Getting Deeper into Problem Solving" Presentation skills at grade levels Rest of day spent in grade-level groups K–5 6–8 9–12 (morning presenter)	Opener: "Something Mathematical You Always Wanted to Know (or Understand) But Were Afraid to Ask" Mini-Asilomar (Day One!) A multitude of magnificent workshop sessions planned, conducted, and attended by participants (like you!) to fill our last two days	Mini-Asilomar (Day Two!), More Wonderful Sessions! An afternoon of epicurean delights at the picnic. The end of the Institute, but the beginning of a beautiful relationship . . .

Figure 5.1. Typical CMP Calendar

Solutions for Math Solutions II, then III). Interested in more than just finding new materials, these teachers became potential leaders:

> Not all teachers want to make that commitment to three years. That's okay. So there are places for the teacher who wants to come and learn a little bit of mathematics or learn a little bit about assessment and how to teach and stuff like that. Those people aren't going to be the leaders. The leaders are people that are going to be thinking about things like: "How do I facilitate this?" "How do I run these workshops?" "What do we do about assessment?" They are people who are looking at the much larger picture.
>
> In most cases, a lot of projects throw out the net. A lot of teachers come, but not many will really be leaders. What do you do with those people who really do emerge? How do you keep them connected?

The commitment to teacher-leadership was not unique to the CMPs; it was a statewide (soon to be national) phenomenon, appearing in the rhetoric of most professional development projects. One director explained:

> Basically what happened is, we started out as a project that brought teachers into the summer and then developed them during the year. Sort of a natural growth was that we eventually said, "Hey, we can't do this forever. We're not going to reach all the teachers." "Teachers Teaching Teachers" is the model we want to go to. So now we've been focusing on leaders. They should be bringing people in and they should be helping other teachers. How that happens varies . . . to different degrees because of who was in charge and how experienced the site is, whether it was a few years old or a million years old. But that's where we're all heading now. . . . It doesn't mean we shouldn't be doing other things. But this has to be a different level. We need to be supporting this level of teacher. Ten years ago we had no idea what this would blossom into. It's amazing now to look at leadership and what it's become.

Nurturing teachers so that they might teach other teachers was not a new idea. Decades of experience and research have suggested that if teachers do not understand or believe in a reform, it is unlikely to take root. In the 1960s, for instance, researchers found it impossible to develop a "teacher-proof" textbook, noting that no matter what a textbook contains, teachers adapt texts to suit their needs, preferences, students, knowledge, experience, and skill.

Educators in the 1980s and 1990s took these lessons to heart, and argued for professional development as the jewel in the crown of reform. Without teacher support, no change would take hold, they argued. Critical to high-quality professional development and reform, they went on to argue, are teacher-leaders whose credibility and knowledge is valued by their peers. This point was made repeatedly in national reports issued around this time, including statements from the Carnegie Commission Task Force on Teaching as a Profession and the Holmes Group (a coalition of deans of schools and colleges of education). Both groups argued that if large-scale change was a national education goal, teachers—especially teacher-leaders—would have to play a central role.

The irony of claiming that teachers had to lead a reform movement aimed more often than not at their own teaching was not lost on reformers. As Judith Lanier, leader of the Holmes Group, noted: "Paradoxically, teachers are the butt of most criticism, yet singled out as the one best hope for reform."[9] Thus, teachers were seen as both part of the problem and its solution. Many elementary school teachers in the United States, for example, lack adequate knowledge of mathematics (and are scared of mathematics as well).[10] Many secondary school teachers do nothing but lecture and assign photocopied readings and worksheets. Still, teachers work with students every day. They may have weaknesses (as do we all), but they're all we've got. Effective professional development programs must walk a fine line between respecting teachers' knowledge and beliefs and challenging them to learn more and change. Outside experts who visit a classroom for a day or two are not compelling enough to catalyze fundamental change. Other teachers might be. And so such organizations as the California Mathematics Project worked to create summer workshops (and meetings throughout the school year) that built on what teachers knew, and pushed them to know more, all the while using other teachers to do the teaching.

During our research, we visited four different CMP sites. Although we observed some variation, the ethos and activities among these sites were more similar than different. As in the Math Solutions workshops, spirits and energy were always high, chatter friendly. Teachers, teacher-leaders, teacher-educators, professors of mathematics, and state department people alike were welcomed and respected for their unique experiences.[11]

Workshop walls were inevitably papered with participants' work. Each day was structured similarly: participants arrived informally each morning around 8 o'clock. Typically, a question, task, or problem would be on the board to greet participants: estimate the number of candies in a glass jar, vote for your favorite summer movie, guess what the next number in a series will be.

The work of the day varied. Whole groups met often, learning about innovations in assessment or changes in policy, discussing reforms, or engaging in mathematics activities. Small groups also met often, designing curricula or discussing grade- or age-specific issues. Typically, a lunch break and bathroom breaks occurred between speakers or activities. Presentations involved new curriculum and new assessments, research findings and policy developments. Mathematicians often taught the teachers about a relevant mathematical topic. The atmosphere was relaxed but serious. Everyone seemed eager to learn, happy to be there, interested.

And mathematics was omnipresent. We found mathematics problems at the beginning of the day and at the end. We saw teachers using numbers or tables, estimating and graphing on a regular basis. In every workshop we visited, between 30 and 60 percent of the time was spent on mathematics-related activities; typically the figure hovered around 50 percent. Other time was devoted to learning about technology, pedagogical philosophies, and various local and national reform efforts.

Activities varied. Generating graphs, collecting data, and surveying participants were staples of every CMP we visited. Artifacts of surveys were taped or tacked to walls—large white sheets of paper filled with bar graphs, pie charts, Venn diagrams, and the like—each capturing tidbits of information about the teacher-participants.

The activities that churned out this mathematical wallpaper often function as opening acts to the day's main attraction. Early morning graphing opportunities got the day going mathematically, inviting participants to "do" mathematics. In many such instances, teachers played multiple roles: offering and gathering data, analyzing and displaying results. Less visibly during our visits, teachers sometimes also played the role of analyst, interpreting the charts and graphs.

Although the activities were mathematical, mathematics seemed not their sole purpose. Graph making sometimes served as an icebreaker. On the first day of one summer institute, for example, participants found three easels upon entering the room. The first included an enthusiastic welcome accompanied by instructions (Figure 5.2).

Food was spread out on a table in the back of the room, and participants deferred graph making until they had some coffee. From 8 until 8:30 a.m.,

Good Morning!
Please
—sign in
—find your name badge
—complete the "have you seen" graph
and the "how you're doing" graph

Figure 5.2. CMP Welcome Poster

teachers and teacher-leaders ate and talked, filling in the sheets on two other easels. One survey concerned two recently released films: *The Flintstones* and *Like Water for Chocolate* (Table 5.1). The second asked teachers to evaluate their "progressiveness" in math reforms (Figure 5.3). The participants were clustered on the right end of these continua, especially in the case of "using some new curricula," "writing in math," and "using models/manipulatives." The only exception to these progressive self-appraisals concerned use of technology. That found most people nearer the traditional end.

During one such workshop, Juanita, the institute's leader, grabbed the group's attention at 8:30. She introduced herself, welcoming everyone with, "Introductions are important, you know." She was careful to model good leadership skills for them, she said, because she was hopeful she would be able to call on them to lead workshops in a similar way over the next few years. Juanita then summarized the movie graph, listing the number of Xs in each table cell. "There are six people who have seen *The Flintstones*," she noted. One participant chimed in, "Those must be parents of small children." Juanita took a poll to check this hunch, only to find that the woman who made the comment was the only one who had young children. Juanita then quipped, "Your conjecture, then, was [pause] not quite. . . ." Her tempo slowed, and her voice trailed off without finishing the statement.

Next, Juanita asked, "Does anyone know what statisticians call this type

Table 5.1. CMP Movie Poll

		The Flintstones	
		Yes	No
Like Water for Chocolate	Yes	xx	xxxxxxx
	No	xxxx	xxxxxxxxx

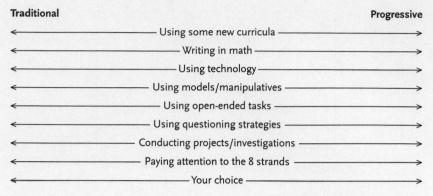

Figure 5.3. Poll: How Are We Doing in Mathematics Education?

of chart?" No one answered. Then one teacher ribbed her warmly, "I bet *you* do." (Teachers know the difference between a question that is fishing for the right answer and an open-ended one.) Laughing, Juanita replied, "This is for your edification: It's a two-by-two contingency table." She briefly discussed other types of tables, explaining that each participant would be required to prepare a similar graph during the course of the session.

This kind of activity appeared to be part of the CMP's standard repertoire. In another workshop we visited, every day a teacher presented a "Question of the Day" accompanied by data from the participants. The walls of this institute, too, were papered with previously completed charts: surveys listing favorite sodas and sports teams; bar graphs and pie charts, a few tessellations. There were also personal surveys of teachers, including number of children (mode: 0; median: 1; mean: 1.49), travel time to the project site (forty minutes on average), highest degree earned (almost half the participants had master's degrees), and political party. There was also a Venn diagram indicating that five participants had email, almost all used computers for word processing, and one-third used computers for both grading and word processing.

A second kind of mathematics-related activity involved discussing (and sometimes creating) open-ended mathematics problems. These problems were often presented in the context of the new assessments. Given the central role that policy makers initially envisioned for alternative and more authentic assessment, it made sense that most CMPs spent time helping teachers learn about those efforts.

At one CMP, for instance, the local math and science coordinator, Ally, arrived as a guest presenter on the topic of "open-ended questions." Ally has had some involvement in the New Standards Project, which she explained as "an assessment system with world class standards that could be used nationwide."[12] She said she was good at mathematics because she could memorize, and she loved mathematics so much that she got a master's degree in it. "I'm not going to talk at you because I don't believe that's the way to teach," Ally began. After putting in a plug for joining the California Mathematics Council (the state affiliate of the National Council for Teachers of Mathematics), she set the participants to work on an item entitled "Design a Corral" (Figure 5.4).

The participants worked quietly on the problem for ten minutes, until Ally asked them to stop. She then explained that fourth- and eighth-grade students did poorly on the item, often confusing area and perimeter. A secondary teacher, Tim, whispered, "I'm sure a lot of teachers in this room did poorly on it, too." There was no discussion of the teachers' work on this problem.

Ally then launched into a discussion of the importance of reforming assessment. Old tests measure unimportant things and we need students to make sense of ideas and explain their thinking, she argued, showing an overhead that explained how and why new assessments would be situated in interesting contexts; involve several math concepts simultaneously; and provide students with several, alternative solution paths. "As a teacher grading them," Ally explained, "you have to value all of these different ways even if they are not your *preferred* way." No one said anything about some answers being right, some wrong. Or what to do about that.

Participants then raised questions. Some were concerned about time limits. Tim went against the progressive grain, saying, "Someone who can use the formula should score higher than someone who counted the squares to find the area." Ally countered with the argument that students might use formulas without understanding them. "But our society values speed," he replied. Tim argued that if a student uses the formula sensibly, he should score higher, since he has a more efficient, general method. Students learn at different rates and in different ways, insisted Ally. "Wouldn't you rather have them forever counting squares and get it right than have them memorize something they don't understand?" Tim didn't respond immediately. Ally added, with a gleeful hint of sarcasm, "Oh this will be fun. But let me

Design a Corral

Tim needs your help finding the best design for his corral. Tim has looked at lots of designs, and he has decided two things:

1) He wants a four-sided corral (a rectangle or a square)
2) He wants to choose the corral design that gives his horse the biggest possible area.

Remember, Tim has 18 units of fence to use.

In the space below, show all the four-sided corral designs Tim can make with 18 units of fence. Label them so that Tim can see which one has the biggest area.

Tim bought his fence units from a store that sells them in sets. Here is a chart from the store:

Small set: 12 units

Medium set: 18 units

Large set: 24 units

Tim shows your design for the 18-unit set to Anne, the store owner. Anne likes your design. She wants you to draw four-sided designs that will have the largest possible areas for the small and large sets of fence units.

On the next page, show the store's customers how to design corrals with the largest area.

1) Make a diagram showing the four-sided design with the largest possible area for each set.

Small	12-unit set
Medium	18-unit set
Large	24-unit set

2) Give the area for each design.

3) Describe how you worked out the designs that have the largest possible areas. Explain how to find the largest possible area for any number of fence units.

Figure 5.4. Corral Problem

go on." She then talked about the politics surrounding the implementation of new assessments.

Next Ally presented examples of student work, soliciting participants' reactions to the scoring. "What will a mathematically powerful student *do* with this problem?" Ally asked, suggesting that teachers need to attend to a problem's central mathematical idea. "What would we expect students to do with such problems?" she asked. "Explore relationships and formulate hypotheses," she continued, "demonstrate understanding through diagrams, graphs, charts or other methods; construct explanations that communicate the findings effectively." Ally did not mention that students also need to, at some point, confirm correctness.

Ally highlighted multiplication as an example of how "old" ways of teaching mathematics do not work for many students. Her assertions were based on teachers' experience—the accepted faculty-room folklore of teaching—not on research, and many participants nodded in agreement (not Tim). She showed some examples of "old" types of multiplication problems, contrasting these with open-ended items designed to tap students' understanding. She mentioned that she wants students to know their multiplication facts; otherwise, how could students make sense of the results on their calculators? "Sometimes memory is just faster than a calculator," a teacher remarked. Ally agreed.

Ally continued putting examples of open-ended items on the overhead projector, explaining variations on the items, occasionally asking questions: "Is there only one answer for this question?" (Yes.) "Are there wrong answers to the question?" (Yes.) Because the discussion of scoring and philosophy took about fifty minutes, there was little time for an in-depth exploration of the complicated nature of these items and the questions surrounding their use.

Then Ally asked participants to "take a curriculum area, and by yourself, for the next ten minutes, jot down some ideas for open-ended items at your grade level. Think about what a traditional problem would look like and how it could be different. Then share these ideas with your group, and then together develop one or two items and put them on a transparency and share them."

After working individually, groups had about fifteen minutes to work together on developing one item. One group of middle school mathematics and science teachers developed an open-ended task about a pizza party. As they talked about the task, there was confusion regarding what they thought the task should be about. No one discussed the relevant curriculum area or mathematical ideas. Instead, the discussion centered on how to make pizza an open-ended problem. When they could not agree on what the constraints of the problem should be, they left the problem with few constraints and asked students to fill in missing information. In the end, their problem read:

> You are inviting 9 friends over for a pizza party. You have $40, pizzas are round and square—which pizza would be the best buy? What additional information would you need?

Groups then shared tasks with each other. Before beginning, Ally announced ground rules about sharing, including the expectation that the tasks could always be improved. With little time left, there was no discussion about such improvements. There was also no discussion about which mathematical areas the groups had worked on and how (or whether) these problems capture the relevant mathematics. In addition to the pizza problem, there were problems that involved arranging tiles and sugar cubes, a brownie recipe problem, a question about the base-10 number system, a probability problem about drug testing, and this problem involving averages:

> The average (mean) of 5 scores is 75. What are some possibilities for individual test scores?

With regard to this question Ally asked, "Does that get at the concept? It sure does!" There was no further discussion. Summing up, Ally said, "Open-ended questions must be part of your teaching all the way through!" She gave an example of a teacher who plans to ask students to explain their thinking in every answer. She encouraged them to try this, too.

A great deal of ground was covered in this session. Ally talked about the solutions to the corral problem, about the value of open-ended assessment questions, about the politics and reality of alternative forms of testing, scoring rubrics. She also seemed interested in helping teachers question their own assumptions: Tim's assumption that using a formula is better, for example. These examples are a small subset of the long list of things California teachers need time to learn about and reflect upon. If the CMP were aiming solely to help teachers get "up to speed" on the *1985 Framework*—a complex document that raised many questions about teaching and learning—the project staff would have a full agenda. But that is not their only aspiration.

At the workshops, teachers were informed about political and educational movements and debates at the state level. They talked about professional organizations like the California Mathematics Council and other professional development opportunities. They explored new curricula. And discussions were not restricted to California initiatives. Teachers also learned about national reform efforts—the NCTM 1989 *Standards*, for example— and they discussed systemic reform initiatives in other states. They talked about the connections between writing and technology with mathematics, the use of manipulatives and open-ended tasks, new questioning strategies and investigations, portfolios and performance assessment. They learned about Family Math, EQUALS, Math Solutions. The list seemed endless.

Teachers need to know about many things in order to make wise professional choices. In a study of another set of California-based networks— the Urban Mathematics Collaboratives—researchers found that teachers need to acquire knowledge of professional community, education policy, and subject matter if they are to become "empowered."[13] There is a lot to learn, and professional development programs like the CMP face the same problem that any teacher faces when deciding about "depth versus breadth." How does one balance attention to a range of topics while not reducing everything to the superficial? How does one create professional development programs that do not become dangerous whirlwind tours in which nothing gets explored in depth and teachers leave with a false sense of confidence, knowledge, and skill?

Complicating things further are potential conflicts between some of the goals and commitments of such professional development. Consider networking: as a goal, it is partially met by bringing in a wide variety of guest speakers, often "experts" in a specific domain. Yet these guest speakers can turn workshops into revolving doors of information and ideas. Consider also the inherent tension between encouraging teachers to take on leadership positions while you also challenge what they know ("Here, be confident and lead other teachers, but, by the way, maybe you don't know your math."). While difficult to talk about at times, teachers leading teachers is a questionable practice when teacher-leaders do not have sound mathematical knowledge.

We might also note the absence of a professional discourse in teaching that would allow, for example, Ally and Juanita to push and to be pushed by, for example, Tim. Schools, especially elementary schools, are places in which teachers have little experience discussing their work and little time to do so. People tend to be polite, keep ideas to themselves, and avoid confrontation and debates. As Seymour Sarason has observed: "Schools have long had reputations as polite places—places where everyone abides by the rules, and no one confronts too directly. Or schools have been places where many engage in covert behavior. Teachers who disagree with decisions complain in private and ignore the decisions in practice."[14]

As Sarason notes, "neither polite places nor covert places" enable reform. Bringing teachers to a summer workshop in which you want them to take risks, explore their thinking, learn new things is no simple feat. Developing the trust, mutual respect, and community necessary for learning and risk taking is hard. It takes time. Asking teachers to challenge the ideas of other teachers is harder still, for it goes against the grain of the culture of most school teaching. Asking teachers—practicing professionals—to examine their own (lack of) mathematical knowledge is often seen as rude and confrontational. Furthermore, participation here is voluntary—these teachers don't have to stay. So how are teacher-leaders and teachers to challenge one another when any one who doesn't like the experience can leave? This is just one of the many challenges that face professional development that aims to help teachers learn and to respect what they bring. CMP staff were masterful at building professional élan and enthusiasm.

High spirits and mutual respect are necessary, but not sufficient, conditions for high-quality professional development. Teachers need to be immersed in and learn about important mathematical ideas. They need to be taught by teachers who are pedagogically skillful and mathematically accomplished. There were occasions when we witnessed sound mathematics teaching by university mathematicians and mathematics educators, but those occasions were not as prominent as one might hope. More frequent were sessions like that led by Ally, chock-full of important information about instruction, reform, and assessment, and weak on mathematics. Teachers need to learn, to use Ally's example, that there is a middle ground between "forever counting squares" and "memorizing something they don't understand." Unfortunately, with so little time and so much to do, we seldom observed work that helped teachers learn about that middle ground in which fluid mastery of an algorithm is accompanied by conceptual understanding.

The pizza party problem is not a good problem. In fact, it is a nonproblem in its current form. You have forty dollars, and you can buy round or square pizzas. The problem's parameters are unclear. It is not a well-designed and conceptualized open-ended problem. The teachers who helped develop it needed to know that, and they needed to learn how to develop better problems. Otherwise, the CMP staff members run the risk of sending teachers with little knowledge and skill back into classrooms to use any old problem in their teaching and call it "reform-minded" math. Similarly, the averages problem is underconceptualized. More conversation would be needed to develop a sense of when and why a teacher might use such a problem. Otherwise, its lack of specificity would lead to wasted curricular time.

For teachers with weak subject matter knowledge and little experience participating in mathematical discussions, challenging their emerging ideas about mathematics problems might be difficult. People close down, tune out, refuse to participate. Facilitating discussions in which teachers confront their own mistakes in public, among other adults, requires grace, skill, and respect (on the part of the teacher-participants and the teacher-leaders). Ally, for example, was not prepared to have such a discussion—maybe because she did not want to scare people off, maybe because her own knowledge of mathematics was not sufficient. We don't know.

My analysis of CMP resonates with the experience of Hung-Hsi Wu, a mathematician at the University of California, Berkeley and member of the CMP advisory board in the late 1990s, who spent one summer visiting several CMP sites on his own. Wu, too, was impressed with what the sites accomplished with their limited budgets and time. Yet he, too, worried about the depth of the pedagogical and mathematical knowledge offered to participants. He noted that the CMPs were able to whet participants' appetites for mathematical explorations, perhaps inspiring them to see and wonder about mathematics in new ways. But inspiration is the first step in a long, often arduous journey in learning mathematics. That longer journey was not made available to participants.[15]

The experienced members of the CMP staff knew how difficult it is to build a teacher-leader cadre that can rise to this challenge. The CMP depended on participants learning over time. And despite its flaws, the CMP did nurture much professional growth. In one study, researchers estimated that teacher-leaders leave the CMP to work with approximately 15 to 30 percent of the state's teachers.[16] Many of these teacher-leaders are more skilled than Ally, who was just starting to learn about teaching teachers. Knowledgeable, reflective, and thoughtful, these more experienced teacher-leaders bring with them knowledge and skill in the areas of mathematics and teaching, teachers' learning, schools, and communities. Like Marilyn Burns, these teacher-leaders (many of whom are women) were nurtured by and then nurtured the very subcultures that contributed to the CDE's efforts to capture professional consensus. It is to those teacher-leaders that I now turn.[17]

Teacher-Leaders

The secret to life is to have a task, something you devote your entire life to, something you bring everything to, every minute of the day for your whole life. And the most important thing is—it must be something you cannot possibly do![18]

Judy Mumme leads teachers into places where they might learn. She graduated from high school in 1961, and spent one term in college before dropping out. For several years, she worked as a "junior engineer" in aerospace, got married, and decided to go back to college. She loved school, breezed through, majoring in biology, while taking a lot of mathematics. She never thought to be a teacher, and had been accepted into a doctoral program at UCLA in vertebrate morphology and paleontology.

It was then that her parents and husband "put their foot down," explaining, "This is ridiculous. Enough is enough. You should do what females are supposed to do, and if you want to do something with your college, why don't you become a teacher?" So Mumme went back to school and got her teaching credentials in the late 1960s. In 1970, she was hired to teach middle school mathematics in a semirural setting in a school where 50 percent of the children were Hispanic.

Teaching surprised her. She loved it—she adored the kids and started to search out ways to learn more about how to teach them. In 1971, she participated in the California Demonstration Schools program, where she learned about individualized instruction. By 1973, when she was department chair in her school, she had instituted the program for all eighth graders, "detracking" the class, even though it meant teaching forty-five kids at a time. Traditionally, children had been tracked into different classes based on assumptions about their abilities. Yet Mumme had witnessed how such tracking (intentionally or not) protected the status quo, enabling white, middle-class students to excel while minority students and students whose first language was not English were marginalized, steered into unchallenging classes with a watered-down curriculum.[19] Mumme saw these patterns play out in action and worked hard to counter these traditions.

Mumme dropped out of teaching for a while to have her own children, and returned in 1977, when she attended a two-week K–8 summer institute. "It was like my awakening," she recalled, realizing that "someday I'd really like to do what these people are doing . . . professional development."

In 1978, Mumme took a year off from teaching and got a master's degree in mathematics education. She then returned to middle school teaching for another five years. She then moved to the high school and quickly became the school's professional development coordinator. This provided her with multiple opportunities to learn: she joined committees, participated in the district's Madeline Hunter training, and, in 1982, received her administrative credential.

The first year of the California Mathematics Project, Mumme attended a summer institute focusing on equity and mathematics education. That, she declares, "was the absolute turning point for me." Shortly thereafter, Mumme left high school teaching to work part time on a National Science Foundation project and part time in one of California's Tech Centers. The next year, she and the CMP director wrote a proposal to the NSF for a project called Project TIME—Teachers Improving Mathematics Education. When the proposal was accepted, Mumme became the project's full-time director. Two years later, she was selected to be on the NCTM *1989 Standards* writing team, and three years after that she was a member of the California Mathematics Framework committee. When Project TIME ended, she took over the California Mathematics Project at her site full time, later leaving that to direct a statewide professional development program called the Mathematics Renaissance Project. As part of that work, she invited nationally renowned scholars to work with teacher-participants. She designed teams of collaborating teachers who visited one another's classrooms and supported one another's learning. She asked James Stigler, a researcher who was just gaining national recognition for a videotape study involving international comparisons of mathematics teaching as part of the Third International Mathematics and Science Study (TIMSS), to teach her how to use his methods in order to study the teaching of her participants. She continued to conceptualize projects related to mathematics teaching and leadership development.

Many women who went on to be teacher-leaders in the mathematics education community in California have similar stories to tell. Judy Kysh, for instance, entered the University of California—Berkeley in 1958. She—like me almost twenty years later—knew she wanted to be a teacher, but was unclear about what she would teach. She took the first three semesters of calculus, but eventually dropped out because the courses were poorly taught and she couldn't remember everything. While she was an undergraduate, the country erupted in concern over the launching of *Sputnik,* and Berkeley was quick to respond to the call for reforms in mathematics and science education, instituting a mathematics-for-teaching major within the mathematics department. Kysh joined the program, eventually doing her student teaching in a local high school one summer.

The program was what we might now call an "alternate route" in teacher education, for it was designed to entice graduates with mathematics and science degrees into the profession quickly, with a minimal amount of interruption by traditional teacher education curricula and requirements. For one summer, Judy Kysh taught every morning and met every afternoon with other interns to both talk about their teaching experiences and to do mathematics. Upon graduation, she stayed in the area, commuting to a nearby school district to teach high school mathematics for two years. The interns from the previous summer continued to meet, talking about their teaching, doing mathematics. Her roommates, all prospective teachers, were jealous of her enthusiasm, her joy. She remembers thinking—clutching her first paycheck in her hand—"And I get paid for doing this!" Moreover, the confidence and pleasure she gained from constantly solving math problems with other interns convinced her that she should get a master's degree in mathematics. In 1964 she took a year off from school to do so. Shortly afterward, she got married. She returned to the same school a year later, became department chair two years after that, and initiated and participated in a summer staff program for reconceptualizing mathematics teaching.

These were boon years in mathematics education of the progressive sort. As an intern, Kysh had learned to teach using materials developed by the School Mathematics Study Group (SMSG) (one of the New Math curricula); as a teacher, she used similar texts. Many teachers retired, and in their places new teachers were hired with similar commitments and enthusiasms. Her department proposed alternative scheduling, bought tables instead of desks so that students could work and sit in small groups. Together with a colleague, she created most of her own curricula.

Gradually, though, the tide turned. Ten years later she took a sabbatical to work on mathematical problem solving. For two years after that, she became increasingly discouraged by the regression in mathematics education. Staff development funds had dried up, a conservative, part-time teacher was hired to be her replacement as department chair, and she began to question teaching as a profession (although she also became president of the teachers union at this time).

Around the same time—1977—some of Kysh's colleagues convinced her to participate in the Bay Area Writing Project (BAWP) one summer, the first summer that the program included teachers from subject areas other than English/language arts. The project reminded her of her internship when teachers sat around and talked about teaching and did mathematics. A practical person who also embraced theory, she loved her BAWP experience.

But Kysh's work as a schoolteacher became more and more discouraging. The more traditional teachers in her department starting taking control, and people began telling her what to do in her classroom. Although she and her colleagues participated in interviewing new teachers, her principal did not take their recommendations.

In 1979, Kysh took a leave of absence, moved to Oregon, and got a degree in broadcasting. On a trip home, she noticed a job opening at the Lawrence Hall of Science for a program coordinator of a project designed to increase the number of minority students interested in mathematics and science and to improve their chances of entering the UC system. And so from 1980 to 1982 she worked in the Oakland schools, creating programs to get and keep more minority students in mathematics classes. At the same time, Jim Gray was working to convince then state senator Gary Hart of the need for a statewide system of professional development subject matter projects that shared the structure, spirit, and commitments of the BAWP—but that spanned the subject matters. As a mathematics teacher who had attended the writing project, Kysh wrote letters supporting the move.

In 1982, she applied for a position directing a university-based project that the following year (when funding became available through a bill sponsored by Gary Hart that created the California Subject Matter Projects) would become one of the sites of the California Mathematics Project. She directed one of those sites and eventually took on a part-time job as statewide director of all the projects (before that position became a full-time job).

While at that CMP site, Kysh applied for a California Academic Partnership Program grant, to create two new courses, one for high school students, another for middle school students. She worked on these courses with seventeen teachers who generated ideas, which she would then write down. After plans were drafted, the teachers piloted the materials in their schools. The effort created a network that focused simultaneously on curriculum development and staff development. And when the funding ran out, the group continued to meet. In 1989, a request for proposals was issued for the development of an entire math curriculum using Eisenhower funding. The Dwight D. Eisenhower Professional Development Program was established in 1985 through Title II of the Education for Economic Security Act. The program provided financial assistance to subsidize professional development for teachers and school staff. At the time, the Eisenhower program was the largest federal initiative using professional development to improve teaching and learning.

Kysh and her colleagues received California Eisenhower funding to develop an integrated mathematics curriculum. In 1993, the group formed a nonprofit corporation so that they could create and distribute the products of that work. All along, Kysh continued to direct her original CMP site, with fingers in multiple curriculum and professional development pies. Eventually, Kysh earned her doctorate and joined the faculty of the College of Education at San Francisco State University.

Each teacher-leader had a similar story to tell. Most started as classroom teachers, all attended summer institutes. Some participated in National Science Foundation projects, others in projects funded by Eisenhower grants. Most went on to get their masters' degrees, most also got administrative credentials. Mark St. John and his associates conducted a survey of teacher-leaders from across the subject matters and found that, while teacher-leaders reported spending some time in national efforts (4 percent), state efforts (13 percent), professional associations (19 percent), and county or regional efforts (23 percent), most of their time was spent focused on leadership activities in their schools and classrooms (72 percent and 80 percent, respectively).

I met many of these men and women in my travels through the state. Many of them were like Judy Mumme and Judy Kysh—people who had entered higher education, and then teaching, in the 1960s, a time of turmoil in American society, a time when many young adults were moved to be more socially committed. One woman, a mathematician, explained how she became involved: "This was the early sixties and all the things were happening in the South and a lot of consciousness was being raised and I wanted to be more relevant than being a math graduate student. This was a very common feeling among the math graduate students and many programs opened up at that time and one was started. . . . [That] was called Project SEED. Based on the work of Robert Davis, it was trying to get graduate students in mathematics to come into elementary schools, all-black elementary schools and teach the kids abstract math. . . . [None] of the black kids made it to geometry and very few made it to algebra, and those that did got wiped out. . . . [The] idea was to teach them algebra in elementary school."

California teacher-leaders are not the only educators whose initiation into education involved the civil rights movement. Robert Moses, head of the Algebra Project, a mathematics project devoted to helping more students—especially minority students—develop mathematical literacy, was also a critical figure in the civil rights movement in Mississippi. Moses writes about the parallels between establishing a political literacy so that African Americans could vote and a mathematical literacy so that all students might become empowered.[20] The work of the California teacher-leaders who came of age in the 1960s was done in the same spirit.

That they entered teaching at a time of heightened social consciousness and awareness may have fundamentally shaped the kinds of teachers—and learners—these people became. "I loved traveling. I thought about being a travel agent," Leslie said. Tears welled in her eyes and voice, "but who in the hell would benefit?" These teachers are not unlike many others who enter teaching for social or religious purposes.[21] And because they entered teaching during the *Sputnik*-induced curriculum reform era, they cut their teaching teeth in teacher education and professional development programs that put a heavy emphasis on mathematics, knowing mathematics, and making mathematics accessible to more children.

Although I met many important leaders who were men—Phil Daro, Walter Denham, and Nicholas Branca among them—I was often struck by the fact that many of the teacher-leaders were women. As women who came of age in the 1960s, all spoke about their limited range of options. Judy Mumme's husband and parents "put their foot down" at the idea of her earning a Ph.D. in paleontology. She listened, for, as she recalls, "I was still at that point, still doing what I thought I was supposed to be doing as a female. Having a baby. After all, I was almost thirty. Gee, I got married when I was twenty-one, and I was supposed to do that. I listened to my parents and my husband and didn't get my Ph.D."

Deirdre, who had always been good at mathematics in high school (and "embarrassed by that fact"), decided to go to a women's college where she could—without fear—major in philosophy and mathematics. But when she graduated in 1962:

> All of the jobs opened seemed to be to learn to type. Or getting teaching credentials seemed to be the way. Or there was a job at a research lab being kind of the lackey of the real male scientist and even though I wasn't liberated then, I didn't like any of those alternatives. So I decided to go to graduate school for a year and maybe I'd get married and I wouldn't have to deal with this. . . .
>
> I mean I grew up believing that a woman should get an education and should go outside the home to be interesting so that she would provide interesting conversation for her husband. My father wanted me to go to school to be an engineer and then the summer afterwards, take a secretarial course because wouldn't it be great for a man to have a secretary who knew some engineering?

These were women of energy, intelligence, and enthusiasm constrained by the social expectations and norms of their time. Each ended up channeling her intelligence and energy into teaching—and its reform. This is a well-documented phenomenon in American education. For much of American history, in fact, women and minorities could aspire *only* to teaching as a career. Consequently, the potential pool of teachers was broader, unthreatened by appeals from competing professions (with the exception of other care-related fields like nursing).

When you meet these women, their commitment to their own continual learning is impressive, second only to their civic commitment, rooted deeply in their enculturation in the 1960s and their personal experiences as parents and teachers. Judy Mumme worked with Hispanic students and saw what they could do, despite the general belief in her school that they should be tracked into the lowest-level mathematics classes. As she recalls: "I thought math was going to be easy, because I thought you do sample problems, you assign them, you give them homework, you spend half the class letting them do their homework, you corrected them every day. I mean, it was pretty straightforward to me, but then I realized that that just didn't do it. And, yes, there were a certain proportion of the students [for whom] that worked okay. But, I was unimportant in the process for them. And there was a huge group of kids for whom that was definitely not okay. And so, I think by the end of my first year of teaching, I realized that I had taken on something that was much more intellectually challenging than any thought of getting my Ph.D. in biology, or what I had thought of at one time . . . being an M.D."

Mumme also had a "pretty graphic realization" that year: "I had not been raised in an environment that was particularly equity conscious, if anything, [it was] quite bigoted. It was real clear . . . it was a three-track system, which is probably better than some places, but three tracks, and the skin color of the kids from the high track to the low track was quite dramatic. I certainly didn't see it in my own conversations with the kids, that that was the way it should've been. And so, I also tried to figure out why the system was doing what it was doing, in terms of putting kids in tracks, designating them in various ways that didn't seem at all appropriate to me."

Most teacher-leaders worried about the underrepresentation of minorities and females in science. As one female teacher-leader explained:

> Part of my motivation for getting into mathematics—a large part of it— and more than an even racial . . . is the gender thing. . . . I think we really limit ourselves as females. And it's very important to me. I think math does that. Math is the filter. I really feel very passionate that my granddaughter, and all kids . . . not just girls . . . I think all kids can have it. It's great for boys too, but I think we all need to be aware of the fact that girls get shortchanged. I totally agree with that. As a result of getting shortchanged, we make all sorts of decisions in our lives that limit us to professions, to jobs, we don't think we can get out of marriages, because we can't handle our own finances, because we've never handled the finances. . . . I want females to realize that they can be very capable in math . . . a lot of my motivation was this gender thing. Math is just a real convenient way to keep females in their place.

As Philip Cusick reminds us, many actors in the education system have different roles—parent and teacher, policy maker and grandparent, for example—and allegiances shift as roles change.[22] Not so with these teacher-leaders whose experiences with their own children (and now grandchildren) reconfirm their commitments to reforming school mathematics.

Leslie worried about her grandchildren. Judy Mumme was heartbroken as she watched her son: "There was one other event, one other circumstance that had a lot of influence on my own thinking. That was my youngest son, in first grade, was identified, or diagnosed, or labeled, 'learning disabled.' And put in special education. I learned the agonies of what that meant for him. I watched. . . . I helplessly watched a very bright, lovely child, be totally demoralized. I desperately tried to change it, and make it better, but couldn't. Saw again, the affects of how again the system doesn't deal with the full range of kids. . . . So, part of the passion in my own work today involves that whole area of equitable access . . . the idea of all kids . . . having access."

One should never underestimate the considerable power of mothers, fathers, or grandparents who object to how their children are being treated. Combine that with the social commitment of young people coming of age in the 1960s, many of them women of intelligence and energy with fewer career options, and the force became formidable. Many of these teachers grew up believing that they wanted to help others. And although contemporary youth culture intermittently resurrects the tie-dyed T-shirts and platform shoes of that period, we sometimes forget that the social commitment for some of the 1960s youth (not all, of course) was not a passing post-adolescent fancy but, instead, the real thing. Those idealistic 20-year-olds grew up, and a handful never abandoned their social commitments. Some became mathematics teachers. In part, they found mathematics attractive because of its history of disenfranchising women and minorities and because mathematics often acts as a gatekeeper for future success.

Because these teacher-leaders spent years (in many cases, two decades) in classrooms, they knew there were no easy answers. It wasn't simply a matter of changing the curriculum or changing teaching. Improving mathematics learning wasn't going to be solved by making sure each child ate a good breakfast. This was a long-term project, and over the course of their careers these teachers repeatedly sought out opportunities to learn more: more about research, more about instruction, curriculum, students and their needs, assessments. They went to workshops at the Lawrence Hall of Science, Marilyn Burns institutes, California Mathematics Project summer sessions. Frequently, they joined such professional organizations as the National Council for Teachers of Mathematics, attending annual meetings, reading professional journals. Many became members of the state affiliate—the California Mathematics Council.

The California Mathematics Council

The California Mathematics Council (CMC) is an umbrella organization for a slew of state affiliates of the National Council for Teachers of Mathematics (NCTM).[23] The organization was founded in 1942 when a small group of mathematics teachers gathered at Stanford University to share information about math teaching. A year later, the group began publishing a house organ, *The CMC Bulletin*, which has since become *The ComMuniCator*. In 1948, the CMC created northern and southern "sections" so as to better serve their members, and added a central affiliate several years later. In 1946, the organization had 425 members. Today, its ranks include over 12,000 California teachers and includes two dozen affiliates.

The group's goals are fourfold: to foster excellence in curricula, assessment, and instructional programs; to promote professional excellence; to strengthen leadership; and to establish and support affiliates. Affiliates have popped up all over the state: Math Educators of the Tri-Counties (METRIC), Sacramento Association of Math Educators (SAME), the Math Council of the Far North, the Bakersfield Mathematics Council, the Greater San Diego Mathematics Council. Sonoma, Stanislaus, San Francisco, Santa Clara all have their own affiliates. Teachers in these associations have multiple opportunities to belong to other groups as well, including the statewide CMC and the NCTM.

Multiple conferences are held each year. Two take place at Asilomar and Palm Springs. Each year, a memorial award is given to teachers in the name of Ed Begle, a mathematician who gave up topology to create and lead the School Mathematics Study Group (at Yale, and later at Stanford), one of the most well known New Math projects. Another award is given in the name of George Polya, a Hungarian-born mathematician who migrated to the United States and eventually settled at Stanford University. Polya, who specialized in probability, complex analysis, and combinational theory, was an active CMC member and a vocal critic of New Math. The umbrella organization and each regional section have their own board and president. Affiliate organizations have independent governing structures and bylaws.

The CMC constitutes a substantial statewide subculture, one that offers members opportunities to learn and talk about mathematics teaching, as well as myriad opportunities for teachers to take on leadership positions. Four times a year, every member receives a copy of *The ComMuniCator*, which includes discussions of current issues and new developments, showcases innovative teaching and assessment techniques, and announces conferences and publications. During the earlier stages of the 1980s reforms, CDE staff regularly used *The ComMuniCator* to post updates from the state department throughout the development of the framework, the model curriculum guide, and the new assessments. In many ways, the journal became a messenger for the reforms. Examples of performance-based assessment were highlighted. Marilyn Burns sometimes wrote articles, and legislative updates were frequently showcased. The majority of the material in any issue concerns instructional strategies, and a careful look at these articles gives one a sense of how teachers were translating the *1985 Framework* and other materials into action. For example, Mary Laycock wrote about teaching third and fourth graders their multiplication facts, explaining an activity that involved children learning the facts ($14 \times 16 = 224$), using algebra to do so, and developing models to support their understanding. "These strategies help children to visualize the number facts that they eventually commit to memory after recording them on three-by-five cards. The experience of problem solving and observing mathematical patterns helps to make the learning of the facts more meaningful," she explained.[24]

These lessons from the field along with announcements about what is going on and how teachers are responding might appear inconsequential. The journal has no glossy cover, no panel of distinguished reviewers or editors. Yet publications like this are often the only ones that busy teachers and administrators have time to peruse. Like the mass-produced pamphlets issued across the United States throughout the nineteenth century, these publications represent a grassroots view of education, and serve as a powerful democratic medium for teachers and others to express their views on mathematics teaching. They are places where teachers write to teachers.

Through its annual meetings and *The ComMuniCator*, the CMC—both the organization and individual members—played a significant role in the reform of mathematics education statewide. The CMC groups reviewed drafts of the *1985 Framework*, and members played critical roles on state policy development committees, serving on the Instructional Materials Evaluation Panels, Curriculum Framework and Criteria Committees, and the Curriculum Commissions, for instance.

In collaboration with the California Mathematics Projects, EQUALS, and the Mathematics Diagnostic Testing Project and funded by a grant from the California Postsecondary Education Commission, the CMC sponsored a "Campaign for Mathematics," launched in 1988 with the goal of attracting leaders in mathematics education to work on "pressing problems." Among its goals was the creation of a consortium of major providers of professional development in mathematics education, increased communication and co-ordination across those enterprises, and the development of a shared vision of mathematics education and professional development.

Task forces were formed to focus on issues of diversity, materials, inservice teacher education, preservice teacher education, reform implementation, and public relations. "Campaign Convocations" were held in 1988, 1989, and 1991. A special booklet on alternative assessments—*Assessment Alternatives in Mathematics*—was prepared and sent to every member of the organization. Unfortunately, the "campaign" never got off the ground and vanished within two years.

One of the largest CMC conferences is sponsored by CMC–North every year at Asilomar, a conference center on the coast of the Monterey peninsula. The setting is rustic and lovely, with winding paths, a view of the ocean, and signs made of wood. In early December 1994, researchers from our project went to observe the event. Over 3,500 teachers and teacher-educators were in attendance, sampling from the over-300 options, ranging from "make-and-take" sessions (where teachers receive materials and instructions that they can take immediately back to their classrooms) to keynote addresses by well-known leaders in mathematics education. Speakers presented on topics far ranging: cooperative small groups and alternative assessment, teacher-leadership, and Family Math. Teachers could go from "Go Fly a Kite!" (learning how to use kite design to explore principles of flight and geometric concepts) to "Demystifying Fractions." Others could go to "A Million to One" (a hands-on workshop to introduce a new instructional unit for developing children's number sense) to "Making Geometric Models by Folding Origami."

Dynamo Marcy Cook, another mathematics education leader who, like Marilyn Burns, operates her own business—Marcy Cook Math—gave an inspiring talk.[25] Burns explained her most recent work in Arizona, which involved—in part—having more contact with parents. She explained how she had taught a unit and what the students had done. She reported on parents' responses, including their concerns. As always, she was engaging and challenging: "You can't teach what you don't understand and you can't teach what you don't love," she argued, noting in her characteristic, straightforward way the troubling lack of mathematical knowledge on the part of many teachers.

In another session, representatives from Family Math ran a discussion

No thoughtless responses to others' comments
No put-downs
Non-judgmental acceptance
No repetition of others just to hear ourselves
Willingness to think
Confidentiality
Separate ideas from people
Non-threatening environment
Equal time
Pay full attention to speaker

Figure 5.5. Rules for Discussion at Asilomar EQUALS Presentation

of teacher leadership. They began by laying down ground rules for discussion, shown in Figure 5.5. As I have noted, teachers—especially in elementary schools—do not work in cultures in which much time is spent on discussion. For those teachers, these ground rules enable participation by declaring that it is okay to take risks and to speak your mind, and that no one will be rude. On the other hand, the same rules can feel constraining: "I can't really speak my mind, if what I want to say is that I disagree with someone," some participants worry. In the extreme, implemented narrowly and dictatorially, such rules result in anything but critical discourse: dissent can be tacitly outlawed, "celebrating diversity" the "one true path." For those of us accustomed to academic conferences or political debates where people speak their minds (sometimes thoughtlessly), these rules seem strange. For critics of the education establishment, these rules reek of political correctness, and of the progressives' tendency to silence difference. As will become clear in later chapters of this book, the clashing norms of discourse across the multiple communities involved in this story became more and more apparent.

Learning Teachers

Taken together, these networks—the CMC and CMP (as well as others I do not explore here)—serve multiple purposes. They educate. Within the networks, teachers learn of new developments and encounter new instructional methods and new curricula. They learn about innovations in assessment and hear about education research. They learn to participate in professional discussions.

All this entails the acquisition of new skills and knowledge. For instance, many teachers talked about learning to listen. These participants were referring to their experiences with one California Mathematics Project director who uses a dyad structure to enable conversation. Elaine explained: "The listening was taught to us there. There was a lot of good listening that went on there. The notion of a dyad. You get to talk for three minutes, then someone else talks for three minutes. You don't have to worry about what you are going to say, because I don't have to respond to what you are saying. It was a very different way of thinking how we communicate with one another."

In addition to learning to listen, teachers reported learning other things: to speak in public, to present their ideas, to argue. Many of the California Mathematics Project sites, for example, required participants to make presentations to groups at their own school, or in other school districts. Teachers then went on to make other presentations at meetings of the CMC and NCTM. Elaine recalled the first time the teachers had to make a presentation and their nervous anticipation. "That gave everyone the presentation skills, the willingness to get in front of an audience. I liked it, frankly. I thought, this is fun!"

Other learning came from the chance for teachers to apply what they had learned during the summer to their own classrooms. Judy Mumme had attended her first California Mathematics Project with a colleague from her school. "Then I really got to play in the classroom with the ideas that I was learning, and try those, and try to craft those better. . . . [Another teacher and I] would run back and forth to each other's classroom, like, you have got to see this. . . . It was an incredible time, and I really loved the teaching."

Other researchers have noted similar findings. For instance, teachers participating in the Urban Mathematics Collaborative in California (sponsored by the Ford Foundation) left their encounters with other teachers and experts with an "enhanced sense of the possible," which often led the participants to incorporate new methods and ideas into their teaching.[26] Some opportunities allowed the teachers and leaders to learn more about mathematics, an observation Judy Mumme made about her participation in writing the NCTM 1989 *Standards*: "I learned a lot about mathematics. Made a lot of [mathematical] connections that were good."

As Gary Lichtenstein, Milbrey McLaughlin, and Jennifer Knudsen note, the increased professional knowledge gained through professional development opportunities in these networks gave teachers a greater sense of power. In part, this power came from increased professional knowledge: of mathematics and new ways of teaching, of policy systems, of professional organizations, of a professional discourse.[27]

Often this empowerment led the teachers into positions more public, sometimes more powerful. Their enhanced knowledge helped them lead. Again, there are connections to the civil rights movement. Robert Moses notes that this "network of people—it was their training ground that allowed them to emerge as political leaders of their state. These were not credentialed people, they were not high school graduates. They were not members of labor unions, or national church associations. Yet through the process, they became leaders."[28]

But these teachers don't simply value these networks for the opportunities to learn that they provide. The networks also provided relationships, as Judy Mumme noted, "It's really been the people. You know, the colleague of mine, Diane, the teacher next door, she had an incredible influence. People like Elaine and Joanne. Elaine was more of a colleague, a teaching colleague. . . . So, those kinds of relationships, I couldn't exist without them. The ten people that I work with now . . . each of them in their own unique way, has incredible influence on me, personally, and impacts how I think about what I do."

A female mathematician's comments echoed Mumme's: "Well, the one thing we haven't talked about is networking and how important that is. And particularly for a woman in a field that doesn't have a lot of male colleagues. Somehow having a base of friends and particularly friends in your field that you can talk to that have the same point of view, is very very important. . . . And this to me was very sustaining."

As a volleyball player, I was nurtured in several ways by my team and its associated activities. We drilled and ran and bumped and set, we occasionally scrimmaged, and we practiced a lot. I became a better volleyball player. That work, done in the margins of the day, was hard to sustain, but the team and the friendships that it generated made the hard work enjoyable, possible. I loved playing volleyball: it made me feel worthwhile, connected, skillful, accomplished.

In their analysis of the "social life" of information, John Seely Brown and Paul Duguid note that individuals who engage in similar practices—

the practice of teaching, the practice of medicine, the practice of photo-copier repair—often spontaneously form networks or communities of practice in order to share and disseminate their knowledge. Drawing on the work of Jean Lave and Etienne Wenger, they argue that learning a practice "involves becoming a member of a 'community of practice' and thereby understanding its work and its talk from the inside. Learning, from this point of view, is not simply a matter of acquiring information; it requires developing the disposition, demeanor, and outlook of the practitioners."[29] These communities are particularly important for professional practices, these researchers argue, because good practice relies not on information alone, but also on knowledge. Unlike information, professional knowledge is "hard to detach," they argue. This explains why practitioners (ranging from Hewlett Packard representatives who visit companies and fix machines to teachers) sustain communities of practice and share their knowledge through stories. In telling their stories, the practitioners generate coherent accounts of messy situations. In this way, they share their individual and collective knowledge, see situations in a new light, generate potential solutions, and generate a framework for interpretation.

The mathematics education networks play a similar role for the participating teachers. They provide opportunities for teachers to learn things about teaching, about presenting their ideas, about mathematics. Teachers told one another stories from their practice, and created a common professional knowledge base and coherent interpretive framework. The networks also provide a social context for the work: teachers find support and friendship, collegiality, respect. And finally, in providing teachers with these experiences, the networks often boost their confidence. Each informant said something that echoed Leslie's observation: "I learned I have something to say. I have ideas that deserve to be heard." These statewide networks were part of a growing national trend in the creation of homes away from home for teachers who were thirsty for new knowledge, skill, and professional discourse.[30] And their ideas were being heard, often by the state department as CDE staff continued to work on California's version of systemic reform.

Lest the reader believe my image of these networks is romantic, I close this chapter with a warning, for I have focused on the positive potential of these networks to enhance teachers' professional lives. But networks can be problematic: participants develop tight allegiances. Colleagues begin to share the same values and worldviews. While these shared beliefs help participants efficiently and effectively communicate with one another, those worldviews can also act like blinders, closing down communication with individuals and organizations who are not part of the network. Many teachers who were members of these professional organizations and networks, who participated in CMC conferences and Math Solutions workshops, found professional sustenance in those encounters with others of like mind. But, as we will see in the later part of my story, outsiders—teachers, mathematicians, parents, policy makers—found no such sustenance and support. Instead, outsiders who did not share the same views, who did not travel in the same circles, experienced these networks as blocs of the education establishment unwilling to participate in reasonable debates about what and how mathematics ought to be taught (see Chapters 8–10).

6 Riding the Tiger: The California State Department, 1990–1992

It's not quite that we have a tiger by the tail.
It's more that we may be climbing up on the back
Of the tiger to ride. It could be frightening; and it could be thrilling.
Wish us luck; we wish you the best!
—Walter Denham

The efforts begun in the mid- to late-1980s by Bill Honig and his staff continued in 1990. Working on all fronts, the state department hoped to change testing, teacher preparation, and available curricular materials. Using these levers and others, the California Department of Education aimed for coherent, consistent curricular guidance. They were a busy lot—surprisingly so, since the CDE had suffered approximately 200 position cuts in the late 1980s.[1]

WYTIWYG

Concern about a rigorous, well-aligned assessment system continued to grow. As measurement gurus sometimes put it, WYTIWYG—What You Test Is What You Get.[2] If tests did not align with extant curriculum, they could distract teachers and students alike, swallowing up precious school time with test preparation activities. As Jeannie Oakes observed: "High stakes test-score indicators will lead most teachers (often through local administrative mandates) to spend a considerable portion of their energy doing whatever it takes to help students raise their test scores. Whatever else they may want to accomplish instructionally is likely to become secondary."[3]

The problem was twofold, for the focus on testing not only shapes curricular content, it also shapes pedagogy: "[Teachers and schools] also tend to mimic how the content is tested. Under pressure to show improved school performance, schools tend to prepare students by spending lots of instructional time on exercises that look just like the test items. In the extreme, an over reliance on multiple-choice testing thus can become a narrow, multiple-choice curriculum, devoid of the complex thinking and communication skills that are essential for students' future success."[4]

For the reformers, who believed that how you teach affects what you teach, this problem—of simplifying content and stultifying pedagogy—was double trouble. Tests were especially important in systemic reform, for they were one of the critical policy levers that needed to be aligned with the *1985 Framework*. In 1990, Governor George Deukmejian vetoed funding for the California Assessment Program (CAP), as the state faced serious financial difficulties. The twelfth-grade statewide testing for that year was canceled, and plans for the rest of the program lay dormant as CDE staff waited to see what the new governor—Pete Wilson—would do. This left the door open for the introduction of new assessments, and through the door walked advocates for innovative "performance assessments" that require students do more than identify facts or recall information.

The ideas were not California-specific, for there was a national move afoot to fundamentally change testing. Rather than assume that all high-stakes tests had to be like the traditional ones of the past—"multiple guess" tests, as some teachers cynically called them—educators were arguing for a radical change in both what was tested and how it was tested. Lauren Resnick and Daniel Resnick's comments captured the popular logic of the time: "First, you get what you assess. Educators will teach to tests if the tests matter in their own or their students' lives. Second, you do not get what you do not assess. What does not appear on tests tends to disappear from classrooms in time. Third, build assessments toward what you want educators to teach. Assessments must be designed so that when teachers do the natural thing, that is, prepare their students to perform well, they will exercise the kinds of abilities and develop the kinds of skill and knowledge that are the real goals of educational reform."[5]

Using such logic—tests will drive teaching and so, if we want a new curriculum, we need new tests—Governor Pete Wilson vetoed CAP. An Assessment Policy Committee (APC) was appointed by Honig and chaired by Tom Payzant, a prominent superintendent of a San Diego Unified School

District who was gaining national attention. Payzant, like Marshall Smith, went on to work in Washington, D.C., as assistant secretary of education. Other members of the committee included Richard Shavelson and Eva Baker, prominent educational psychologists in the field of measurement and assessment, as well as administrators, teachers, and school board members.

The APC issued a report asserting that tests had to provide individual test scores for every child, be based on performance standards, provide opportunities for students to demonstrate what they know, and be tied to the curriculum frameworks. The recommendations of that committee became the blueprint for a new assessment system—the California Learning Assessment System (CLAS)—which was put into law with SB 662 in 1991. Support for the effort came from three directions: the governor, the state superintendent, and Gary Hart, then chair of the Senate Education Committee.

Despite their agreement that the state needed CLAS, Honig, Hart, and Wilson had very different expectations for the test. Wilson wanted every parent to receive test scores for their children so that parents could evaluate individual teachers. In fact, Wilson's goal was to create a merit pay system for teachers with high-scoring students. Senator Hart believed that a more appropriate assessment system was necessary to enable site-based management: a good assessment system would allow the state to hold schools accountable for their results. In exchange for this accountability, schools could then have more autonomy. Honig, on the other hand, saw the assessments as an essential piece of a curricular system that tied standards to assessments to instructional materials (and later, to teacher preparation and professional development).

There was very little legislative oversight. The CDE staff met with the APC to report on work, but the policy committee never exercised much leadership, relying instead on the CDE's expertise and experience.[6] This meant primarily that the assessment developments followed the protocols established by the CDE more generally, including strong teacher participation and an attempt to tap into the expertise of the education leadership.

The development effort was led by Tej Pandey, a longtime state department staff member who was on the NCTM *1989 Standards* writing team, as well as a member of the Technical Advisory Committee of the National Assessment of Educational Progress (NAEP). Through these associations, Pandey (like many of his CDE colleagues) was part of both California-based and national discussions of curriculum, standards, assessment, and systemic reform. CLAS was to be a student assessment written by teachers, one that broke new measurement ground and aimed for ambitious tests that went beyond assessing basic knowledge. The proposed changes in assessment met with widespread approval, including that of the California Teachers Association.[7]

Development work on CLAS resonated with more general statewide trends toward alternative assessments. Teachers rallied around the calls for "authentic" assessment (even though it remained unclear what that meant). Teachers were hungry for other assessments, believing that anything had to be better than the traditional multiple choice tests of basic skills. The argument went something like this: assessment tools need to be designed to measure the knowledge and skills teachers value most (conceptual understanding, mathematical reasoning, flexible use of math knowledge). They also need to be aligned with curricula, and—in the best of all possible worlds—readily and smoothly integrated into instruction. (With good assessments, teaching to the test becomes a nonproblem.) Publications began appearing, including the California Mathematics Council's Campaign for Mathematics *Assessment Alternatives in Mathematics*.[8] The message echoed one being communicated nationally. Grant Wiggins, on his way to becoming the "guru" of authentic assessment, was writing about "more authentic and equitable assessment."[9] The National Research Council (an arm of the National Academy of Sciences) was sending similar messages: "As we need standards for curricula, so we need standards for assessment. We must ensure that tests measure what is of most value, not just what is easy to test. If we want students to investigate, explore, and discover, assessment must not measure just mimicry mathematics. By confusing means and ends, by making testing more important than learning, present practice holds today's students hostage to yesterday's mistakes."[10]

"Open-ended problems" began appearing in school districts. Some didn't look radically different from the ubiquitous ones we had in school, save the emphasis on "explain your thinking":

> A train starts with 163 passengers. On its route it makes 6 station stops before the final stop. At each of the station stops 50 passengers get off the train and 32 get on the train. At the final stop, how many passengers are left on the train? Explain in detail how you arrived at your answer. The number of passengers left on the train is _____ .

Or:

Tell what the next three numbers would be in the following table:
x 2 3 4 5 9 12 16
y 7 12 19 28
Explain the pattern that you found.

Others seemed less familiar:

You are at an oasis and in need of exactly 7 gallons of water. The only containers available are a 3-gallon and a 5-gallon container with absolutely no markings on them. How can you measure out exactly 7 gallons of water? Explain your answer.

Or:

You are the caretaker of a baseball stadium. The season will begin soon and you must paint the outfield wall. Here are some important facts about the baseball field: The baseball diamond has 90 feet between each of the bases; the baseball field extends 90 yards from home plate down the right field line to the outfield wall; it is 90 yards to the left field wall also; at every point along the base of the outfield wall it is the same distance to home plate; the outfield wall is 8 feet high.

The paint will cover 300 square feet per gallon, and you will require only one coat of paint. Write an explanation of how you will determine the proper number of gallons of paint to buy.

Teachers were encouraged to use such items both to teach and test.[11] The push was for more problem solving, more focus on conceptual understanding.

While some advocates for the reforms talked exclusively of problem solving, others argued for a balance: a retreat from the overemphasis on skill development, but not an abandonment of those skills. For example, in one California Mathematics Council report, the authors analyzed standardized tests that were currently on the market, examining the full battery of questions that publishing houses used on their tests. The analysis showed that *only* arithmetic computation skills were tested thoroughly and rarely were there items that required students to reason. Moreover, most of the strands of the *1985 Framework* were ignored, with the heaviest emphasis placed on "number" (67 out of 100 items on a test focused on number, 6 on measurement, 7 on geometry, 5 on algebra, 8 on word problems). The small number of items for the other strands made those measurements fragile at best. The authors suggested that "publishers of standardized tests should reduce the number of rote computational items, increase the number of items calling for higher level thinking skills, and provide clear descriptions of the skills tested."[12]

The report's authors argue not for the elimination of computational problems, but rather for a reconsideration of the lack of emphasis and attention to problems that require a demonstration of mathematical reasoning. The request echoes Alfred North Whitehead's argument from years earlier: "In this sense, there is no royal road to learning. But it is equally an error to confine attention to technical processes, excluding consideration of general ideas. Here lies the road to pedantry."[13] For the most part, throughout the reform, participants were calling for a balance of facts and procedures on the one hand and problem solving and conceptual understanding on the other.

New Curricula Turn into New Professional Development

Meanwhile, CDE staff members were frustrated with their experiences fighting the textbook companies. Walter Denham, Joan Akers, and others searched for other ways to get their hands on new kinds of curricular materials. A major problem in the earlier round of textbook adoptions was that publishers would do market research and ask teachers what kinds of materials they wanted. Teachers, whose experiences were largely limited to the familiar two-page, master-a-new-algorithm-today-and-then-practice-it format, asked for what they knew: more of the same. So the challenge for the reformers was to find ways to introduce to teachers new materials, so that their options were broadened. The group searched for good ideas. Hugh Burkhardt at the Shell Centre in Nottingham, England, was developing curricular materials that could be used to replace traditional mathematics. One of the leaders of the mathematics education community, Phil Daro, heard of this work and discussed it with his colleagues, including Walter Denham in the CDE. Out of their brainstorming came a new strategy called "replacement units."

The logic went something like this: if you provide teachers with smaller, more innovative pieces of curriculum, they are more likely to agree to try them. Once they try them, they'll fall in love with what the students learn and what the teaching and learning feels like. This will create more interest in alternative curricula. Slowly, but surely, teachers will begin to demand alternative materials. This will change not only teaching and learning but also market demands, and textbook companies will eventually have to bow to teachers' demands for better, more mathematically challenging materials.

Strapped for funds, the CDE could commission only one such unit. So they subcontracted with the Massachusetts-based Technical Education Research Centers (TERC) to develop a replacement unit entitled Seeing Fractions.[14] TERC is one of many small organizations that work outside the formal education system. These organizations consist of educators and researchers who conduct research, design and offer professional development programs, develop innovative curriculum and assessments, and conduct evaluations for school districts and states.

The five-module unit that TERC developed for the CDE began with an explanation of why fractions are so hard for students to understand. The authors urged teachers to move slowly through the unit, to emphasize "explaining and justifying solutions" rather than simply focusing on "getting the correct answer." The introductory pages are strikingly different from the typical pages in a teachers' manual. Section titles include: "Teaching Is not Telling" and "The Role of Frustration in Learning Mathematics." Teachers are encouraged, also, to branch out and to use the materials flexibly. The page-by-page, lockstep progression is not presumed.

As part of their replacement unit strategy—officially called the Fifth Grade Mathematics Unit Project—the CDE sponsored a series of professional development seminars that focused on helping teachers learn about Seeing Fractions. Using a teacher-leader model, the CDE hoped to teach teachers about the unit; the teacher-leaders would then teach other teachers in their home school districts. Thirty master teachers participated in a pilot year: taught by the TERC authors, the teacher-leaders returned to their classrooms and trial-tested the unit. The following summer—in 1990— those 30 master teachers taught approximately 1,700 fifth-grade teachers in 2 ½ -day workshops throughout California. The following year, many of those teachers then used the unit in their teaching.

A survey of over 200 teacher-participants indicated that teachers changed their practices during their use of Seeing Fractions: they used small groups, urged students to write about their understanding, and made more use of manipulatives during the implementation of this replacement unit. Teachers reported that students were more enthusiastic, that students acquired knowledge they needed to work with fractions, and that the unit—overall— led to a higher level of understanding of fractions than students typically demonstrate. Teachers also expressed some reservations about the unit: 25 percent of the respondents worried about the time it took, 15 percent were concerned about how well the unit prepared students for standardized tests, and another 15 percent reported difficulties in using the alternative assessments that accompanied the unit. Overall, the respondents thought "the pluses outweighed the minuses," and, as the evaluators reported:

> The majority of teachers found *Seeing Fractions* to be a valuable teaching tool. They found the hands-on, inquiry approach to the activities to be effective; they noted increased student involvement; and they felt that integrating language (e.g., oral explanations, writing, reading) with mathematics instruction was critical to increasing students' learning and to evaluating students' thinking.
>
> Moreover, teachers valued their new role in the classroom. They felt that learning was deeper when they acted as a coach and guide to their students' thinking instead of explaining answers and demonstrating operations. They were able to adopt inquiry methods and use them to their satisfaction in the classroom. . . .
>
> Teachers were also enthusiastic about their students' learning. . . . They reported that the unit improved their students' understanding of fractions and, importantly, they indicated that it was more effective in this regard than traditional textbooks. They reported that the hands-on, open-ended approach allowed all students to learn about fractions.[15]

The State Department hoped that others would develop similar materials that could be distributed as replacement units. They were in luck. Given the national emphasis on teaching mathematics for understanding, a wave of curriculum development projects had already begun. Another Massachusetts-based, soft money laboratory, Educational Development Center (EDC), had developed a unit called Gulliver's Travels, funded by a National Science Foundation grant. And Marilyn Burns developed (with the assistance of her friend and collaborator Bonnie Tank) a third-grade unit on multiplication. Over 400 teachers attended a two-day workshop funded by the Exxon Educational Foundation, the Department of Education, and Marilyn Burns Education Associates that was designed to launch the multiplication materials as another "replacement unit" option.

No mathematics education reformer we spoke to ever saw the reform of mathematics education in simplistic ways. From the beginning, they saw it as a complex technical, pragmatic, political, intellectual, historical problem for which one needed to mobilize groups, write new policies, develop new resources, and persuade many constituencies. Rather than identifying one activity as the engine that drove the reform—for example, change the tests to change the teaching—all the leaders presumed one needed to do lots of work in parallel: curriculum development and professional development, assessment revision and parent communication. However, sometime in late 1989 and early 1990, a subtle shift occurred—both within California and nationally—toward placing professional development at the center of reform. Rather than regarding professional development as one of many strategies to be aligned with other levers or reform "drivers," scholars, policy makers, and reformers alike began treating it as the reform's linchpin.

With this shift toward more emphasis on professional development and teacher learning, the work on replacement units became opportunities for teacher learning, as much as they were opportunities for new curricula to infiltrate the system. And in 1991, the CDE created the Mathematics Renaissance, a middle school initiative that built on the lessons learned through the past six years of reform activity. Initially tapping seventy-eight middle schools statewide, the project invited teachers and schools to participate. Replacement units were used as the medium for discussion, and teachers met regularly—and were visited regularly—to discuss curriculum and student learning. Seven full-time teacher-leaders were hired as staff, providing assistance to the teachers and schools signed up to be part of the enterprise.[16] The ideas behind the effort—school-based, teacher-led, long-term professional development among them—were very much in the air, both nationally and within California. The calls for reform, heard early in the 1980s, had only increased. Schools needed to change, and standards—for curriculum and teachers, for opportunities to learn—were necessary. Common wisdom argued that if any of these changes were to take root, teachers needed to be central, active contributors.

A State of Emergency? The National Conversation

Professional development was not the only item on the national agenda. In the late 1970s, federal studies reported sharp declines in achievement of American students in mathematics, science, and foreign languages. SAT scores were also in decline. Reports were issued declaring a state of emergency; commissions met and considered alternatives. For example, in 1981, the Educational Excellence Network was established. Between 1983 and

1984, approximately twenty national commissions reported on the ills of American schools. Prominent among these reports was *A Nation at Risk,* which warned of a "rising tide of mediocrity."[17] The authors made a slew of recommendations: Raise high school graduation requirements. Upgrade the elementary curriculum. Adopt more rigorous academic standards in assessment. Use standardized tests of achievement at critical transition points. Improve the preparation of teachers, as well as the desirability of the work as a profession. Use time more efficiently, have longer school days and years. Strengthen incentives for attendance. Create master teacher programs. Allow citizens to oversee reforms and provide financial support.

Many states (including California) responded. Nearly every state joined in a national movement to address the recommendations. States made significant efforts to provide students with more, and better, content. Student testing requirements went up. States instituted higher standards for prospective teachers.[18] California did a lot. In addition to Bill Honig's focus on the frameworks, textbook adoption, and revisions in assessment, the Hughes-Hart Educational Reform Act, or SB 813, an omnibus reform act, set new graduation requirements, and lengthened the school year. The act also called for the creation of the California School Leadership Academy, an effort to enhance the knowledge and skills of administrators (the potential instructional leaders for teachers embracing reforms). Hughes-Hart revised textbook adoption and standard setting procedures so that each piece of the bill was tightly aligned. The frameworks, as William Firestone and James Pennell noted, were treated like a "meta-policy," providing standards and guidance for the rest of the system of reforms.[19] Charter school legislation was passed, incentives were provided for schools to restructure, and the California Assessment Collaborative (CAC) was created to provide local districts with funding to experiment with alternative assessments.[20] Most of the reforms mapped directly onto recommendations in *A Nation at Risk.* In addition to the legislation, the CDE issued its own state-specific reports: the *1985 Framework, It's Elementary, Caught in the Middle, Second to None.*[21] Other frameworks in other subject matters, other assessments in those areas, and professional development plans were also in place. Mathematics education was clearly not the only target of education reform in California.

In addition to the national discourse on excellence and accountability in teaching, a parallel line of activities was taking place within the mathematics teaching community. In 1980, the National Council for Teachers of Mathematics issued *An Agenda for Action: Directions for School Mathemat-*

ics for the 1980s.[22] In 1981, the National Research Council appointed the "David committee" and charged its members with a comprehensive review of the status of mathematical research in the United States. The committee issued a report and a national plan for renewal, *Renewing U.S. Mathematics: A Plan for the 1990s*. In 1985, the NRC created the Mathematical Sciences Education Board (MSEB) with the intent to provide a continuous assessment and evaluation of the state of mathematics education at all levels. The MSEB appointed a group of twenty representatives from mathematics, higher education, industry, and public policy to the Committee on the Mathematical Sciences in the Year 2000. The purpose of this three-year project was to reconceptualize and revitalize mathematical sciences education in American higher education.

In 1989, the NRC issued another report—*Everybody Counts: A Report to the Nation on the Future of Mathematics Education*. "Wake up, America!" the authors urge, "Your children are at risk. Three of every four Americans stop studying mathematics before completing career or job prerequisites. Most students leave school with insufficient preparation."[23] The substance of the reports echoed messages sent through California policies. The authors wrote about the need for mathematical power ("It is the students' acts of construction and invention that build their mathematical power") and mathematical literacy. They spoke of the demands of the changing workplace and a commitment to teaching all children. Near the end of the report, the authors detail seven "transitions" that reforming mathematics education entails:

Transition 1: The focus of school mathematics is shifting from a dualistic mission—minimal mathematics for the majority, advanced mathematics for a few—to a singular focus on a significant common core of mathematics for all students.

Transition 2: The teaching of mathematics is shifting from an authoritarian model based on "transmission of knowledge" to a student-centered practice featuring "stimulation of learning."

Transition 3: Public attitudes about mathematics are shifting from indifference and hostility to a recognition of the important role that mathematics plays in today's society.

Transition 4: The teaching of mathematics is shifting from a preoccupation with inculcating routine skills to developing broad-based mathematical power.

Transition 5: The teaching of mathematics is shifting from emphasis on tools for future courses to greater emphasis on topics that are relevant to students' present and future needs.

Transition 6: The teaching of mathematics is shifting from primary emphasis on paper-and-pencil calculations to full use of calculators and computers.

Transition 7: The public perception of mathematics is shifting from that of a fixed body of arbitrary rules to a vigorous science of patterns.[24]

The NRC then went on to declare 1990 "The Year of Dialog." Other reports followed, including *Reshaping School Mathematics* and *On the Shoulders of Giants,* a set of essays about "big ideas" in mathematics. In 1991, the Committee on the Mathematical Sciences in the Year 2000 released its report, *Moving Beyond Myths: Revitalizing Undergraduate Mathematics,* which described the weaknesses of undergraduate and graduate university preparation in mathematics.[25] Simultaneously, the NCTM was convening panels to write its three sets of standards.

Another national conversation concerned assessment. In 1990, funded by the Pew Charitable Trusts and the MacArthur Foundation, the National Center on Education and the Economy (a not-for-profit, Washington-based group) and the Learning Research and Development Center (LRDC) at the University of Pittsburgh (a research center known for its high-quality, largely psychological research in education, led by Lauren Resnick) collaborated on the creation of the New Standards Project. This project would develop a multiple-method national assessment system that consisted of portfolios, student performances on tasks, and timed tests. In 1996, the project published a set of performance standards that built upon professional standards like those published by the NCTM and the National Council for Teachers of English, as well as other missives from the National Academy and the National Research Council. Accompanying materials were dedicated to helping schools reach out to parents in their standards-based reform efforts. Performance tasks in mathematics and language arts were developed, along with curricular and professional development materials.

This was a dizzying array of reports and organizations and activities, characteristically American and grousing: the documents call for dramatic change, the authors speak of a crisis. American prosperity depends on sci-

Table 6.1. Old and New Views of Mathematics

Previous View	Newly Emerging View
"Mathematics" is about symbols written on paper.	"Mathematics" is a way of thinking that involves mental representations of problem situations and of relevant knowledge . . .
Knowledge of mathematics is constructed from words and sentences.	These mental representations are built up from pieces learned as a result of previous experience . . .
"Teaching mathematics" means getting students to write the right thing in the right place on the paper.	"Teaching mathematics" is a matter of guiding and coaching . . .
The point of learning mathematics is to learn a few facts, a few standard algorithms for writing symbols on paper, and a few definitions . . .	The goal of studying mathematics is to learn to think in a very powerful way . . .
Students would not be able to invent algorithms themselves.	Students often invent their own algorithms . . .
"Assessment" means finding how well students conform to the prescribed orthodox rituals . . .	"Assessment" or "evaluation" means finding out how a student thinks about some interesting problem.

ence and technology, which, in turn, depend on mathematics—"the foundation of science and engineering . . . a key to our nation's future."[26] The reports note inequities in the distribution of mathematical "power"; white males learn more, women and minorities less.[27] Students drop out of the mathematics pipeline at a high rate. In 1972, 3.6 million ninth graders took courses in math; in 1976, the number was 294,000. Of those freshmen, 11,000 received undergraduate degrees in mathematics in 1980, 2,700 received master's degrees in 1982, and 400 received Ph.D.s in 1986. On average, women receive one in five doctorates in mathematics.

The reports also argued that students must learn more than just facts, that their "understanding" must be more flexible, more conceptual. Robert Davis (of New Math days and by then professor of mathematics education at Rutgers University) characterized the differences between "old" and "new" understanding in mathematics in a two-column chart (Table 6.1).[28]

In response to the national calls for improved mathematics and science teaching, the National Science Foundation began sponsoring a number of curriculum and teacher development projects, starting in 1989. Among these projects was the Connected Mathematics Project (CMP) at Michigan State University, a five-year project that led to the development of a middle school mathematics curriculum. Another middle school curriculum project, Mathematics in Context, was developed at the University of Wisconsin—Madison and the Freudenthal Institute at Utrecht University. Yet another, the Interactive Mathematics Program (IMP), is a four-year secondary, comprehensive, problem-based curriculum that integrates traditional content, such as algebra, geometry, and trigonometry, with other topics such as statistics and probability. Across these projects, curricula were developed that asked students to investigate nonstandard problems; look for and articulate patterns; make, test, and prove conjectures; discuss their answers and explorations; and model the work of mathematicians.

Progressive mathematics educators hungrily snapped up these curricula, anxious to have instructional materials that might help more children learn mathematics. California was no different. Little did anyone know at that time that less than a decade later, some of those innovative curricula would come under heavy attack, for it was these curricula that were the subject of the letter to Secretary of Education Riley that was run as an advertisement in the *Washington Post* (see Chapters 1 and 8).

Part of the national dialogue also concerned systemic reform. The idea had gained such popularity that the National Science Foundation initiated a grants program for states interested in pursuing systemic reform initiatives. California, given Honig's early efforts, was a logical candidate, and the state applied for a State Systemic Initiative (SSI). The NSF gave California a five-year, $10 million grant in 1992. Honig and Maureen DiMarco (state secretary of child development and education) were to be co-principal investigators. Marshall Smith, co-author of the essay that introduced the language of "systemic" reform into the national discourse, was to head the evaluation effort. The SSI was to be named the California Advocacy for Mathematics and Science. Renamed the California Alliance for Mathematics and Science (CAMS), the initiative was to expand two extant networks of teachers: in mathematics, the Mathematics Renaissance Project and, in science, the California Science Implementation Network (CSIN).

During its first year of operating, CAMS offered summer institutes for teachers, introduced innovative instructional materials, and provided on-going support for teachers throughout the school year.[29] The project was conceptualized as a "river of reform": "Organizations interested in promoting change can learn from the water analogy. Isolated from each other, they may form a tight, cohesive group, but over time, their future could be ill fated. On the other hand, partnering with like-minded organizations that share common visions and policies can make an impact. By designing and maintaining systemic plans for implementation, reform efforts become a reality that move forward, not backward."[30]

The boundaries between the national and California discussions of mathematics education and its reform were porous and permeable. It was hard—as observers—to separate those discussions and to determine where ideas originated. Actors like Marshall Smith, Bill Honig, Tej Pandey, Elizabeth Stage, Phil Daro, and others moved back and forth between Washington and Sacramento. They picked up ideas at national conferences and imported them to the state as often as they shared Californian innovations with their colleagues in other state departments. In 1990, for example, the MSEB gave California seed money to start a statewide coalition—the California Coalition for Mathematics—that would bring together a diverse constituency: teachers and administrators, higher-education faculty and staff developers, representatives from industry, parents. Elizabeth Stage, Nicholas Branca, and Walter Denham (among others) participated in writing the proposal to the board. Elizabeth Stage went off to Washington, D.C., to work on the National Science Education Standards. Daro left the California Mathematics Project to work for the New Standards Project. James Smith and Francie Alexander, both CDE staff when the study started, moved to national positions (Smith as senior vice president of the National Board of Professional Teaching Standards, Alexander as deputy assistant secretary for policy and planning in the U.S. Department of Education). Marshall Smith, co-author of systemic reform and Stanford University professor and dean, had by this time become undersecretary of education. Judy Mumme, Joan Akers, and Walter Denham all regularly attended national meetings about curriculum, standards, and alternative assessment. Many California schoolteachers were part of the writing of and the reaction to the development of the NCTM 1989 *Standards*. The times were exciting, the conversations invigorating. And those California educators carried their enthusiasm and energy—as well as new ideas—back to California.

The *1992 Framework*

> Publication of the *1992 Mathematics Framework for California Public Schools* answers a call from the President of the United States, the nation's governors, the National Council of Teachers of Mathematics, the Mathematical Sciences Education Board, and the teachers and mathematics educators who served on the Framework Committee. That call is to change what mathematics we teach, how we teach it, and to whom.[31]

Because frameworks are on seven-year cycles of revision, the next framework was to be reissued in 1992. Again, the Curriculum Commission nominated a committee that was then approved by the State Board and that work began in 1988. The Curriculum Framework and Criteria Committee this time had fifteen members, including Alan Schoenfeld (from the University of California—Berkeley) and Philip Curtis (from UCLA) representing mathematics, six teachers from across the state, Judy Kysh, Judy Mumme, and Elaine Rosenfield (all teacher-leaders with extensive experience in the California Mathematics Project), and several other curriculum specialists. In the final stages of the process, Phil Daro—at that time executive director of the California Mathematics Project, and shortly thereafter a member of the New Standards Project in mathematics—took over.

Daro was another of the central players in mathematics education reform throughout the 1980s and 1990s. A high school kid during the *Sputnik* era, Daro was like me—a successful test taker; raised in New Jersey; encouraged to pursue mathematics and science by teachers and family alike, based almost completely on his test scores. Admittedly "carried away with the fervor," Daro went off to Berkeley to become a particle physicist. "They were just starting an honors math program there at Berkeley," Daro explained to me, "which was also part of *Sputnik,* and I got into the honors program. . . . It was taught by a mathematician, a small seminar, it was extremely formal. All we did is prove things, and I loved it."

Based on this experience, he decided to become a math major instead— that is, until he decided to drop out of school for a year and work in New York. By the time he returned to Berkeley, he had changed his mind again and eventually graduated with a B. A. in English, committed—as many students were at that time—to free speech and rejecting the establishment. Convinced that he was going to become a poet, he wrote a sonnet every morning before he had his coffee. But sonnets didn't pay the rent, and he eventually returned to New Jersey, enrolled in a teaching credential program at Trenton State, and was immediately assigned to teach math and chemistry classes based on his undergraduate transcript (my own emergency credential to teach high school mathematics was based on my high SAT scores).

Daro returned to California as a graduate student, finally ending up in the CDE, working in research and statistics. Called by some colleagues a "polymath," Daro has done a lot: he was director of the California Mathematics Project, as well as executive director of the mathematics portion of the New Standards Project. Currently, he is executive director of the California Institutes for Professional Development and the director of research and development for the National Center on Education and the Economy.

Daro's leadership role in the *1992 Framework* was different from the role Stage played in the *1985 Framework*. The CDE had hired a professional writer in this round, and so the draft was much more coherent by the time Daro stepped in. Instead, Daro played a crucial role in opening lines of communication, and making sure that relevant interest groups, including University of California mathematicians, had input on the draft and its revisions. In 1991, the draft was sent out; over 500 reviews were received, compiled, and used in the editing. Several insiders told us that the draft *1992 Framework* had to be "toned down." According to Honig—and others— some "zealots" wished to push the reform beyond "sensible" boundaries, and the review process was meant to result in a more reasonable stance.

The final *1992 Framework* was intended as an elaboration of the *1985 Framework*. It was considerably longer (217 pages, as opposed to 46 pages in 1985). An eighth strand—discrete mathematics—was added to the original seven. The authors changed "logic" to "logic and language," to emphasize the importance of language in mathematical communication, and they edited "patterns and functions" to be "functions," noting that there are relevant patterns in all the strands.

"Mathematical power" had figured prominently in the *1985 Framework*, which the authors defined as "the ability to discern mathematical relationships, reason logically, and use mathematical techniques effectively."[32] In the *1992 Framework*, the committee expanded that discussion and offered a diagram, shown in Figure 6.1.

Mathematically powerful work was defined as "purposeful." The concept was so central to the *1992 Framework* committee members that they devoted an entire chapter to it, including discussions of the dimensions of mathematical power (thinking, communication, ideas, and tools and techniques),

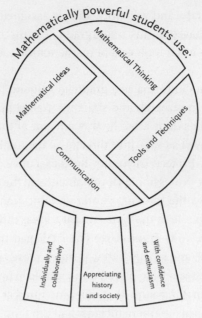

Figure 6.1.

goals that support mathematical power (collaborative work, positive dispositions toward mathematics, connections to mathematical history and to society), expectations for student work, and how mathematics is learned in ways that support the development of mathematical power.

In another chapter, the authors explain how to develop mathematical power in classrooms, including discussions of "the gift" of diversity, the role of the teacher, the place of technology and manipulatives, why teachers need to move away from tracking and ability grouping, and how one assesses student work for mathematical power. The final three chapters discuss the curricular content: the place of the strands, the relationship between the NCTM 1989 *Standards* and the 1992 *Framework*, the role of units of instruction and their "unifying ideas."

The document is sprinkled with three-column charts that contrast "traditional practices" with "some alternative practices" with "recommended practices." Teachers are urged to engage in messy mathematical work, to act as guides and pacers, and to model positive dispositions and problem solving attitudes toward mathematics. The authors propose a dozen "guiding principles" for "teaching for understanding" that were originally proposed in the 1987 *K–8 Model Curriculum Guide*. The principles clearly emphasize constructivist theories of learning and a progressive view of the teacher's role (almost to the exclusion of anything that smacks of the traditional and familiar). The list is full of exhortations: "Our top priority should be the development of students' thinking and understanding," "We must know that understanding is achieved through direct, personal experience," "Students need to verify their thinking for themselves rather than depend on an outside authority," "We should encourage students to work together in small groups," "We must be interested in what students are really thinking," "We must value the development of mathematical language."[33]

The *1992 Framework* concludes with a series of appendixes. One appendix lists traditional, alternative, and desired classroom practices. Another summarizes changes in the curricular content and lists topics in two-column charts that show which topics will receive "increased attention" (number sense, estimation, mental computation, collection and organization of data) and which will receive "decreased attention" (naming geometric figures, memorizing equivalencies between units of measurement, isolated treatment of division facts, long division, paper-and-pencil fraction computation, for example). The document assures teachers that change takes time and that the authors of the framework did not intend it to be a detailed roadmap. Instead, the authors invite teachers to "summon the courage to see where we are and the courage to begin the journey" forward.

The document is everything critics of the education establishment abhor. It's wordy and speckled with educationese ("problem solving," "mathematical power," "investigations," "unifying ideas"). It mixes descriptions of content with descriptions of teaching. It deemphasizes traditional practices and encourages innovation and progressive ideas. It makes claims based on the folklore of teaching and educational philosophy, and treats those statements like empirical truths (while I might agree that "Memorizing definitions without understanding interferes with thinking," this is not something that has been proven through scholarship). It urges teachers to teach "unifying ideas" even though not all teachers have solid mathematical knowledge of the building blocks of those ideas.

Overall, however, for the reformers the document is a hopeful one: "There is overwhelming agreement that this framework appropriately and accurately describes the mathematics programs that should be established in our schools."[34] It was, perhaps, the last hopeful document the reformers would get to pen.

7 The Tide Turns: 1993–1995

And nothing really changes if the dream turns into a nightmare. California owns, and promotes, its own dystopia, too.
—Richard Wright

The disasters we create in response to true belief.
—William Kittredge

By 1992, California had many pieces of the reform puzzle in place: a framework and aligned assessment system, a theory of professional development, innovative curricula. This was a systemic reformer's dream come true, surprising in any context, especially surprising in a state as diverse and large as California. But then things started to disintegrate.

It is hard to pinpoint where and when the unraveling began. In 1991, tensions arose between Bill Honig and the State Board. Insiders spoke of "power struggles." In 1991 and 1992, upset with Honig's unwillingness to implement some of their policies, the State Board sued him. This led to a court of appeals decision in 1993, which gave the board more power and directed the superintendent to implement board policy. At the same time, the board was reprimanded for "micromanaging" and overstepping its legal authority. The decision was appealed to the Supreme Court, which decided not to hear it.

Things got worse. It was revealed that the California Department of Education had contracted with Honig's wife's nonprofit organization. Honig was brought up on conflict of interest charges, found guilty in record time, and, in 1993, removed from office. Rumors ran wild: maybe the charges were a convenient way to rid the governor of a high-profile, nationally respected, obstinate public figure.

Although the CDE staff was remarkable and tireless in their commitment, enthusiasm, and experience, without Honig's leadership, the systemic effort to transform mathematics teaching in California became vulnerable to attack. The first target was the controversial and innovative testing system, California Learning Assessment System (CLAS).

The Demise of CLAS

In the spring of 1993, CLAS mathematics and language arts performance assessments were administered statewide to more than 1 million students in grades 4, 5, 8, and 10. Because the CLAS tests contained multiple choice and open-ended items, the items were harder to score and much more labor intensive. This required the use of a technique called "matrix sampling," which entails divvying up portions from a larger pool of questions into separate booklets. These different subsets are given to equivalent samples of students. The strategy minimizes the time taken for testing while also allowing for complete coverage of the content being assessed. However, every child is not equally tested for every content item in equal depth and breadth.[1] Thus, using this strategy means that not every child receives a score, a practice to which Governor Wilson was committed. Exacerbating the problem was the decision to score only 42 percent of the open-ended test items because of budget and time constraints (all the multiple choice items were scored).

Questions began to be raised about the test. What did it look like? What were some example questions? Why was it so different from traditional tests? In response to this first wave of critical questions, one informant told us that the CDE "hunkered down in its bunker," adopting a "siege" mentality, and refused to release test items, insisting that maintaining secrecy was essential to the assessment's integrity.[2] This defensiveness fanned the flames and lost the CDE potential public and political support. As sample CLAS questions began to leak out, opposition mounted. Small groups of parents (and several conservative legal organizations that backed them) initiated lawsuits against school districts. The test—which repeatedly asked students to explain their reasoning, think critically, perform experiments, and write essays—was accused of invading students' privacy.

Much of the opposition focused on questions from the language arts portion of CLAS, most notably selections that involved controversial literature, like the work of Richard Wright, Dick Gregory, Alice Walker, and Maxine Hong Kingston, minority authors who wrote of the sometimes troubling lives of minorities, the oppressed, and women (long before Oprah Winfrey's book selections gave authors like these a more popular, national stature). "Roselily," a short story by Alice Walker, evoked controversy because it was interpreted as offensive to the religiously observant. An excerpt from Annie Dillard's *An American Childhood*, which involved children throwing snowballs, was criticized for supporting violence.

One item that was circulated asked students to explain their reasoning. A picture of a head (with nothing in it) accompanied the question. Children were to fill in the head with their thoughts. Critics declared this "open mind question" inappropriate because it "delved into individuals' psyches." Schools are responsible for providing students with knowledge and skill, not for invading their privacy and asking them about their innermost thoughts, the critics argued. One's thoughts are a private matter between parents and children.

The critics declared, "We want mastery of academics, not student attitudes."[3] As the criticisms became more public, phony test items were circulated as examples of what might be on the test.[4] No differentiation was made between actual items, piloted-and-rejected items, and imagined items. It would not be the last time that media coverage inflamed the discourse with strategically selected examples that fanned passions rather than furthering deliberation. Of particular note was the growing dominance of reasoning by anecdote. A columnist, reformer, or critic would tell a story of something that happened to someone they knew that represented the very worst thing that could happen and treat it like the norm. This would become a characteristic of later discussions. The "war" had started.

As it turns out, California was not alone in experiencing a backlash against innovative assessments. Opponents to Indiana's statewide testing program went to court to block the use of essay questions they labeled as "too personal" and "psychologically intrusive," complaining that the essay questions were about "attitudes, not academics."[5] Similar controversies erupted around Kentucky's alternative assessment (KIRIS), with criticisms being leveled at test prompts and scoring rubrics that were pro-women's rights, pro-environmentalism, and pro-multiculturalism. The "train wreck" of the Arizona Student Assessment Program died before it was ever implemented.[6]

Six statewide groups led the first wave of the California backlash: the Traditional Values Coalition, based in Anaheim and part of a national network of churches that have lobbied for prayer in schools and anti-abortion and gay rights legislation; the Capitol Resource Institute, located in Sacramento and affiliated with The Focus on the Family, a conservative Christian coalition based in Colorado; the Eagle Forum, the national organization founded by Phyllis Schlafly; Parents Involved in Education, a statewide group committed to reinstituting parental power and rights; the Rutherford Institute, a Virginia-based Christian legal organization that solicits volunteer lawyers willing to litigate cases involving trespasses on constitutional liberties; and the United States Justice Foundation, an official-sounding, conservative legal foundation based in Escondido, California.

Concerns have a way of snowballing. Pursuing information about one concern sometimes leads to the discovery of another. Anxieties rise, emotions elevate. Parents were originally concerned with the invasiveness, but as they learned more, their worries multiplied: Where was the *content?* One opposition leader explained:

> We were opposed to [CLAS] for two reasons. The first concern was the one that had a tendency to catch the attention of the media. It was that the test seemed to be delving into areas of students' psyches. The types of questions and the types of stories were emotional ones. It appeared that the people making the test had a philosophical agenda. The test was an invasion of student and family privacy.
>
> But there was a much deeper concern that we didn't see until we delved into the test much more. CLAS was not challenging enough for kids academically. The standards being tested were unclear and not rigorous. I would define rigorous as testing kids for a knowledge of facts, but more than just a regurgitation of facts. A rigorous test would also challenge students' intellectual abilities. . . . We've been told by a math expert that in the CLAS test, basic skills were skipped over, but students were expected to do problems that college physics students can't complete.[7]

Note the concerns about rigor, for they would resonate with later concerns about education establishment, the predominance of process, and the erosion of a classic, traditional education.[8] More concerns arose. Bill Honig had overpromised what CLAS could do. Governor Wilson wanted individual test scores; Honig promised that he would have them, even though it was beyond the capacity of the CDE to develop, pilot, and implement a completely new, cutting-edge test with the time and money allotted. The project's time line was much too short for the development necessary, the costs considerable.[9] Researcher Lorraine McDonnell estimates that in its first years, CLAS cost at least $30 per student tested (as opposed to the costs of between $2 and $20 per pupil typically charged by commercial testing houses for off-the-shelf tests).[10] The large-scale education necessary to train scorers, or to adjust expectations of teachers, administrators, parents, and students, could not be planned and mounted thoughtfully.

Between them, the Rutherford Institute and the United States Justice Foundation filed lawsuits against more than thirty school districts in an attempt to block the administration of the 1994 CLAS. The opponents lost their cases, but a provision was made that allowed California students to opt out of taking the statewide test. The opposition—a small minority of parents and teachers—was concentrated in the southern parts of the state, most notably in rural and suburban areas. Of the 1.2 million school children to be tested, 61,000 opted out (about 5 percent). Given the conservative character of these organizations and the small size of their albeit vocal constituency, many of the original reformers were quick to dismiss the objections as marginal, raised by the religious, fundamentalist right, not John Q. Public. Like the problems they had encountered with textbook companies when those companies refused to make major curricular revisions, the reformers saw these criticisms as a bump in the relatively steady road to progress.

More complaints were registered. School district personnel complained that the testing procedure was complicated and, in some districts, poorly organized. Journalists wrote of angry parents of children who traditionally did well on tests, yet did poorly on the CLAS. The *Los Angeles Times* conducted an investigation of the sampling procedures, claiming that there were more than 11,000 methodological violations in 1993 alone (a claim that was later disputed by Acting Superintendent David Dawson).[11] The president of the California Teachers Association wrote a scathing letter to the CDE.

Dawson appointed the Committee on Sampling and Statistical Procedures, a panel of three highly regarded measurement specialists—including Norman Bradburn from the University of Chicago, Daniel G. Horvitz from the National Institutes for the Statistical Sciences, and Lee Cronbach (the committee's chair) from Stanford University—to review the test. The panel submitted a report applauding the "energy and imagination" that went into the CLAS's development, and saw many of the initial problems as predictable growing pains for an innovative and radically different assessment system. While the authors were critical, they did not suggest the state abandon the CLAS; rather, they recommended that the state appoint a single contractor to oversee its administration, as well as full-time technical coordinators to analyze and interpret results.[12]

From Bellwether to Bottom of the Barrel

Meanwhile, other storms were brewing. California has always taken pride in a world-class education system, so, in 1992, when the media reported that California students had done very poorly on the National Assessment of Educational Progress (NAEP), tying with Louisiana (just ahead of Guam) and at the bottom of the state heap for test scores, parents and politicians alike were alarmed.[13] Things got worse: in 1994, NAEP scores ranked California near the bottom in mathematics and reading. For a state that took pride in leading the pack, having a state score lower than the national average every year was a blow.

The public was outraged, and the new language arts and mathematics frameworks quickly became the scapegoat. In some ways, this assumption would make sense—after all, weren't the frameworks responsible for what children learned? But the history of education reform in the United States casts doubt on this facile analysis. Over and again, research has demonstrated that teachers do not change their practice simply because a new textbook, curriculum guide, or framework arrives at the classroom door or because a far-removed policy maker announces a new mandate. Instead, if teachers change their practices at all, they combine old with new, creating, as David Tyack and Larry Cuban argue, "pedagogical hybrids": "Reformers who adopt a rational planning mode of educational reform sometimes expect that they will improve schools if they design their policies correctly. They may measure success by fidelity to plan, by whether predetermined goals are met, and by longevity. Such a technocratic and top-down approach, however, slights the many ways in which schools shape reforms and teachers employ their 'wisdom of practice' to produce pedagogical hybrids . . . schools are not wax to be imprinted."[14]

In part, these hybrids arise because teachers are not blank slates; rather, teachers interpret and react to new mandates drawing on past experience and current knowledge. Milbrey McLaughlin argues that this "muddling through" might be for the best, for "there are few 'slam bang' policy effects. This is because policy effects are necessarily indirect, operating through and within the existing setting. Thus policy is transformed and adapted to conditions of the implementing unit. . . . But we also have begun to understand that this kind of incremental, creeping, locally defined change is often for the best. . . . 'Muddling through' then can be seen not only as an adaptive response to demands for change but also as the more beneficial response in the long term."[15]

Most teachers take seriously their obligations as civil servants, and they responsibly follow mandates. But they do so prudently, mixing old practices with new, seldom completely abandoning what they consider to be sound practice. California teachers in the 1980s were no different. In fact, a national survey funded by the National Science Foundation found that teachers' classroom activities were more traditional than not, and were not aligned with the recommendations of the National Council for Teachers of Mathematics or National Research Council. Over 6,000 K–12 teachers in approximately 1,250 schools reported a heavy emphasis on helping prepare students for standardized tests (40 percent) and on learning algorithms (54 percent of high school mathematics teachers). The researchers also found that traditional methodologies still dominated science and mathematics teaching, and while many teachers reported that they were in favor of more "hands-on" instruction, they nonetheless thought that "students must master arithmetic computation before going on."[16] (I return to this issue in Chapter 9, when I briefly consider what classrooms looked like while this tempest was brewing in the public arena.)

So if teaching did not change dramatically, why the drop in test scores? Since the discussion went immediately to blaming the frameworks, there was no systematic analysis of the many factors that might have accounted for what the public perceived as a precipitous and alarming drop in NAEP scores.

We do know some things, however. California's public education system had been suffering from serious neglect for nearly twenty years. Per pupil spending had taken a nosedive: in 1964–65, California was ranked fifth in the nation, spending 20 percent over the national average per pupil. In 1994–95, it was ranked forty-first, roughly 20 percent below the national average. (In 1999, it was still well below the national average.) In *Education Week*'s 1997 report cards for states, California was given a D− for school climate and resource adequacy.[17]

Teacher salaries kept pace with inflation (largely owing to a very powerful California Teachers Association), so belts were tightened by deferring building maintenance and the purchase of new equipment, and by slashing arts and music programs and counseling and nursing services. This dive in state support for education was related to larger financial dramas being played out in the state, most notably Proposition 13.[18]

Researchers differ as to the connection between per pupil spending and student achievement, and I am not offering one facile explanation to replace another.[19] But it seems reasonable to think that overcrowded classrooms, outdated textbooks, buckling floors, leaky roofs, and too many portable classrooms do not enhance learning, especially when combined with a steadily increasing student enrollment, and especially in urban, high-poverty environments. The poverty rate in the state—25 percent in 1998—had doubled since 1969.[20] As Peter Schrag wrote: "No one can accurately measure the accumulated effects of a generation, more or less, of rotting public services, of noninvestment and disinvestments, or the cost of the deferred maintenance, much less the consequences of the economic opportunities missed, or the damage to confidence in the most basic public services. Nor can anyone really calculate the cost in community and in human health, social pathology, and miseducation. But some signs—dismally low reading and math scores of California students on the National Assessment of Educational Progress, for example, or high dropout rates, crime rates, and teen birth rates that are all among the ten highest in the country—are hard to miss."[21]

Complicating things further is the fact that one out of every four Californians is born outside of the United States. For the overwhelming majority of California schoolchildren, English is not their first language. In 1996, over 1.3 million students were identified as limited-English-proficient. And analyses of the NAEP math items, especially items designed to assess more than simple recall, suggest that, especially on longer items, students who spoke a language other than English at home performed significantly lower on the NAEP than students who spoke only English at home. Thus, there is a serious confounding of language and performance on NAEP math items.[22]

Given this tangle of forces, it is unlikely that curricular reforms of the 1980s—"whole language" and "new new math," as critics were calling them—were the sole culprits in plummeting test scores. But the public debate largely ignored these other circumstances. One long-time lobbyist told the *California Journal* that the language arts framework "was the single most-damaging education reform effort in the history of the state—and it may have overwhelmed the good of all the rest. The state should've required scientific evidence that [the framework] worked before subjecting the entire state's student population to this experiment."[23]

The call for "scientific evidence" would continue. By the summer of 1994 when Gary Hart, the state senator who sponsored the original authorization of the CLAS, was writing its reauthorization, the uproar reached a crescendo. In August, at an anti-CLAS rally at the state capitol, Senator Bill Leonard, a Republican from Redlands, called for the impeachment of interim State Superintendent of Instruction Dawson for administering the CLAS to California children. Governor Wilson withdrew $26.4 million in funding, refusing to authorize its expenditure until the assessment system was revised. Among the revisions that Wilson demanded were changes in oversight, development, and scoring, following up on the recommendations of the measurement experts. Wilson also demanded that teachers be pulled out of the process and that "experts" from contracted testing houses score and develop the test. He wanted the State Board to approve the test rather than the state superintendent of schools, and he wanted to appoint a parent advisory panel that would have the right to modify, reject, and alter the test.[24]

Teachers and teacher-leaders were worried and offended. California had a long history of heavy teacher involvement in the development of curriculum and assessment policies. After all, teachers worked in the trenches, and they brought to state policy making a wealth of practical knowledge. One teacher noted that Wilson was "coming from a completely different philosophical view. What's being proposed is taking teachers completely out of the loop, and that was the magic that made CLAS work. It reflects the best classroom practice."

Measurement specialists were also concerned, in particular about the governor compromising the integrity of standardized tests by allowing the State Board to tinker with carefully crafted items that had been piloted and normed for reliability and validity. The inclusion of parents and the State Board—as equals with the educators and the measurement experts— in educational decision making was a significant shift away from the professional process toward a more public one.

In part, the push for a more inclusive process was fueled by the sense that the CLAS tests had been written by a group of insiders. One member of the governor's staff noted, "I think they [the CLAS tests] stink; they're instructionally horrible. They got that way because the curriculum Nazis—

the content folks in the [State Department of Education] and the people they used on committees—had an agenda. These people are a very insular, in-bred group. . . . That wasn't a problem when Bill [Honig] was there. I'm convinced that *Black Boy* and the open mind question would not have been on the test if he had been there. I know I sound like I'm saying, 'if only Bill, if only Bill. . .' But it's true, it would have been different if he had been there."[25]

Others, too, felt that Honig had become distracted by the attacks on his administration, failing to rein in an overly zealous group within the education establishment who wanted to replace all basic skills testing with authentic assessments. While unkind, the accusation of an "insular, in-bred group" is, in some ways, fair, if by that one means the leaders of mathematics education in the state. But those leaders were not all zealots. When Honig's staff wanted to put some "bite" into California's frameworks and remedy the past problems of a watered-down framework weakened by consensus, they drew upon the extant professional consensus, which was not dominated by zealots, although there were zealots within the ranks.

Perhaps the more serious problem was not fanaticism, but a lack of public engagement in the entire process. Teachers and teacher educators—the education establishment, as some like to call us—dominated the process (although a few mathematicians had also participated). As Susan Fuhrman and Diane Massell noted, "Highly regarded teachers, scholars, and other state and national experts were selected for the framework writing committees. Draft frameworks would circulate to networks of professional educators for review and comment. Unlike some other states where lay citizens are actively involved in setting broad goals for education and for curriculum prior to the drafting of frameworks, citizen participation in California largely occurs during the process through regular meetings or public hearings of the Curriculum Development and Supplementary Materials Commission. . . . The state also requires lay citizen input during district reviews that compare local curriculum to the state frameworks and decide upon matters like state textbooks."[26]

Although the system that I described earlier—with its Byzantine and confusing structure of the SB, CDE, CC, SMC, CFCCs, IMEPs, review processes, open meetings, public hearings—appears to be a system with permeable boundaries, offering textbook publishers, the public, and others multiple opportunities to participate, the system was not designed to *guarantee* diversity of perspective. Instead, it was possible that one group could control the process by "stacking" the relevant committees. This was done not malevolently, but in the name of making progress, by finding committed mathematics teachers and leaders in the state (people who had spent their careers trying to make schools better places for children) and asking them to establish standards. But without others—teachers who opposed the reforms, mathematicians who worried about the content, parents who did not recognize the mathematics their children would encounter— the formal process did not serve as a forum in which different parties could, over time, work out their fundamental differences. Further complicating the issue was the fact that many very good mathematics teachers did not participate, for they chose not to be part of the progressive educator networks. Finally, experience is not equivalent to expertise; thus, the expertise of the experienced educators who participated was uneven.

As David Cohen would write several years later: "Public education about public education is especially critical, because public schools are locally and popularly controlled and thus quite vulnerable to public pressure. But the reformers who pressed standards-based reforms spent little time or energy on efforts to build a broad constituency. Like the 1950s reformers, they were members of political and professional elites; they worried about the lack of a broad constituency for the reforms they advocated, but they did little about the problem. That was probably a fundamental mistake."[27]

Similar problems were fermenting on the national level as the NCTM *1989 Standards* drew their own share of criticism, ranging from accusations that they were—alternately—too conservative and too progressive. Education scholar Michael Apple called the NCTM standards a "slogan system," arguing that such systems are vague enough to attract support from multiple—sometimes differing—communities yet focused enough to offer some concrete suggestions and ideas. Apple suggests that such systems have the ability to charm, to "grab us." As a slogan system, the NCTM *1989 Standards* might have attracted people with very different ideologies (and different goals), only then to be used by the most powerful subgroups within the initially broad coalition for a singular, more narrow set of goals. Apple worried that those goals would further a conservative education agenda, maintaining (rather than toppling) the status quo and extant inequalities, perpetuating a system in which mathematical knowledge is *intentionally* not accessible to all, and a system in which standards are used as an excuse to keep some people out.[28]

Meanwhile, other critics saw the NCTM *1989 Standards* as too radical and progressive, arguing that they were written by a group of insiders unwilling to listen to dissenters. Frank Allen, a former NCTM president, posted several criticisms and letters of complaint on the Internet, including a quotation he attributed to Lord Stockton: "Again the Liberals have come forward with many good and new ideas. Unfortunately none of the good ideas is new and none of the new ideas is good." He called for open debate and raised questions about some of the underlying assumptions of the NCTM 1989 *Standards:* Was it really true that many teachers emphasize drill without conceptual understanding? Is complex assessment a good idea? Does research support the vision of mathematics education in the *Standards?* He posted a poem on his website:

Pity the NCTM today
A worthy group that's gone astray
A group completely under the sway
Of theoreticians, far away
From schoolroom events of everyday
It matters little what they say
This is the message their deeds convey:

"Standardized tests are an awful bane,
They reveal little or negative gain,
And we regard them with disdain.
A little logic might cause some pain,
From proof that's tough we will abstain.
We'll appeal to the hand instead of the brain.
Subject teacher time to a terrible drain,
With an assessment system that's hard to explain.
We'll repeat sixth grade, like an old refrain,
Recycling the facts all over again."

"If you disagree with us at all
You are a Neanderthal."

If we can't stop them then let us pray
For secondary math in the USA.[29]

Other websites materialized, some in support of the *Standards,* others in opposition. *Education Week* ran an article by Chester E. Finn, Jr.: "What if those math standards are wrong?" "Has this new approach been fully tested?" he asked. "Do we have enough qualified teachers? Are we throwing the baby out with the bathwater?": "We oughtn't dump all our eggs into [one] basket. . . . Or any other. No single container is capacious enough. Diverse classroom strategies should be welcome—so long as solid learning occurs. The reason for standards isn't to impose a regimen of what Diane Ravitch terms 'pedagogical imperialism.' Rather, it's to be clear and prescriptive about ends—and then laid back and versatile about means. I doubt this was intended, but the NCTM may have given a boost to such imperialist tendencies in math."[30]

John Saxon, publisher of a curriculum series for traditional math instruction, bought an advertisement in *Education Week:* "Proposed Math-Testing Standards Damaging to Minorities," the headline ran, "We have had three generations of non-productive nonsense from NCTM. Enough is enough!"[31]

At the national level, some reformers tried to engage in discussion (unlike the dig-in-your-heels reaction of the CLAS test developers). A central bone of contention was the reformers' position on basic skills. The then-president of the NCTM went on record: "First, we believe that students need basic skills and that they need to develop algorithms to help them do mathematics efficiently and effectively. Perhaps we have not stated those needs clearly enough. We do not want teachers to throw away everything that has worked well for their students in the past, but we do want them to understand that the nature and content of mathematics is changing."[32]

Unfortunately, the ferment and politicization was beginning to spin out of control, obscuring nuances like reform-as-shifting-emphases versus reform-as-full-scale-replacement of one ideology with another. Meanwhile, things weren't quieting down in California and the public concerns about the CLAS (and the associated frameworks) continued to appear in newspaper headlines. Hart rewrote the CLAS reauthorization bill (SB 1273), which passed both houses despite opposition from a number of conservative Republicans. But in September 1994, Wilson vetoed the legislation, and all state-level testing was called to a halt.[33] Governor Wilson argued that he wanted a testing program that would yield reliable individual scores for every California schoolchild, noting that performance-based assessment might become a legitimate aspect of an accountability system that had "multiple measures," another assessment idea that was growing in popularity.[34] However, he noted, the reauthorization of CLAS proposed that such a system would not be in place until the spring of 1999. "That's not good enough," he claimed, "It's too long a wait."

Lorraine McDonnell posits five factors that led to the premature deconstruction of this elaborate and innovative assessment system. First, she notes, the participants in the development process were curriculum experts, psychometricians, and teachers who subscribed to a constructivist view of learning and teaching. (We already know the labels that harsh conservative journalists were beginning to assign to this group: "pedagogical imperialists," "educrats," "the educational establishment," or "curriculum Nazis.") Thus, the process included a relatively narrow range of educators and little to no public discussion. Second, time and budget constraints seriously limited what the reformers were able to do, given the radical shift in assessment (and content) that the new test required. The secrecy around the test only helped to fan the flames. "It makes you wonder what people are doing to your children if you have no right to see the test," one opposition leader noted. McDonnell also notes that there was a lack of legislative oversight, a problem compounded by very little political leadership, as Honig resigned and was replaced by Dave Dawson, a career civil servant. A final factor was timing: the controversy occurred in an election year. With every move, Pete Wilson had the potential to attract or repel potential voters.[35]

Nine Plus Three: Adopting New Textbooks

Meanwhile, in the wake of the 1992 *Framework*, yet another round of textbook adoption occurred. The Curriculum Commission nominated a group of mathematics teachers and educators, and this time around, nineteen publishers submitted twenty-five different programs. Many of the large publishing houses—given their experience in the last round of adoptions— had invested heavily in creating "California-friendly" textbooks. Houghton Mifflin alone invested $20 million in an overhaul that started in 1991 and lasted until spring of 1993. Other publishing firms began investing in innovative curricula including materials developed by National Science Foundation–sponsored projects.[36]

The Curriculum Commission (based on recommendations from the reform-dominated Curriculum Framework and Criteria Committee) rejected Houghton Mifflin's submission to the next round of textbook adoption, as well as the Encyclopedia Britannica materials. California was expected to spend approximately $130 million on mathematics textbooks alone after

this round of adoption, and losing California as a market would cost
Houghton Mifflin alone approximately $10 million over the next three
years. Heavy lobbying ensued. Publishing analysts slashed their earnings
projections; one cut $13 million from her earnings figure. Rumors flew
about whether State Board members might be swayed by bribes from the
textbook publishers (not a totally paranoid notion, given Richard Feynman's
experience). Houghton Mifflin and Silver Burdett both brought in public relations firms to help lobby for a change.

Of particular concern to several mathematicians were some of the "innovative" curricula on the list, particularly MathLand, which they found
incoherent and mathematically compromised. (Concerns for MathLand
eventually compelled concerned mathematicians to write their open letter
to Secretary of Education Richard Riley in the *Washington Post*.)

As was standard practice, the CC recommended a list of approved texts
to the State Board. In an unprecedented move, on October 14, the board
voted 6–1 to *add* three math programs to the list of approved texts:
Houghton Mifflin, Silver Burdett, and Encyclopedia Britannica. One board
member reported that she had met with the Houghton Mifflin people at
least twice and had been persuaded by their logic: "Teachers should have
the option of using a more traditional math curriculum such as Houghton's," she explained.[37]

Staffers at the CDE were appalled and discouraged. Dawson, then acting superintendent, said, "It's as if a bunch of wealthy parents came in to
lobby the principal to get their kids' grades changed." Delaine Eastin, a state
assemblywoman who was then running for the state superintendency,
was cutting in her criticism, calling the move "a real pollution of the process."[38] The reformers were shocked. Rumors included one that went so
far as to suggest that word had been leaked to Wall Street ahead of time
that the "fix was in." After all, Houghton Mifflin stock had taken a dive (on
October 13, shares were at 40 ¾, down ¼), only to recover the next morning; yet the decision had been made on California time, three hours later. Indeed, the stock prices did rise. On the 14th, shares were up by 3 ⅛ to 43 ⅞,
and on Monday the 17th, the stock had risen again, this time to 47 ⅛ per
share.[39] Meanwhile, critics of the adopted curricula were horrified. Math-
Land, for example, was a fatally flawed curriculum in their eyes, lacking in
both mathematical rigor and pedagogical prudence. Of particular concern
was the fact that there was little empirical data demonstrating that the innovative curricula led to higher student achievement.

Opposition continued to grow. Debra J. Saunders, a self-proclaimed "conservative journalist" for the *San Francisco Chronicle,* began writing scathing columns. In "Duck, It's the New-New Math," she wrote that the curricula the commission had recommended to the State Board could "deprive children of a foundation necessary for strong math skills and replace basic absolutes with 'meaningful'—not necessarily correct—ways of computing." Quoting from one of the approved curricula, Saunders was appalled at the claim that there was more than one right way to solve a problem, that children need to learn how to describe their reasoning, and that teachers might need to probe students thinking. Saunders called the new curricula "fuzzy crap" and "edu-think," sarcastically questioning the reformers' belief that "people will understand a 25-percent sale better if, as children, not if they memorized basic math, but if their classes were meaningful."[40] In another article entitled "There Is No One Answer," she railed on: "Apparently state educrats have decided that there isn't enough uncertainty in the world, so they needed to inject some extra ambiguity into junior high mathematics."[41] In yet another column, she described her view of the process: "Process-Firsters used their consensus-loving committees to control thought and suppress opposition. After a panel wrote the new-new math framework, another panel happily enforced it. The Instructional Resources Evaluation Panel blacklisted traditional texts and penalized those that featured lessons that called for 'predetermined numerical results,' were 'repetitive' or were taught 'generally under the direction of the teacher.'"[42]

Many of the teachers and teacher-leaders we interviewed were stunned by these commentaries. Teachers are not typically political veterans; most live relatively quiet lives working in modest classrooms, on modest salaries. To see their ideas and professional processes ridiculed in this way alternately hurt and enraged them. Few had abandoned the basics, all believed in strong foundational knowledge, and few saw the pedagogical potential of exploring multiple solution paths as *necessarily* in opposition to getting a right answer.

But anecdotal "horror stories" became popular newspaper fodder statewide, with stories of teachers neglecting the basics, of children being taught that algorithms are evil, of parents being told not to teach their children how to solve problems with tried-and-true rules. As with the CLAS items, some stories were no doubt true—or at least remotely related to something that had happened to someone's son or granddaughter. Other stories were not. But it was impossible to sort fact from fiction, and the discourse deteriorated further, moving from one in which critics reasonably called for evidence and raised critical questions, to reasoning or—in the case of some of the Saunders articles—ridicule by anecdote.

A month after the textbook adoption debacle, Delaine Eastin was elected the new state superintendent of schools, and California Republicans regained control of the Assembly. Eastin began her administration by reorganizing the Department of Education, in part to replace the "old guard" (advocates for, as one person put it, "too radical a shift away from 'pen and pencil computation'") with people who had a more balanced perspective. Eastin was rumored to be "pulling back," and some CDE insiders reported that they had heard her say, "We don't always have to be out there to make change." The leaders of the earlier reforms began to worry.

A Call for "Focus"

In the winter of 1995, one of Eastin's first acts as state superintendent was to call together two task forces—one for reading, one for mathematics—to examine the frameworks. Eastin did not, however, ask for the State Board's feedback about this process, thus planting seeds for a "lukewarm" reception by the board to Eastin's administration. Ever since Bill Honig's administration, the relationship between the superintendent and the State Board had remained unclear, with no one quite knowing how much latitude the state superintendent had to implement his or her own ideas, programs, and agendas, or how much congruence to expect between the wishes of the State Board and the work of the CDE.

Eastin appointed all the members of the task forces. Appointments included insiders and outsiders to the "education establishment." Her charge to the group was clear: "Let's do what needs to be done to turn education in mathematics around—to prepare all of California's children for success in the future by providing them with the knowledge and skills they will need. And let's do it now."[43]

From the start, the mathematics task force had problems. The committee was chaired by Phil Daro (who had polished the final version of the 1992 Framework). This led some people to be suspicious of just how "balanced" the committee was. Debra Saunders wrote: "Eastin's appointees to her new math task force overwhelmingly loved new-new math. A math advisory draft written by her staff is pro-new-new math. And a group she appointed to revise the draft is stacked with new-new mathers."[44]

Other members, however, were not associated with the earlier reforms, including Kathryn Dronenburg, a member of the State Board of Education, several school district superintendents, teachers, parents, and representatives from IBM and Hewlett Packard. The task force also included several prominent education researchers, including Berkeley professor Alan Schoenfeld and UCLA professor James Stigler, as well as teacher-leaders from the mathematics education community, among them Elaine Rosenfield and Ruth Cossey. The committee's mixed membership was intended to shift ownership of the process from the education establishment to a more diverse, democratic group, one that included parents, business representatives, and community leaders.

Daro reported that although the task force had originally wanted to "get rid of constructivism," eventually it came out calling for balance, "skills, problem solving, and concepts." From Daro's perspective, the history of debate about mathematics education has involved three factions: the "mathematical skills" people, who push for computation; the "mathematical concepts" people, who claim that without conceptual knowledge of mathematical ideas you cannot apply those ideas to novel situations; and the "real life applications" people, who lobby hard for "real life" problems so that students won't forget what they have learned. The task force tried to strike a balance, believing that "if any one of those groups loses, it is a disaster and if any one wins, it is a disaster."

The task force made five recommendations. It urged Eastin to take immediate steps to establish clear and specific content and performance standards; to establish a "stable, coherent, and informative" assessment system; to provide adequate resources—time, instructional materials, "mathematically powerful" teachers; to establish a management, research, and information system about the state's mathematics policies and programs; and to urge administrators and teachers to work with parents in the identification of the responsibilities of school and home. Both the mathematics and reading task forces issued reports calling for more balance, arguing for more "basic skills" and traditional mathematics instruction but not at the expense of problem solving. However, what anyone meant by "balance" remained unclear. One member of the task force eventually resigned out of frustration with the "mushy" characteristics of balance.

These calls for balance were nothing new. Eliakim Moore had called for "Evolution, not revolution" in his 1902 presidential address to the American Mathematical Society. Alfred North Whitehead had warned of the pedantry that comes with a narrow focus on drill. New Math reformers had called for more attention to inquiry and problem solving, but not to the exclusion of the basics. The *1985 Framework* had used the language of more and less "emphasis" on teaching for understanding and traditional rote instruction, respectively.

Eastin sent bundles of the reports—*Every Child a Reader* and *Improving Mathematics Achievement for All California Schools*—to every superintendent in the state. Although some members of the press put a "back-to-basics" spin on the report, Eastin explained: "While some headline writers seem to want to simplify this message to say it signifies a return to basics, the task forces made it very clear that our instructional program needs to *balance* reading comprehension and analytical and problem-solving skills with basic skills, such as phonics, spelling and computation of numbers. We do not want to throw out the wonderful aspects of a rich literature program or hands-on mathematics learning to return to rote memorization and repetitive worksheets."

Oppressive Progressivism

Despite calls for balance, the situation became more inflamed and was not helped by what Chester Finn and Diane Ravitch call "the tyranny of dogma." From their perspective, contemporary discourse about education is dominated by a "pedagogical correctness":

> When it comes to instructional philosophy, however, all the dominant approaches can be traced to a common ancestor: the progressive-education movement that arose in the early part of this century.
>
> Strategies that heed this orthodoxy are described with such phrases as "student-centered," "child-centered," "learner-centered," "developmentally appropriate," "discovery-based," "self-directed," "constructivist," and the like. Their names, details, and emphases vary. These features, however, are less important than what their common dogma excludes. Practices that are deemed "teacher-directed" or "knowledge-based" or that involve "direct instruction" are most certainly not welcomed by contemporary instructional theorists. The pedagogical tent, it turns out, is not very big at all.
>
> The reigning orthodoxy demands not only obeisance, but also the exclusion of dissenters. The results of rigorous studies and pilot projects

that don't conform to progressive ideology are dismissed, while airy speculation, vacuous theories, and sloppy evaluations that buttress the prevailing wisdom are published in Ivy League education journals.[45]

While rhetorically slippery ("orthodoxy" and "dogma" are carefully chosen words here), Finn and Ravitch's concerns are real. Some educators hold to their ideas firmly, refusing to acknowledge other perspectives. What Ravitch and Finn fail to mention is that these enthusiasts are readily found among constructivists and traditionalists alike. Dogmatism was not limited to the education establishment. These "true believers" (whatever their position) border on the evangelical, and find it very difficult to engage in deliberative discussions.[46] Conservatives find it particularly ironic (and perhaps annoying) that educational progressives espouse egalitarianism but the dogmatic among them practice what Diane Ravitch has called a "pedagogical imperialism."[47]

Concerns about constructivism are completely legitimate. In the case of any learning theory, it is important to differentiate between the idea and its implementation. As several scholars have pointed out, some uses of constructivist theory can be anti-intellectual. As Zalman Usiskin, a professor at the University of Chicago, noted, "Some (not all) of constructivism is rooted in a dangerous anti-intellectualism, a nihilism that denies the knowledge that has been developed by previous generations and our present one, a nihilism that denies that an adult might be able to transmit knowledge directly to a child, a nihilism that considers books as evil."[48]

When reasonable ideas become dogma and theories are treated as truths, they become conservative forces rather than liberating ones. In the case of California, it seems reasonable to assume that some people encountered a questionable constructivism, and others—when they raised questions—felt dismissed. Meanwhile, some progressive educators also felt that they were encountering an oppressive traditionalism. Eventually, the either-or dogmatism that some critics and reformers encountered would exacerbate the "war," heightening passions on every side.

The Parents of Palo Alto

The opposition's momentum snowballed and seemed unstoppable. A group of parents in Palo Alto became concerned about the implementation of reform-minded curricula in the middle schools. They started attending local school board meetings to air their complaints.

A mathematician from Stanford University was one such parent. He had a child in middle school before the implementation of the new curricula, and a son in middle school during its implementation. He recalls a problem his son was given: How many Friday the 13ths would you expect to encounter in any given year?

The mathematician's son started sensibly enough: Friday is one of seven days in any week ($1/7$). In the week that contains the 13th, therefore, there is a $1/7$ chance that it will be a Friday. If there are 12 months in the year, then the expected number of Friday the 13ths will be $12 \times 1/7 = 12/7$. Twelve sevenths is between 1 ($7/7$) and 2 ($14/7$), so you would expect to have between one and two Friday the 13ths in any year.

But then his son thought some more. What about a non–leap year? What about the fact that some months have 30 days and some have 31? There are 5 Tuesdays in the March I am writing this book, and only 4 Wednesdays. The probability of a day being Tuesday, therefore, is different from the probability of a day being Wednesday. And as it turns out, in some years there is a Friday the 13th in February, which means—automatically—that there will be a Friday the 13th in March. The events are not independent of one another. Thus, the problem is much more complicated than it appears initially. The mathematician's son turned in his homework, explaining everything he had worked through and how he could not answer the problem.

On a scale from 1 to 5, the young man got a 3 because the teacher thought the child's answer was insufficient. The mathematician was concerned about the quality of the mathematics instruction. Now, one would expect that a Stanford mathematics professor would be able to find things wrong at some point in the work of a middle school teacher. Teachers have nowhere near the expertise that mathematicians do, especially middle school teachers, who often need to be generalists.[49] The mathematician wasn't so much concerned with errors as he was with his son's seemingly perpetual state of confusion. Yes, the class worked on some interesting problems, but more often than not, these problems left the students perplexed. Meanwhile, the mathematician worried that the students were not acquiring important knowledge and skills. What troubled him most was that the curriculum was so teacher-dependent: to use it well, teachers needed to know a lot of mathematics.

Other parents had similar experiences. Saunders wrote about two students who answered a CLAS question concerning replanting a forest. One student who answered the question with the correct mathematics but did not explain his reasoning received 2 out of 4 points. Another student, who answered with a preposterously wrong answer but wrote a nice note along with her wrong answer got 3 out of 4 points. The example, Saunders explained, "demonstrates the major problem with the new-new math: it's real short on math. Students are indoctrinated under the credo that it's just fine to be wrong as long as you can articulate your wrong thinking."[50]

Hung-Hsi Wu, a mathematician at the University of California at Berkeley, took a decidedly different approach to critiquing the "reformed" mathematics curricula, choosing in-depth analysis over sarcastic reasoning by anecdote. He, too, worried about the mathematics of some open-ended problems that were gaining popularity. Analyzing several problems in an essay in the *Journal of Mathematical Behavior,* Wu wrote: "It is necessary to emphasize that one faults this problem not for its good intentions, but rather for its very real potential of being abused in a classroom situation. . . . With a little more care, one could alter the problem so as to achieve essentially the same goals while minimizing the potential for abuse." Analyzing three such problems, Wu goes on to show how each could be adjusted so as to make it more mathematically acceptable.[51] Thus, instead of rejecting the work out of hand or calling the authors of the problems fuzzy-headed educrats, Wu enriches the discussion by focusing his considerable expertise on the problems and offering ways to improve them.

This is what the debate needed: not antagonism, but deliberation. "It is impossible to disagree with this drive to open up mathematics by changing its façade," Wu wrote, "Mathematics *should* look more attractive and hospitable than it had up to now."[52] Then, using his mathematical knowledge, he also carefully addresses the mathematics and explains how the problem could be tinkered with. His discussion details how and when a teacher's mathematical knowledge would come into play, rightfully noting that in several instances, a teacher who did not know the subject matter related to the problem might mislead students. This focused analysis—concrete in its attention to particular problems rather than a generalized attack (as was the case in many local school board meetings, newspaper articles, and the like) that did nothing to further the discussion—had enormous potential for pushing the reform of mathematics education forward, critically but constructively. Perhaps Wu's analysis was helpful because he had a history of working with education, in both the California Mathematics Project and the NCTM.

But such discussions did not occur often enough in California. Instead, sides started forming in Palo Alto, and labels followed: the reformers vs. the traditionalists, the educrats vs. the conservatives. Soon, the parents organized themselves into a group—Honest Open and Logical Debate (HOLD). They gathered information about the jargon they encountered: "constructivism," "standards," "NCTM." They looked for education research on different kinds of curricula, instruction, and assessment. The Stanford mathematician whose son explored the Friday the 13th problem did not join the group; he didn't want to get involved in the politics.

One catalyst for the formation of HOLD was the report that Palo Alto students' scores on the Stanford Achievement Tests computational dimension for eighth graders had dropped from the 86th percentile in 1992 to the 58 percent percentile in 1994. Parents and teachers traded letters to the editor, attesting to their children's successes and failures, often recalling their own poor experiences with a new math curriculum when they were schoolchildren. Some worried about the lack of right answers, others were concerned that their children would not be properly prepared for college.

The members of HOLD began posting information on their website, including commentary on the 1992 *Framework* and the NCTM 1989 *Standards*. A group wrote a memo to the NCTM about suggestions they had for the next revision of the standards. The suggestions are telling, for they target many of the more generalized concerns. The group argued for a reversal of the goals for students: "The most important thing is learning mathematics, not appreciating mathematics." They wanted clarification of reasoning as a goal, so that it was clear that it was "mathematically correct reasoning." They wanted the document edited so that teachers would not interpret it as telling them not to "teach, but instead only facilitate": "HOLD strongly believes that the role of the teacher should be first and foremost to teach, which includes direct instruction and immediately responsive constructive criticism, in addition to coaching. The new Standards must make the point that it is crucial for the teacher to achieve closure of ideas in the class and not let students leave the class full of erroneous math as a result of student 'brainstorming.'"[53]

The group also wanted to edit out the "whole math" philosophy that permeated the NCTM 1989 *Standards,* to clarify the stance on calculators (which "destroy the ability to calculate"), and to have performance standards embedded in the next version of the document. Finally, the group suggested that alignment of assessment with curriculum was wrongheaded. First, the

NCTM *1989 Standards* should weather the test of producing students who could do well on traditional standardized tests: "The Standards must prove their effectiveness based on the original assessment that called them into existence, before trying to espouse new assessment."[54]

Sides began solidifying. In Palo Alto, one group of parents argued for a "direct instruction" track for eighth graders. Several parents who wanted a traditional mathematics program collected 600 signatures and petitioned the school board.[55] "I think there's a great concern about 'one size fits all' challenging students. . . . How can we put together the most advanced students with the less advanced students and maintain a pace that challenges them all," one parent said. Earlier, this same parent had commented: "I think we cannot afford to experiment too much with the kids who have the greatest abilities, the ones we need most for our competitive world."[56] As issues of what mathematics to teach got mixed in with issues of whether it is right to "track" students, emotions were inflamed, for it became obvious to parents that among their ranks, they had fundamentally different perspectives on the purposes of schools, differences that were not typically made obvious at bake sales and in conversations on the sidelines of after-school soccer games. "Sorting and selecting children is not one of our missions," a school official said.

The press had a field day. At one meeting, 200 parents, teachers, and students showed up. Some wore neon green nametags, declaring themselves "ProBalance." They spoke of the new mathematics program as liberating. It "changed my life," one student attested. A HOLD parent then offered an alternative view: "It's a travesty. My daughter was cheated by the experience."[57] The critics won out, and parents could choose traditional or less traditional tracks for their children.[58] The event left a bitter taste in the mouths of many participants. Parents and teachers alike felt vilified, blindsided by what they considered an uncivil discourse. This, unfortunately, was not unique in California. Capistrano Unified School District, in the southern part of the state, would eventually pass a "civility policy" targeting adults (teachers and parents alike).[59]

Mathematically Correct

In some ways, then, HOLD became a parallel network, made up of parents, mathematicians, teachers, and concerned others instead of the teachers and teacher educators who attended their NCTM, California Mathematics Council, and California Subject Matter Project meetings. Other networks arose. One website that would gain national recognition in subsequent years was "Mathematically Correct." Its slogan: "There Is a Mathematically Correct Solution." The website comes complete with a dedication:

> Over four score and seven decades ago philosophers brought forth into this world a new mathematics, conceived in correct computational formulae and dedicated to the proposition that two plus two equals four.
>
> Now we are engaged in a great educational war, testing whether algebra I or any form of mathematics so conceived and so dedicated can long endure. We are met on a great virtual battlefield of that war. We have come to dedicate a portion of that field to those who are giving up the quality of their education so that California's Math Framework might live. It is altogether fitting and proper that we should do this.
>
> But in a larger sense, we cannot dedicate, we cannot consecrate, we cannot hallow their loss. The brave children who now must struggle to learn math outside of the classroom have consecrated it far above our power to add or subtract. The world will little note nor long remember the actions of a few irate parents, but it can never forget what fate has befallen the children. It is for us, the mathematically competent, rather to be dedicated here to the unfinished work, to the battle to save basic math skills that has thus far been so nobly advanced. It is rather for us to be here dedicated to the great task remaining before us—that from these honored children we take increased devotion to the cause for which they gave up their weekends and vacation time—that we highly resolve that these children shall not have suffered in vain, that this state shall have a rebirth of computational skills, and that a mathematics of algebra I, geometry, and algebra II shall not perish from our schools.[60]

Mathematically Correct, however, is not the same kind of "community" that we have explored thus far. Instead, it is a website that acts as a resource for interested parties who have concerns about mathematics education. It has no membership, no dues, no annual meetings. Because the site includes links to the writing of many critics of the earlier reforms, some of those critics were then presumed to "belong" to Mathematically Correct, even though there was no actual community. The website did act, however, as a network, for it linked concerned citizens (albeit virtually) to resources, news updates, and the like. It became a modern-day samizdat, circulating a sometimes fugitive literature critiquing the earlier reforms and coaching parents on how to resist the "new math" onslaught. Thus, the new network, too, became a statewide actor.

Visitors to the site can look up definitions for "new math," "whole math," "complete math," "New-new math," "fuzzy math," "fuzzy crap," "Mickey Mouse math," and "Algebra Lite." The concerns of the founders of Mathematically Correct were many: that the "new new math" ways of teaching were untested and unproved; that the only large-scale empirical work done on mathematics instruction demonstrated that direct instruction is more effective; that the frameworks emphasized mathematical appreciation, not mathematical content knowledge; that the new tests being advocated were "subjective." As one parent explained, the 1992 *Framework* is "essentially empty of any mathematical content. What it contains instead is a social vision of how our teachers should teach mathematics, and how our children should feel about mathematics. Not what they should teach. Not what our children should learn."

Other critics of the 1992 *Framework* agreed. Henry Alder—who had raised doubts about the 1985 *Framework*—spoke to the State Board in December of 1995: "Common sense would indicate that the prescription of one teaching strategy over another is wrong, but this is exactly what the 1992 California Mathematics Framework does. Different teachers excel in different teaching strategies. Every teacher should be allowed to use the strategy with which he or she feels most comfortable. To force a teacher to use a strategy clearly not appropriate for him or her can only negatively impact the learning of students."[61]

On the Mathematically Correct website, someone has listed the problems with "touchy feely," "fuzzy," "whole," or "new new math":

In practice . . . this approach:

1. Reduces the material that students are expected to learn ("dumbsdown math")
2. Virtually eliminates the teacher role as an information provider.
3. Demands a very large time commitment to writing about math at the expense of doing math.
4. Demands group work and group grades, and restricts questions of the teacher from individuals.
5. Reduces knowledge and accuracy in the parts of math that actually do get done.

6. Greatly reduces practice and drills so basic skills don't become automatic.
7. Promotes dependence on the use of calculators, and basic arithmetic suffers as a result.
8. Has been reported by teachers to produce inferior results.
9. Leaves students poorly prepared for later science and math courses.[62]

Reasonable concerns all. But here the Mathematically Correct lobby commits the very crime it accuses the progressive reformers of: making sweeping claims based on limited empirical evidence. Not all progressive minded mathematics teachers reduce practice and drill and thwart the development of automaticity in students. Not all teachers report that the methods used produce inferior results. Not all teachers see the approach as eliminating their need to lecture or direct, but rather see their work as more balanced— sometimes being more directive, sometimes less. The problem, however, was that there were anecdotes and instances of very poorly implemented progressive curricula and instruction. And so critics could find a case to point to for each and every one of their concerns. Seldom did people attempt to make more nuanced analyses, differentiating problems of design from those of implementation, noting when claims were made based on "common sense" and when they were made on empirical results, discussing at length what constituted "research."

What Counts as Research?

The issue of research quality is essential, and over time it manifested as a chorus of criticisms of recent education reforms. Where is the research that supports these ideas? And is it high-quality and rigorous? For some, that meant: Is the research "scientific" in the narrow sense of undertaking traditional psychological experiments, controlling most variables, isolating one event, conducting tests prior to and following the administration of a "treatment"?

Teachers have long sneered at such research, for classrooms are messier than psychological and scientific laboratories. Experimental research paradigms often try to control for the complexity of the real world, but no experiment can be easily and readily conducted in real schools. Thus, historically, complaints have abounded about the disconnect between education research and real classrooms. In addition, there have been significant social and intellectual shifts away from thinking of "science" as the only way to generate knowledge. Fields as far ranging as economics, political science, history, and psychology have expanded their use of research methods to include more qualitative and quantitative methodologies. Complaints about the disconnect between education research and classroom practice, combined with the cultural shift from research modeled on science to research rooted in a wider range of disciplinary methodologies have led education researchers to embrace other research paradigms—traditions rooted in anthropology, sociology, history.

Unfortunately, much research published in the name of "new" methods has not uniformly met high, rigorous standards. Sometimes quality has been compromised because of what E. D. Hirsch called "an insistence upon ideological conformity which makes for unreliable science."[63] At other times, the problem has been not so much that the research has lacked quality as that studies limited in their generalizability have been used to make claims too far-reaching. Thus, issues of quality have been confounded with issues of qualitative methods. So when calls for "replicable, rigorous research" are made—justifiably so—there is some confusion: Does that mean returning to experimental and quasi-experimental research, isolated from classrooms? Or does that mean conducting good research from a host of disciplines, drawing on methods as far ranging as clinical interviews and ethnographies, experiments and protocols?

This debate was also the target of caricatures and oversimplified generalizations. Critics were accused of being scientistic. Progressive educators were accused of disregarding rigor. Neither caricature seems appropriate, for many participants in the debates were persuaded by quasi-experimental and interpretive work. The TIMSS analyses serve as one such case, for that research involved both large-scale surveys and analyses of videotapes. Liping Ma's *Knowing and Teaching Elementary Mathematics,* a study that drew heavily on interview data with prospective teachers in the United States and Taiwan, is another case in point.[64]

The debate has also been poorly served by the introduction of even more questionable evidence, like the shaky claims made on some websites. For example, according to the Mathematically Correct website, "July 11, 1996— Al Gore commends all members of Mathematically Correct for a concerted effort to promote math education." Teachers from the California Mathematics Council, concerned about this citation, called Washington, D.C., to track down the records. No one they contacted had any recollection of such a commendation.[65] Instances like this remind us of the lack of accountability of the Internet to its users. As Peter Schrag (among others) noted, "For the first time in history, the unfounded rumor, the fragment of suspicion, the wildly false 'fact,' is something not just shared over the back fence but spread through megabytes and milliseconds, without editing, review, or check, to an audience of millions—peasants with pitchforks on the Internet."[66]

Defining Balance

It was a thoroughly confusing time. Parents did not know what to think, and were amazed at what they heard in local school board meetings. Teachers who had participated in the reform were stunned by what they considered to be unfair representations of their thinking and practice. Other teachers were relieved, for they had been feeling oppressed by their progressive colleagues for too long (recall Tim's lone voice in support of traditional teaching at the California Mathematic Project summer session). Mathematicians were amazed at what they considered sloppy thinking about policies concerning mathematics curriculum and instruction. Participants in the earlier waves of the reform were depressed and saddened, as their hopes for improved education dwindled.

Many journalists represented the controversy as a war. Participants from every corner picked up the language quickly and unreflectively, and the jarring experience of participating in emotionally charged debates sometimes led to the formation of adamantine sides. The one thing everyone "agreed" about was the need for "balance," for no one saw himself or herself as being ideological or unreasonable, and almost everyone was trying to do the right thing for California schoolchildren or for their own children.

But no one stopped to define "balance," and it was clear from the discussions that the participants were talking about many different things, including the purposes of frameworks and the place of content and pedagogy in those, the content and character of statewide assessments, the questionable legitimacy of constructivism theories of learning, the nature of research and what should count as trustworthy scholarship, and who should get to participate in decisions about what and how California students should learn mathematics.

In the midst of this dizzying array of issues, no one—not the reformers, the press, the critics, the parents—successfully called a halt to the increasingly divisive discussions and tried to analyze the myriad issues that ran under the surface of these arguments. Before continuing with the story, let's consider a few of the undercurrents.

Let us start with considering the multiple meanings of balance: the astrological Libra or blindfolded Justice holding her scales; the balance of powers in our government, so that no one branch upsets the democratic course; balancing one's checkbook; a balance beam performance at the Olympics. Thus, balance can alternatively be thought of as a state of equilibrium or parity; a harmonious or satisfying arrangement; an amount on the credit side of an account; an attribute of a shape; the exact correspondence of form on opposite sides of a dividing line or plane, as in *symmetry* or *correspondence* in mathematics; an equivalent counterbalancing weight; or a scale for weighing.

It is impossible to tell from the calls for balance what kind of balance the participants had in mind: parity, canceling out, symmetry, justice, grace. To complicate things further, it was unclear what was to be balanced. Some participants were concerned about a balanced *mathematics*, some basics, some concepts, some problem solving, some real life applications. Indeed, in the Mathematics Program Advisory, the CDE explained: "In a balanced mathematics program, students become proficient with basic skills, develop conceptual understanding, and become adept at problem solving. All three areas are important and included—none is neglected or under emphasized. . . . Balance does not imply that set amounts of time be allotted for basic skills, conceptual understanding, and problem solving. At times, students might be involved in lessons or tasks that focus on one aspect, while at other times lessons or tasks may focus on two or all three aspects."[67]

But when these issues were discussed in the public domain, they were quickly reduced to an oversimplified and dangerous dichotomy of all process versus mindless rote memorization.

Other participants were worried about a balanced view of *pedagogy*, and argued for some traditional teacher-directed instruction (lectures, for example) and some more child-centered instruction (small groups, for example). When these issues were discussed publicly, they too were reduced to oversimplified misrepresentations of drill-and-kill versus mindlessly entertaining, feel-good activities lacking substance or structure.

But the argument for balance went further, for the disagreements were not simply about mathematics and instructional technique. When some participants called for balance, they meant it in the sense of *voice and rep-*

resentation, and they argued for the inclusion of multiple perspectives. Here, at least three distinctions were important. Sometimes the issue was one of including parents, policy makers, business leaders, mathematicians, teachers, and teacher educators, among others. But all parents and all business leaders are not of like mind, and so, at another level, the call for representation was a call for equal representation of varied educational philosophies: some more progressive, others more conservative. Because some of the policymaking bodies were political entities, appointed by the governor and others, another important issue of representation became political affiliation: Democrat and Republican, Libertarian and Independent.

So the calls for balance could mean at least three different things: calls to ensure that the various aspects of mathematics were represented (conceptual knowledge, skills and basics, problem solving); calls to ensure that varied educational philosophies were present; calls to ensure that different constituencies (parents and teachers, Democrats and Republicans, research mathematicians and mathematics educators) were present.

Complicating things further was the fact that these differences—in what kind of math, what kind of teaching, what kind of politics, what kind of social position—masked other important differences. Several are important here. First, there were contrasting views concerning what counts as knowledge. Teachers and some education researchers held more liberal views of knowledge, tending toward a more "generous" interpretation of knowledge (one that included teachers' experience, qualitative research, more traditional quantitative research, and the like). Critics of the earlier reforms tended to have a narrower view of what counts as knowledge, dismissing qualitative research and looking only for experimental, quasi-experimental, and large-scale research that followed the traditional scientific approach to social science inquiries. Even when critics had more liberal views of knowledge, they had legitimate concerns about the difference between experience and expertise.

These differences are not just about methods—whether one surveys or interviews, gives pre- and post-tests or takes field notes. Below the surface are substantial differences in what researchers believe about the nature of knowledge. We live in a world that is conflicted about whether or not we can confidently claim to know anything. Academics argue about positivism, instrumentalism, idealism, critical realism, critical theory, postmodernism, pragmatism. Although these debates seem far removed from K–12 schools, school board meetings, and the like, we all hold tacit views of knowledge that account—in part—for how we react to claims about what and how children should learn and know. For example, some of us hold more positivistic views—a philosophical position characterized by an emphasis upon science and scientific method as the only sources of knowledge. In a positivist view of the world, science is a way to get at truth, to gain knowledge that will help us predict what happens in the world and thereby control it. In this view, the world is deterministic—operated by laws of cause and effect. Positivists believe in empiricism—that observation and measurement are central to the scientific endeavor.

Positivism came under serious attack in the late twentieth century, and I cannot do justice to the issues at play here. Let it suffice to say that some teachers and scholars held more interpretivist views, seeing knowledge as more situated and socially determined. Scholars with interpretivist assumptions about knowledge aim to determine the meaning that actors make of events.

Debates about whether something can be known or not are part of a larger American social, political, and intellectual debate. For many, as Philip Cusick and Jennifer Borman note, hold "a contemporary suspicion of objective knowledge, and a hermeneutical suspicion of the relation between knowledge and interest. As a set, these ideas emphasize the personal over the communal, multi- over mono-culture, critique over catechism."[68]

In addition to disagreements over knowledge and scholarship, there were dissenting opinions about the purposes of schooling in the United States. This issue was an undercurrent to all the discussions, but seldom was it explicated and discussed. Yet we know that Americans differ dramatically in their views of what public schools should provide for their children. In fact, the history of education in the United States is a schizophrenic tale. On the one hand, our young nation made a bold move by arguing for a universal literacy. Horace Mann of Massachusetts, John Pierce of Michigan, John Dewey, and E. D. Hirsch, among others, have argued that the soul of American democracy depends on a quality education for every child. On the other hand, it has never been clear—and scholars have spent considerable time debating—whether schools are meant to sort children for society's needs or to provide children with the power that comes with academic knowledge. We differ, individually and collectively, in our views of whether schools are meant to control or to liberate.

In part, this is because, as a nation, we are divided in how we value knowledge and intellectual work. In Richard Hofstader's classic *Anti-intellectualism in American Life,* he claims that Americans possess a "national disrespect for mind," arguing that while we admire intelligence (an "excellence of mind" that can be directly applied to practical problems), we also find intellectuals "wordy," "pretentious," "subversive," possibly immoral eggheads who lack common sense and (sometimes) intelligence.[69]

Indeed, our national ambivalence about intellectual work and intelligence plays itself out time and again, as school boards and parents, policy makers and teachers debate about the content of curricula. Our ambivalence about the value of knowledge pops up in the most unusual places. In the winter of 2001, for example, Vince Carter, a strong and accomplished African American basketball player, chose to attend his graduation from college during the national basketball championship playoffs. He didn't miss a practice or a game, but critics quickly came out of the woodwork, claiming that it was a publicity stunt, that he was paid too much money not to put his team ahead of his graduation. (If he really cared about the team, the critics argued, he would have focused exclusively on preparing for the game.) Few mentioned the fact that Carter's graduation from college was an important academic act for him, for his family, and for the many African American athletes who never graduate from the colleges whose basketball and football teams they star on.

David Labaree talks of the three-way tug of war that plays out in our schools as our three national goals—"credentialism," sorting, and democratic equality—pull for first place.[70] Although we seldom speak of such things in these politically correct days, the parent who said that "We cannot afford to experiment too much with the kids who have the greatest abilities, the ones we need most for our competitive world" took the breath away from parents whose goals for their children did not include sorting them from other children and making way for the elite (intellectual or otherwise) to march forward.

These multiple—often conflicting—views about the value of intellectual work and the purposes of acquiring knowledge, mathematical or otherwise, get tangled up in talk of schools. Parents, teachers, mathematicians, policy makers all come to the table to talk about mathematics for children, but typically each has his or her own ideas about what "mathematics" means—ideas that, commonly, do not get discussed or clarified.

Finally, the centrality of the conservative/traditional versus progressive/liberal distinction means that—even though it was seldom raised explicitly—race and equal opportunity was also an issue in the discussion of mathematics education. As Russell Baker notes in an essay about Barry Goldwater and the conservatives: "It would be silly to pretend that racism is not a factor here. Racism has always been the unmentionable guest at conservatism's table. Conservatives insist it is principle, not bigotry that compels them to oppose civil rights bills, affirmative action, and all such soft-hearted and fuzzy-minded attempts to equalize the distribution of America's boons."[71]

Many of the teachers and teacher-leaders (not all, of course—nothing is that simple) were committed to social justice and action rooted in liberal assumptions about the role of government and the place of bureaucracies. When confronted with a conservative's spin on their ideas (Saunders's columns, for example), they were unprepared to talk explicitly about issues of equality and race, for on the surface the discussion appeared to be about mathematics. But many educators were working toward a better world, and they had differing opinions about what kinds of social policies (including education policies) would expand educational and social opportunity.

Differences in instructional preference, in views of mathematics, in hopes for schools, in political preference, in assumptions about what counts as knowledge, in views of race, class, and society—all were obstacles to discussion. As was the language of war, and ossified sides, as well as the tendency to caricature positions and those who held them. There weren't two sides in this discussion. This wasn't a debate between the Republican-Conservative-Traditionalist-Positivist-Math-as-Skills-Direct-Instruction-Social-Efficiency Camp and the Democratic-Progressive-Constructivist-Interpretivist-Math-as-Conceptual-Understanding-Child-Centered-Instruction-Democratic-Equality Camp. Few people are that easy to pigeonhole, for our political preferences, educational philosophies, epistemologies, and social commitments don't line up predictably like ducks in a row. We Americans are more complicated than that.

And so the debate raged on, reduced, as Joan Didion once wrote of another debate, "by politicization to a factitiously moralized rhetoric," with no one able or willing to stop it.[72]

8 Dueling Standards

By 1995, the legislature was taking its own measures. A pair of bills emphasizing a back-to-basics move toward a more balanced curriculum—the ABCs bills—was passed in October. They required that "the state board of education 'shall ensure that the basic instructional materials that it adopts for mathematics and reading in grades 1 to 8, inclusive, are based on the fundamental skills required by these subjects, including, but not limited to, systematic, explicit phonics, spelling, and basic computational skills' (AB 170); and . . . the state board of education 'shall adopt at least five basic instructional materials for all applicable grade levels' and shall approve such materials on the basis that they are 'consistent with the state framework' and are factually accurate and incorporate principles of instruction reflective of current and confirmed research (AB 1504)."[1]

In that same October, Governor Wilson signed a bill—AB 265 (the California Assessment and Achievement Act)—creating a new statewide assessment system—the California Assessment of Academic Achievement. Intended to replace the California Learning Assessment System, the bill provided incentives for districts to use off-the-shelf standardized tests in the following year to test basic skills mastery and also provided funds for the development of a new statewide testing program in academic subjects for grades 4, 5, 8, and 10.[2]

The bill also demanded the creation of a twenty-one-member commission—the Commission for the Establishment of Academic Content and

Performance Standards—to write rigorous academic content and performance standards for all grade levels and all subject matters. Mathematics and language arts would be the first subject areas covered. The statewide assessment would be tied to these new standards. The public would participate in the standards development and in the review of aligned assessments. A six-member Statewide Pupil Assessment Review Panel would review the assessments to make sure they contained no questions about a student's or parent's personal beliefs about sex, family life, morality, or religion, and no questions designed to evaluate such personal characteristics as honesty, integrity, sociability, or self-esteem.[3]

The new legislation clearly bore the thumbprints of past experience. The legislature was determined not to repeat the mistakes of the CLAS. Insiders claimed the bill was written in a way to make sure that the staff of the California Department of Education could not get their hands on the assessment.

Throughout this time, the teachers who were members of the mathematics education community began mobilizing their resources. Using their extant networks, they began corresponding electronically, strategizing how to lobby for a more balanced curriculum and assessment system. They experienced the criticisms of the reforms as an attack, and they did not know how to "fight back." Much of the dynamic between the leaders of the mathematics education community and the critics was not one of dialogue, and the groups became polarized. Hearings were held in which educators and researchers were assigned to "pro" and "con" sides and asked to present "research" and not simply opinion. The State Board sponsored many of these hearings, in search of information that would clarify what constitutes a "balanced mathematics program."

The CDE and the Mathematics Program Advisory

Meanwhile, the CDE, under Delaine Eastin's leadership, was also working to provide guidance to teachers and schools. In 1996, based on the work of the task force, the CDE, together with the State Board and the California Commission on Teacher Credentialing, issued a *Mathematics Program Advisory*. By this time, Walter Denham had been labeled, as he later put it, "damaged goods in mathematics education," so he was reassigned to other, less high profile assignments. Joan Akers continued to work on mathematics, however, which included the *Advisory*. The *Advisory* described a "challenging, rigorous mathematics for all students": "This advisory is based on the premise that all students are capable of learning rigorous mathematics and learning it well, and all are capable of learning far more than is currently expected. Proficiency in mathematics is not an innate characteristic; it is a consequence of persistence, effort, practice, support, and encouragement."[4]

The *Mathematics Program Advisory* described "balance" as a mix of basic skills, conceptual understanding, and adept problem solving. A page was devoted to describing basic skills, their development and maintenance: "Students must practice. . . . The practice should be varied. . . . As students learn a basic skill, it is necessary that over time they understand the reasoning behind the skill." Conceptual understanding is discussed in two paragraphs: "Students who have conceptual understanding make sense of mathematics. . . . Mathematical concepts are at the heart of mathematics and are important at all levels of study. . . . Students with conceptual understanding . . . see the structure and logic of mathematics." Problem solving was described on yet another page: "Solving problems involves applying skills, understandings, and experiences to resolve new and perplexing situations. . . . Real problems, mathematical or otherwise, are not usually stated in precise or easy to identify form. More often they are embedded in vague descriptions of puzzling or complex situations." The *Advisory* also noted the need for high-quality, sustained professional development programs so that teachers might learn the mathematics they need in order to teach to the high standards.

The press continued having a field day. MathLand—one of the progressive, innovative curricula that had been approved in 1994—became the focus of much attention. Articles claiming that California children were "lost in MathLand" popped up throughout the state, with parents and educators weighing in on both sides: no computation vs. balanced computation; not enough substance vs. lots of substance. Creative Publications, the publishing house for MathLand, established an assessment consortium of school districts willing to examine student test scores on basic skills and conceptual understanding, and gathered data to demonstrate student gains. In her newspaper column, Debra Saunders reported on news from some Department of Defense schools that had adopted the curriculum:

> BUY A bunker. For two years, the U.S. military has been teaching new-new math to the 80,000-plus students of parents who serve overseas. Department of Defense schools have gone touchy-feely. Their math goals,

according to Stars and Stripes, include teaching eighth-graders to "write poems or journal entries about relationships between math and real life."

DOD schools have adopted the trendy MathLand series for grades K–5 and Glencoe Interactive series for grades 6–8.

MathLand's approach? "When children are allowed to pursue topics of personal interest, their math experiences become more meaningful to them." Think of it as math among the daffodils. Me-me math.

With math goals such as the one calling for fifth-graders to "work co-operatively to reach agreement about the meaning of words and definitions," the military is helping create a next generation of engineers who are able to confab about how they feel a bomb ought to behave, without knowing how to calibrate it.

Do not expect accurate computation. The new-new math motto is: There is no right answer.

(Relax, they're only bombs.)[5]

The debate hit the national press. In the *New York Times,* for example, Lynne Cheney, former chairman of the National Endowment for the Humanities, dueled with Tom Romberg, a professor of mathematics education at the University of Wisconsin—Madison and chair of the committee that wrote the NCTM *1989 Standards.*[6] Reporting on California parents' complaints, Cheney used some questionable reasoning. First, she related a story about an article that reportedly was refused publication in a major education journal because the authors were "debunking" constructivism. From this one example, readers were to believe the educational establishment had been taken over by an ideology that refuses to publish any critical scholarship. She went on to lambaste Creative Publications, publisher of MathLand, for not identifying the districts in their evaluation sample or their sampling method. From this example, readers were to conclude that the publisher was using sloppy social science. Cheney concluded the piece by reminding readers of the crisis in education, drawing an analogy to medicine: "When medical researchers administering a protocol find it has negative consequences for human subjects, they do not ignore those results and change their test. They end the experiment to avoid imposing further harm. Surely it is time for educators to realize that the same ethic should apply to them. In the face of strong evidence that constructivist mathematics does not help and even hurts, they should consider closing down the whole-math experiment."[7]

Cheney did not mention the fact that textbook publishers have seldom been required to show proof of impact. Instead, traditionally, textbooks have been sold on their appeal to review committees that seldom asked for or looked at data about student growth. This tradition changed during the mathematics education debates of the 1980s and 1990s, and curriculum developers were asked to produce "proof" that their materials led to improved student achievement.

This legitimate demand for student achievement data put curriculum developers in a double bind. They could use standardized tests, but those tests typically measured superficial knowledge and skill, not the kinds of robust mathematical understandings to which the reformers were committed. Dissatisfied with those traditional measures and still wanting to respond to the calls for student achievement data, curriculum developers used other measures: student grades, locally developed assessments, and alternative assessments developed especially for the curricula. Unfortunately, those assessments were often not standardized, which led the critics to wonder whether inflated grades and high test scores were the result not of improved knowledge of mathematics, but of a progressive ideology aimed at bolstering students' self-esteem.

Worries heightened as researchers from the Third International Mathematics and Science Study (TIMSS), the largest-ever piece of international education research, began releasing their results in 1996 (analyses continued to be released through 2001). Students' scores in mathematics and science were compared across 5 continents, 48 countries, 102 education systems.[8] The TIMSS database is extraordinary. The researchers analyzed textbooks and curricular policies, and developed country-level and school-level surveys, as well as teacher and student surveys. Under the direction of James Stigler, videotapes of teaching in 231 eighth-grade mathematics classrooms—100 in German, 50 in Japan, and 81 in the United States—were also collected.[9]

Among the study's several conclusions were that, while American fourth graders are competitive with their international peers, our eighth graders rank twenty-eighth in mathematics and seventeenth in science and that the curricula and texts in the United States cover more topics with less focus than do curricula and texts in other countries. This lack of focus is reflected in the teaching, with American teachers covering more material but with less organization than teachers in the countries where students scored higher. Teachers in the United States have diffuse learning goals and carry that diffuseness into their classrooms. They emphasize familiarity with many rather than fewer topics, and offer a curriculum that is—according to researchers on the Second International Mathematics Study (SIMS) and TIMSS researchers—"a mile wide and an inch deep." Furthermore, the study reported that no one is in charge of mathematics and science education in the United States. Admitting that several states have a larger student population than that in many of the TIMSS-participating countries, the researchers found that in the United States, the education community had no single, commonly accepted vision of what school mathematics is or how to teach it.[10]

In sum, in both survey and videotape analyses, researchers found that American students were exposed to a curriculum that was thin and fragmented. "The content appears to be less advanced and is presented in a more piecemeal and prescriptive way," James Stigler and James Hiebert note.[11] In videotape analyses of eighth-grade teachers in Germany, Japan, and the United States, Stigler and his colleagues found that lessons in the United States appeared to place more emphasis on definitions and less on conceptual understanding or the underlying rationales. In effect, American students seem armed with technical vocabulary but lack significant understanding about how to reason mathematically.

The study caught the eye of educators and policy makers alike, promising to serve as an important resource for local, state, national, and international discussions about teaching, curriculum, professional development, and concomitant policies. Major publicity included articles in the *New York Times* and a cover story in *The Economist*.[12] Both pieces paid particular attention to the fact that the countries where students scored the highest in mathematics—Japan, Hong Kong, Singapore, and South Korea— are also among the world's most successful economies. (Three of the four—Singapore, Japan, and South Korea, along with the Czech Republic— scored the highest in science.) Noting the connection between a country's student scores in mathematics and science and its economic success, President Clinton called for new and higher standards at a meeting of government, business, and education leaders.[13]

New Frameworks, New Standards
Back in California, the State Board called for a rewriting of the *1992 Framework* before its seven-year cycle was up. Ninety-four people applied to be on the new Subject Matter Committee, and the Curriculum Commission

selected for its nominations—with only one exception—people who either had been involved in writing the 1992 *Framework* or were known to be supporters of the earlier reforms. When the commission sent the slate for the framework writing committee to the State Board of Education, the board removed ten of the recommended appointees and replaced them with fourteen others from the application pool (the board appointed eight of the original candidates from the CC slate). Some reformers regarded the replacements as staunch critics of the earlier reforms. In part, the reformers were right, for a few of the new appointees were either members of HOLD or people whose names had been linked with the Mathematically Correct website.

The reformers saw this development as a corruption of process; the board saw it as an attempt to "balance" the committee, concerned that the framework writing process not repeat the same mistake made with the 1992 *Framework,* in which only one view of mathematics teaching and learning was represented. Among those the board named was Henry Alder, now professor emeritus at UC Davis who had been on the State Board when it all began in 1985. Deborah Haimo, a mathematician and former president of the Mathematics Association of America, was elected as chair. Haimo asked everyone to focus on discussions of content, and to avoid discussions of pedagogical preference. "This framework focuses squarely on content," the final document reads. The committee wrote a new framework in record time (6 months instead of the typical 18 months); 3,000 copies of the draft—according to due process—were sent out for field review in the winter of 1997.

But process was not followed to the letter of the law. State Board–appointed advisors made significant revisions, introducing them at the last stages of the process, and not vetting them with a broad audience of concerned citizens. In part, these revisions and the truncated process could not be avoided. By law, the new framework had to align with the new state standards. But since the state standards were not yet completed, the board asked several mathematicians to help align the framework with the emerging standards.

Complicating matters further were rumors that a small group of extreme traditionalists on the framework committee had set out to sabotage the process and derail any effort to reconcile the concerns of the earlier reformers with those of the emerging critics. These interpersonal and political struggles were not made public, yet they are important to note. All communities in this story had their extremists. All groups—progressives and traditionalists, mathematicians and schoolteachers—were not of a single mind. Consequently, each group experienced internal struggles to respect the diversity within their ranks while at the same time mitigating the impact of extremists. And because they did respect the right of colleagues to hold different, sometimes radical positions, these internal struggles were quietly handled, seldom publicly acknowledged or discussed.

The published 1999 *Framework* looked very different from the earlier frameworks. Balance is defined, basic computational and procedure skills enumerated, conceptual understanding illustrated, problem solving redefined as aiming more at applying knowledge than at exploring unfamiliar situations. Chapters 2 and 3—in which content is described and elaborated—constituted almost half the entire document, all 350 pages of it. It is as thorough a treatment of content as exists in contemporary standards documents. It is clearly written and, although the focus on content remains a priority in those chapters, the authors also described different kinds of instruction teachers might use to explore content with students. One message is consistent: teachers teach (rather than "coach" or "facilitate"), and they direct students' attention to the matter at hand—math.

The content chapters are followed by other—much shorter—chapters, including one on instructional strategies (sixteen pages); assessment (sixteen pages); universal access (nine pages); and responsibilities of teachers, parents, students, and administrators (five pages). When research is cited, it is research that fits—for the most part—a narrower paradigm of experimental and quasi-experimental research. Research is presented as definitive and authoritative. No mention is made of disputes over certain practices (like tracking). No mention is made of highly regarded research (among mathematics educators) that draws on other research traditions that are more qualitative. In this regard, the authors took a stance similar to that of the authors of the NCTM standards, who also failed to make nuanced distinctions concerning the empirical bases for many claims.

In the wake of the 1999 *Framework,* there was another round of textbook adoption. This time, the approved texts were no surprise: no "questionable" NSF-sponsored curricula were on the list, a list that testified to the dominance of traditional, rather than innovative, instruction. Among the texts selected were several published by Saxon Publishers, the firm established by John Saxon, a longtime critic of the progressive ideology that had dominated public statements of the National Council for Teachers of Mathematics.

The framework committee was not the only group writing standards. A virtual flurry of California-based standards writing erupted. In the fall of 1995, the California Education Round Table, for example, announced a partnership between the CDE, California State University, the University of California, the state's community college system, and other higher education officials to improve the state's education system. The process they proposed would start with the development of standards and competencies, move to a task force on ways to assess student progress, followed by efforts to assess teacher preparation programs, develop technological supports for all this work, and involve the community. As a first step, the round table convened a task force on mathematics and English graduation standards and issued their own content standards.[14]

Meanwhile, when Delaine Eastin was elected she announced yet another initiative that involved the development of standards—the "Challenge Initiative." This was a voluntary program for which the CDE developed model Challenge standards that participating school districts could then use in the development of their own local standards. The CDE's model standards were to be aligned with the New Standards Project, but the state department was seriously understaffed (with one mathematics specialist and one science specialist) and the quality of the standards issued was heavily criticized. Districts that agreed to participate would receive a waiver from the state department for certain requirements. These waivers were intended to free up districts from the bureaucracy in exchange for a promise that they would raise student achievement (using multiple measures) by 5 percent annually. Contributing to the problems in implementing this initiative was the more limited role of the state superintendent and the CDE since the court order concerning the need to follow State Board policy. By announcing this initiative without discussing it with the board, Eastin alienated them even more—especially since, historically, the board is the body that makes decisions about waivers.

The Dixon Report

A central concern continued to be about what we "know" based on research. According to the California State Education Code, the state's framework had to "incorporate principles of instruction reflective of current and confirmed research," but no one could agree on what counted as "research." In 1997, the State Board contracted with Douglas Carnine, a professor at the University of Oregon, to review high-quality research.[15] But because no one could agree on what counted as "research," it was even more difficult to agree on the criteria for "high quality." According to the researchers, the board had "quite specifically requested that we locate experimental studies in mathematics."[16] This meant that only true or quasi-experimental research studies were included in the review that resulted—the Dixon Report.

In the end, the authors reviewed 110 studies (out of 968 identified articles). With that limited number of studies, it was nearly impossible to discuss trends or what the research demonstrated generally. For example, 4 studies were found that investigated the impact of manipulatives; 5, the impact of grouping; 5, the impact of calculators. The authors concluded that "the jury is still out" in terms of the use of manipulatives ("Studies are needed that control well for the many variations possible in the use of manipulatives").[17] They also found that the research on cooperative groups is "quite positive" and that such groups serve both motivational and mediational purposes. That is, groups help students want to work and learn, and group work creates bridges between teachers' explanations and independent student work. From the three studies that compared didactic instruction and guided discovery, the authors found a "slight advantage" to guided discovery. Three studies found that calculators helped with computation instruction.

Overall, the report's tone is equivocal. "Conventional teaching"—teacher explains an algorithm, students practice it in homework problems—was found wanting, and "effective interventions" consisted of three phases (summarized in Table 8.1). In the first phase, "Teachers not only demonstrated, but explained, and asked many questions, checking for understanding, or conducted discussions. In sharp contrast to the conventional model, students were almost always quite actively involved in the instruction during the initial phase." Instruction then moved into the second phase, one that "varies considerably, from students helping one another collaboratively to high levels of teacher help with feedback and frequent 'correctives.'"[18] A third phase involved students working independently or being evaluated by the teacher.

It is not an unreasonable exercise to ask the question: "What does research tell us when we use high standards of quality?" Nor is it unreasonable to summarize research within traditions (considering, for example,

Table 8.1. Phases of Instruction from the Dixon Report

Phase 1	Phase 2	Phase 3
Teachers demonstrate, explain, question, and/or conduct discussions	Teachers, individual peers, and/or groups of peers provide students with substantial help that is gradually reduced	Teachers assess students' ability to apply knowledge to taught and/or untaught problems
Students are actively involved, through answering questions and/or discussion	Students receive feedback on their performance, correctives, additional explanations, and other forms of assistance	Students demonstrate their ability to independently recall and/or generalize and transfer their knowledge

what quasi-experimental research suggests). Examining the products of certain research traditions can tell us much. As it turns out, we "know" very little based on this limited research base, for there were too few studies about most instructional strategies to make any claims about trends. Nonetheless, the report's conclusions should not have been particularly troubling to progressive educators: students should be active, and teachers should use a variety of different organizational and instructional techniques.

But some progressive reformers were appalled that the Dixon Report (alternatively known as the "Carnine Report") was used as the major source informing the State Board's deliberations, and emails were sent across the state criticizing its conclusions In one analysis, the author wrote: "There are numerous inaccuracies in the report itself and the applicability of the research chosen to inform the SBE on instructional practices is highly questionable. . . . We ask everyone using this report to actually look at the research designs from each study, read the researchers' conclusions as stated in the actual articles, and think through for themselves what implications for mathematics instruction can be drawn, instead of accepting the summary statements in the Carnine report at face value, many of which provide inappropriate advice."[19]

Picking up on the practice of open letter writing used repeatedly by the reform's critics, the American Educational Research Association's Special Interest Group for Research in Mathematics Education wrote an open letter to the State Board, objecting to the numerous mistakes. Seventy-three educators endorsed the letter.[20] In addition to questions about the validity of the analysis, some progressive educators were concerned about the narrow view of what was deemed legitimate research. While experimental research has been highly regarded and used extensively in fields as far ranging as medicine and education, there has been (as I have mentioned) a growing awareness that other kinds of research—ethnographic and interpretivist among them—have a great deal to contribute to our understanding of teaching and learning. This has been especially true in education research, since classrooms are noisy and human places, and it is virtually impossible to "control" for all relevant variables. Of particular worry to teachers has been the tendency of experimental research to ignore long-term impact. Pre-tests and post-tests are often given within six months of the "treatment," leaving us with little understanding of what students learn more permanently.

But it was not just concerns about a narrow view of research or errors in the report that motivated this reaction. Carnine, second author on the report, was seen as a political conservative, having written a paper criticizing the education establishment for the Thomas B. Fordham Foundation (whose president, Chester Finn, had clearly come out on the side of educational conservatism).[21] Carnine was also seen as close to at least one politically conservative State Board member who consistently worked to champion the critics' agenda. Later, Carnine would become involved in advising then-Governor George W. Bush about education policy in Texas.[22] While the talk remained at the level of erroneous findings and what the report considered legitimate research, these political undercurrents were a considerable factor in understanding the more progressive reformers' concerns.

The Commission
Meanwhile, the AB 265–mandated Commission for the Establishment of Academic Content and Performance Standards was also busily producing reading and mathematics standards that, by law, had to be ready by January 1, 1998.[23] Governor Wilson, Superintendent Eastin, and the Senate and Assembly made the appointments to the commission. Nine of the original members were experienced K–12 teachers; others were university faculty and researchers and several business executives. The appointments also included Joseph Carrabino (former SBE chair when Bill Honig was in office, and then a professor of management at UCLA); Daniel Condron (statewide

public policy coordinator for K–12 education and a public affairs manager for Hewlett-Packard); Bill Evers (outspoken member of HOLD, and research fellow at the Hoover Institution at Stanford); Dorothy Jue Lee, a retired elementary school teacher and member of the SBE; and La Tanya Wright (a writer who home-schools her three children).

The group met and consulted with experts (including E. D. Hirsch and TIMSS researchers William Schmidt and James Stigler). The process was difficult for a number of reasons, according to researchers Lorraine McDonnell and Stephen Weatherford. In particular, two commissioners butted heads and seemed unwilling to deliberate about decisions, seeing their role instead as advocates for a particular stance. The researchers also noted that there were "profound intellectual disagreements over the balance between basic skills and conceptual learning, between direct instruction and discovery-based learning, and over the degree to which traditionally separate subdisciplines within mathematics (e.g., algebra, geometry, trigonometry) should be integrated in student coursework. Further disagreement centered on the amount and specificity of the content that students should be expected to learn."[24]

Discouraged with the standards that were accepted, one commissioner, Evers, took his complaints to the editorial page of the *New York Times* in an op-ed article arguing for "platinum standards" rather than the proposed "gold standards."[25] Despite his concerns, the commission voted 15 to 2 (with two abstentions and two members absent) in favor of adopting their last draft and sent it forward to the State Board in October 1997. The draft document included over a hundred model word problems, which were meant to communicate the kinds of intellectual work that students should be engaged in.[26]

But the board rejected the standards, for several reasons. For one, the model problems were examples from teaching practice, and they seemed too close to the classroom. Such standards sounded suspiciously like prescriptions for how to teach rather than descriptions of what to teach.

Making matters worse was the fact that some of the problems were wrong and needed to be removed. For example, consider the definition of an asymptote that was offered in the October 1997 draft of the content standards: a straight line to which a curve gets closer and closer but never meets, as the distance from the origin increases. This definition says that $y = -1$ is an asymptote for $y = \frac{1}{x}$, since the curve gets closer and closer as x goes to plus infinity. This is wrong, since the definition offered fails to say that the distance not only decreases, but decreases to become arbitrarily close to zero.

In addition, the definition contradicts the term "asymptote" as commonly used by mathematicians, who would call the x-axis the asymptote to the curve $y = (\sin(x))/x$. In this case, the curve meets the x-axis infinitely often as x goes to infinity, so that the distance between the curve and the x-axis is neither consistently decreasing nor always nonzero. While this use of "asymptote" contradicts the literal meaning of the word (in Greek, "asymptote" means "not capable of meeting"), linguistic considerations cannot override a scientific practice. The definition of asymptote in the draft therefore jarred mathematicians' sensibilities in more ways than one, and it was mistakes like this that the State Board wanted to avoid at all costs.[27]

Other considerations were raised as well, both about missing content (Where was long division?) and about unnecessary use of educationese. The board asked four highly regarded mathematicians to rewrite the standards on a very short timeline, for it was already October and the standards— by mandate—were to be completed by December.

The board-revised standards went back to the full SBE (not to the commission, which had been charged with standards development), with no time for public review and discussion. One commissioner resigned in protest. The board voted 10 to 1 (with one abstention) to adopt the revised *Mathematics Content Standards for California Public Schools.*[28]

The revised standards drew even more public attention. Perhaps because they read so simply, some reformers felt that this was a return to the basics— to the algorithmic, skill-and-drill driven classrooms of the past. The removal of the problems was seen as the removal of problem solving. The state superintendent expressed her disappointment with the standards publicly, as did William Schmidt (who later changed his mind). The revised standards received national publicity, with two pieces in the *New York Times,* one of which quoted an assistant director of the National Science Foundation who claimed that: "The wistful or nostalgic back-to-basics approach that characterizes the board standards overlooks the fact that the approach has chronically and dismally failed."[29] The assistant director was later reprimanded and asked to apologize to the board.

Delaine Eastin, among others, claimed that the standards offered a "dumbed down" version of K–6 mathematics (and too rigorous for grades 8–12) that went too far in the direction of basic skills, stating, "Math instruction, if it only emphasizes basic skills, will put us at a terrible competitive disadvantage in the global economy." She went on to say, "I'm disappointed. I think this is a half a loaf. I guess that's better than none, but we went from a real world-class set of standards to one that cannot be characterized as world-class."[30] Other critics of the new standards rejected them because of the process. Some progressive teachers felt disenfranchised. As a result, they condemned the standards.

Others disagreed. In February 1998, over 100 California mathematicians endorsed the newly rewritten standards in the form of yet another letter to the State Board. In addition, in an evaluation of standards across the states sponsored by the Thomas B. Fordham Foundation, Ralph Raimi (a mathematician) and Lawrence Braden (a schoolteacher), gave California an A for the commission's standards. Only two other states—North Carolina and Ohio—received As, and California was the only one of the three to get sixteen out of sixteen points in the scoring system the authors used (even Japan got a lower score, fifteen out of sixteen). Raimi and Braden claimed that, "If teachers and textbooks can be found to carry it through properly, this Standards outlines a program that is intellectually coherent and as practical for the non-scientific citizen as for the future engineer. . . . Initial reaction to the adoption of this document included a widespread apprehension that this 'return to basics' represented an anti-intellectual stance: rote memorization of pointless routines instead of true understanding of the concept of mathematics. The opposite is true. One can no more use mathematical 'concepts' without a grounding in fact and experience, and indeed memorization and drill, than one can play a Beethoven sonata without exercise in scales and arpeggios."[31]

All true. In the ideal world. But the earlier reformers had worried about what typically happens to a list of topics to be taught. Well-intentioned teachers respond to the myriad pressures of school (high-stakes testing, parents who want their children taken care of, children who are uninterested in—or worse, frightened of—mathematics, too little time, increasing responsibility) by doing what comes naturally: conventional teaching, which largely entails marching through the content with uninspired instruction. In part, this is due to the uneven mathematical knowledge of teachers, especially elementary and middle school teachers. So we have poor teaching and poorly prepared teachers.

It is understandable, then, that participants in the debates differed in terms of how they conceptualized what the problem with mathematics education was. To some, the problem was instruction. These educators identified a stultified and oppressive pedagogy as the reason so many children and their teachers do not know or like mathematics. To other participants, the problem was that the mathematical content of K–12 schools had become compromised. To them, policies like the content standards and frameworks needed to focus on mathematical content, and teachers (some of whom did not know the mathematics) should not be left to their own devices to determine the content of the curriculum. Furthermore, since traditional teaching had been implemented poorly, critics of the progressive platform argued, we do not know that traditional teaching is inadequate; we only know that poorly implemented traditional teaching is inadequate.

The Road to Pedantry?

By this time, California's struggles were once again receiving national press. In November 1997, the *Wall Street Journal* ran an article, "Numbers Racket" (journalists could simply not resist the temptation to play on the mathematical language), about the debates. Parents were concerned about the "undisciplined, dumbed down . . . and fuzzy" nature of standards-based mathematics, highlighting the hostilities over multiplication tables.[32] Other parents, equally concerned, supported the earlier reforms, arguing that math for them had been long on memorization, short on understanding.[33] Some journalists continued their tirades, full of the seemingly ubiquitous hyperbole: "A generation of innocent and helpless children is being educationally crippled and California will feel the effects for decades in terms of crime, welfare dependency and lack of workers for the highly technical jobs of the twenty-first century. It will take years, untold billions of dollars and a top-to-bottom overhaul of curriculum to set things right. But nothing, absolutely nothing, is more important to the future of this state."[34]

The controversy expanded. More articles appeared, including several in the *New York Times*. I heard about the debates on National Public Radio's Morning Edition one day as I was working out in the gym.[35] The National Science Foundation threatened to pull funding—over $50 million in grants that had been made to California school districts—if school districts moved away from a commitment to "deep, balanced, mathematical learning" to more basic skill-and-drill. This created even more ado among the critics of the earlier reforms, who quickly claimed that the NSF was also intellectually bankrupt.

Mathematicians were divided. One Stanford professor argued that California students would be better prepared, with strong skills and strong problem solving abilities. "I'm a mathematician," he explained, "how could I possibly be anti-problem solving?" Another mathematician from San Francisco State worried that students would be limited, strong in "number crunching," weak in more analytical thought. Many educators felt that learning for understanding was, indeed, once again becoming an "endangered species of cognition."[36] And the discourse seemed to spin out of control. One reporter noted, "The accusations being slung are as ugly as they are heartfelt: that in her zeal to get reelected, state schools chief Delaine Eastin is peddling a movement popular with teachers, but dangerous for children. And from the opposite camp: that State Board of Education members are pawns in a two-year conspiracy manipulated by a political scientist at the Hoover Institution. That they are engineering statewide standards that will exclude poor and minority students from advanced mathematics."[37] Insiders who knew the board members found such claims laughable, for the State Board was composed of strong-willed members not easily swayed by capricious forces.

Reports of Eastin telling school districts to "ignore" these standards and aim for higher ones hit the press. When Eastin denied she told districts to "ignore" the standards, someone produced a tape of a speech she gave in San Diego to prove it. One reporter quoted the SBE chair: "If Eastin continues the rebellion, I would think that we could make some activities that would get her attention." There were rumors that there might be cuts in Eastin's budget.[38] More public comments appeared about the "contentious, mean-spirited environment" in California.[39]

New Assessments

As initially conceived, the commission's *Content Standards* would be used to guide the development of a new assessment system.[40] Governor Wilson, concerned with the lag time involved, wanted accountability immediately, not later. After the CLAS was abolished, the state offered districts financial incentives to buy off-the-shelf standardized tests to measure student achievement. Assessment reformers saw this as a step backward, for these tests had never been substantially improved to test for higher-order thinking or deeper understanding, nor were they aligned with the state's instructional guidance system.

At the same time, Eastin's Challenge Initiative required that participating school districts use multiple measures to assess student progress. Within California and nationwide, language concerning assessment had shifted again. Recognizing the rhetorical, practical, and conceptual flaws arguing for only performance assessment, the testing field also began speaking about balance; in this case, "balanced assessment." The logic? If the curriculum is balanced, assessment tasks should also be balanced. The NSF funded the Balanced Assessment Project, based at the University of California—Berkeley, and collaborating with Harvard, Michigan State University, and two British universities—the University of Nottingham and the University of Lancaster. Within the project, "balance" was conceptualized as multidimensional: balance in mathematical content (among the topics of number and quantity, algebra and patterns, geometry and space, data and statistics, probability, as well as other mathematical topics); balance in mathematical process (modeling and formulating, transforming and manipulating, inferring, evaluating and checking, reporting); balance in task type (nonroutine problems, open investigation, design, plan, review and critique, technical exercise, definition of concepts); balance in goal type (pure mathematics, illustrative application of mathematics, and applied power over a practical solution); and balance in circumstances of performance (task length, modes of presentation, modes of working, modes of student response).[41]

While the California policy climate included talk of "balance," the idea of balance was not nearly as complex as this, nor was there—as of 1998— much attention to a balanced assessment at the state level. Governor Wilson wanted every student in the state tested, and he wanted the scores to be comparable across districts. But the tests that districts chose varied wildly, normed on different populations, testing different knowledge and skill. In fact, some of the tests were norm-referenced, others criterion-referenced. After convening consultants to examine the possibility of comparing different test scores, Wilson chose another strategy and insisted that the state contract with one testing house and use one test for every California student. This test would then become the centerpiece for the new California Standardized Testing and Reporting Program (STAR).

Tests were submitted for review. Again, the School Board and Eastin differed: Eastin had recommended the Comprehensive Test of Basic Skills/ Terra Nova published by CTB/McGraw-Hill of Monterey, California (which the majority of California's districts were using by that time). But on November 14, 1997, the board chose instead the Stanford Achievement Test 9th Edition (called the SAT9 or Stanford 9), published by San Antonio–based Harcourt Brace Educational Measurement. Eastin did not quarrel with the decision, stating publicly that she had preferred one over the other because she felt it was stronger for elementary school students, but that the test selected by the board was equally strong, especially for high school students. The president of Harcourt Brace Educational Measurement announced the triumph of "back to basics": "All across the country, educators are getting back to basics, returning to trusted concepts in the classroom and raising academic standards."[42] No mention was made of the fact that testing houses are for-profit enterprises, and that there is a considerably higher profit margin when the testing house can sell an existing test rather than do the research and development necessary to develop more innovative assessments.

Of significance was the fact that the SAT9 is a norm-referenced test, designed to compare students and schools to each other (both in the state and in the national norm group). The test, thus, was in some ways antithetical to the systemic drive to align policy levers, for a standards-referenced test would have been more appropriate. One report quoted James Popham and Bob Schaeffer, measurement experts, who had evaluated the test for the *Los Angeles Times:* "The truth is it's a fundamentally flawed testing system. . . . Students' scores are almost certainly meaningfully contaminated by factors that have little to do with the effectiveness of a teaching staff's instructional efforts."[43] In part, these concerns led to the "augmentation" of the SAT9 with additional items aligned to the state standards. The augmented items were crafted and tended to by a Content Review Panel. Insiders suggest that Harcourt Brace officials have been badgered by members of the panel to make sure that the items are mathematically accurate and adhere to the *Content Standards.*

The mandate went out: Every school district in the state was to cooperate with Harcourt Brace and administer the SAT9 by May 25, 1998. Every parent would receive individual scores for their children, and scores were to be reported by school and district. Harcourt Brace posted a $2 million bond, assuring that it would have all school and school district scores on the Internet by an agreed-upon deadline. A year later, in 1999, "augmented items" were added to the SAT9 in the first of many steps to pull the state's assessments closer in line with the state's standards.

Concerns arose. The "hurry-up" nature of the testing program was worrisome to many teachers. As Dan Walters of the *Sacramento Bee* wrote, "California schools need deliberate, thoughtful reform that will serve for the

long run, not the political one-upmanship that has marked so much of recent policy-making and has ill-served California's children."[44]

School districts struggled to respect the mandate. San Francisco Unified
simply refused, taking a stand for the non-English-speaking children and
risking as much as $11 million in funding. Other districts, trying to re-
spond, found themselves in tangles. Children with special needs often go
to special schools outside the formal system but receive support from the
public school district in which they live. These small schools can have children from any number of districts simultaneously. According to the policy, all children had to take the test, and all the related districts had to administer the test. In southern California this meant that nine districts had
to send teams to one school for children with special needs; this was a
nightmare for the school and, according to some in the central office, a
waste of everyone's time and money. Furthermore, while districts were required to administer the test to children with special needs and limited-
English speakers, much to their dismay and frustration, Harcourt Brace
supplied only raw scores for any child who took an altered form of the test
(the most frequent alteration is the removal of all time constraints). The raw
scores were nearly impossible to interpret and use. The obvious waste of energy devoted to an enterprise that had little payoff aggravated an already
edgy situation. "Why do it? Why make us jump through hoops that don't
help anyone?" educators asked.

The release of the scores in 1998 and 1999 was sobering. California students scored below the national average in almost all subject areas and almost all grade levels. However, if one controlled for language proficiency,
California's English-proficient students in 1999 were scoring at or above
the national average.[45]

As of 2001, the assessment saga continued. Further attempts have been
made to align STAR with the state's standards. Another test—the "Matrix"
test (officially known as the California Assessment of Applied Academic
Skills, or CAAAS), will eventually assess problem solving skills. It has
been dubbed the "Matrix" test because it will entail a matrix sampling
framework (like the CLAS did), whereby some students in one school respond to one set of items, while others respond to parallel items. A high
school exit examination (CAHSEE) was also under development (that students will have to pass beginning in 2006), as was an English language development test.[46]

In 1999, the legislature signed the Public Schools Accountability Act

(PSAA) into law, and authorized the creation of a new education account-ability system. The Academic Performance Index (API) was considered the cornerstone of the legislation, for its purpose was to measure a school's performance and growth. The API was supposed to include multiple measures (graduation, attendance, or dropout rates, SAT9, other standardized test data, and more). However, since there were no other reliable measures at this time, the API was calculated using SAT9 data only. In July of 1999, the State Board of Education adopted a framework of criteria to use in the development of the API—criteria that resonated with lessons learned from previous assessment and curricular reforms. According to the board, the API must be technically sound; emphasize content, not process; be aligned with the state standards; include as many students as possible; and be understandable to both teachers and the wider public.[47]

A Parallel National Debate

All the while, there was more national news. The twelfth-grade TIMSS results were released: twelfth graders in the United States performed below the international average and were among the lowest of the twenty-one TIMSS countries on the assessment of mathematics general knowledge. The United States was one of three countries that did not have a significant gender gap in mathematics general knowledge among students at the end of secondary schooling. While there was a gender gap in science general knowledge in the United States, as in every other TIMSS nation except one, this gap was one of the smallest.

Education Secretary Richard Riley commented:

> These results are entirely unacceptable, and absolutely confirm our need to raise our standards of achievement, testing, and teaching, especially in our middle and high schools—and to get more serious about taking math and science courses.
>
> Let me outline five basic steps we need to take. First, we need to build a firm foundation for our students during the middle school years; second, state assessments and standards must be raised; third, we must expect more high school students to take four years of math and science, including physics, chemistry, trigonometry, and calculus; fourth, more teachers must be prepared to teach these subjects; and fifth, as a nation we must make sure that all students—not just the elite or the brightest—understand the importance of math and science in their lives.[48]

Secretary Riley called for the development of a firmer foundation of mathematical knowledge in elementary and middle school, and he challenged states and schools to raise standards, measure student performance, reduce the number of teachers teaching out-of-field, and offer high-quality professional development. He urged that teachers, too, should take tests measuring their mathematical knowledge and that higher education improve the preparation of new teachers. A public engagement campaign, including parental involvement, was seen as central.

Part of the plan involved a proposal for a voluntary national mathematics test for eighth grade. But what would be the content of the test? Committees met; their discussions echoed those in California. What was the place of basic skills? Was there too much dogmatic constructivism? Where was problem solving, and what did it look like? Mathematicians and mathematics educators were called in, and the hearings were broadcast on C-SPAN. Attempts were made at engaging a broad range of perspectives. And according to Hyman Bass, the committee developed an "open, generous, and respectful working ethos." Hearings were called across the country, open to anyone with concerns and commentary. The committee worked hard to listen and respond to many comments. Bass paid special attention to the thorough and critical analyses offered by two Stanford mathematicians, Richard Schoen and James Milgram.[49]

But all the responsiveness in the world could not assuage some people. A group of critics wrote yet another open letter to President Clinton, explaining how inadequate the test was and raising concerns about the integrity of the committee that had developed the test:

> The committee which is drafting the exam specifications is biased. First, nearly all of its members are strong advocates of the NCTM Standards and of programs that repute to be aligned with the NCTM Standards. There is not a balance of different viewpoints regarding mathematics education. Second, members of the committee have significant conflicts of interest as they are actively involved in the writing or promotion of particular mathematics curricula. Even the slightest suspicion that the authors would bias the test toward material covered in their programs, or that their authorship of the test would be used to sell their programs or to help them get grants, undermines the credibility of the exam. Conflict of interest protections should be in place for those writing a document as important as the national math test.[50]

To the committee members—who did not see themselves as a homogeneous group—the accusation of bias and a conflict of interest stung. Especially given the care they felt they had put into the process and the revisions. As professionals, they were constantly confronted with potentially complex "conflict of interest" cases—reviewing articles by colleagues, writing letters for the promotion of former students, deciding whether to use textbooks they had contributed to or written—and they took pride in negotiating such situations with integrity. The accusation of bias, for them, cloaked the real problem: that in the ranks of mathematicians, mathematics teachers, teacher-leaders, curriculum developers, and education researchers there were profound, perhaps incommensurable, differences. While some people—despite these differences—seemed willing to listen and perhaps learn from one another, others wanted to "win" by gaining majority rule of important committees. For them, nothing less would do. And when asked, everyone explained—whether they were for majority rule or for deliberation—that it was their moral imperative.

In January 1998, Education Secretary Riley called for a cease-fire in the "math wars" in a speech to the Joint Mathematics Meetings of the American Mathematical Society (AMS) and the Mathematical Association of America (MAA), urging the assembly to "bring an end to the shortsighted, politicized, and harmful bickering over the teaching and learning of mathematics":

> This undeniable and critical increase in the value of challenging mathematics for both individual opportunities and our society's long-term economic growth leads me to an issue about which I am very troubled—and that is the increasing polarization and fighting about how mathematics is taught and what mathematics should be taught.
>
> . . . This is a very disturbing trend, and it is very wrong for anyone addressing education to be attacking one another in ways that are neither constructive nor productive.
>
> It is perfectly appropriate to disagree on teaching methodologies and curriculum content. But what we need is a civil and constructive discourse. I am hopeful that we can have a "cease-fire" in this war and instead harness the energies employed on these battles for the crusade for excellence in mathematics for every American student.[51]

The Letter

But civil discourse was not the norm. In October 1999, the U.S. Department of Education (USDE) issued a list of ten "exemplary" mathematics education programs. On the list was MathLand and College Preparatory Math, two curricula that had raised such ire in California, primarily because a number of mathematicians were appalled at their lack of mathematical rigor and integrity. According to some insiders, it was especially the decision to call these curricula "exemplary" that annoyed them, for—according to their analyses—even the most noteworthy curricula among those nominated were, at best, "promising."

Several mathematicians decided to write a personal letter of protest to Secretary Riley. But as the draft letter circulated through the electronic networks of concerned participants, a number of teachers and administrators urged the mathematicians who were writing the letter to "go public." The authors saw the USDE's decision to publicly award the title of "exemplary" to a handful of curricula as a political act. They thought of their letter as another political act in response. They enlisted as many signatories as they could among the ranks of K–12 teachers and higher education faculty in mathematics and science they knew.

The result was that nearly 200 mathematicians, scientists, and others scholars signed the letter, which ran as an advertisement in the *Washington Post*, urging Riley to withdraw the department's approval. It was an expensive gesture, costing almost $67,000 to run and sponsored by the Packard Humanities Institute in Los Altos, located not far from the home of HOLD.[52] The authors of the letter included David Klein (one of the founders of Mathematically Correct); Richard Askey (a University of Wisconsin mathematician with a long history of concerns about progressive-oriented mathematics reforms and curricula); James Milgram (one of the Stanford mathematicians who had been asked to rewrite the commission's standards); Hung-Hsi Wu (the Berkeley mathematician who had been so prominent in the California story as well); Martin Scharlemann (a professor of mathematics at the University of California—Santa Barbara); and Betty Tsang (a research physicist at Michigan State who worked in the National Superconducting Cyclotron Laboratory). The signatories included E. D. Hirsch, Henry Alder, and Chester Finn, with Nobel Prize–winning signatories duly noted.

The authors note that "It is not likely that the mainstream views of practicing mathematicians and scientists were shared by those who designed the criteria for selection of 'exemplary' and 'promising' mathematics curricula."[53] They target one mathematics educator in particular: "The strong views about arithmetic algorithms expressed by one of the Expert Panel members, Steven Leinwand, are not widely held within the mathematics and scientific communities." They list a series of curricular analyses and papers written by the critics.[54] They conclude:

> While we do not necessarily agree with each of the criticisms of the programs described above, given the serious nature of these criticisms by credible scholars, we believe that it is premature for the United States Government to recommend these ten mathematics programs to schools throughout the nation. We respectfully urge you to withdraw the entire list of "exemplary" and "promising" mathematics curricula, for further consideration, and to announce that withdrawal to the public. We further urge you to include well-respected mathematicians in any future evaluation of mathematics curricula conducted by the U.S. Department of Education. Until such a review has been made, we recommend that school districts not take the words "exemplary" and "promising" in their dictionary meanings, and exercise caution in choosing mathematics programs.[55]

The networks, both those of the traditionalists and those of the progressives, were abuzz with emails sent fast and furious about the letter. Some saw it as a grandstanding gesture, with the letter's authors and their endorsers interested only in attacking the progressive wing of the mathematics education community. Others saw it as their moral obligation to raise critical concerns. Deborah Saunders quoted Wu's explanation that he was driven to write the letter out of his "sense of duty."[56]

Others saw it as an attack on the elites. Steve Leinwand, the mathematics educator on the expert panel who was targeted in the letter, was quoted as saying, "This is an issue of who mathematics is for." The mathematicians disagreed, arguing that a watering down of a classic mathematics curriculum is "liberal paternalism" that ends up only hurting poor kids.[57]

The only thing that was clear was that the letter did not encourage further deliberation. Glenda Lappan, then president of NCTM and coauthor of one of the exemplary curricula, said, "It's such a sad thing that we can't harness the incredible interest of the mathematicians and get them to sit down alongside of math teachers and figure out how to make a real difference."[58] Hyman Bass, then president-elect of the American Mathematical Society, echoed her comments: "What disturbs me about the open letter is that it throws an important discussion into an arena where nothing can be accomplished, and a lot of damage will be done."[59] Some signatories have since the publication removed their names from the letter, feeling that they were misinformed. (Those signatures have not, however, been removed from the Mathematically Correct website posting of the letter.)

But such collaborative work was increasingly more difficult to imagine. Although there had been heated debate for several years, none of the vocal critics of the earlier reforms had been invited to sit on the panel for the review of exemplary programs. Yet the experiences of California—most of which had a national viewing audience—suggested that any and all decisions about standards, assessments, and curricular guidance (textbooks, instructional programs, materials, and so on) would be critically appraised both for their content and for the processes used to develop and evaluate them. Hindsight suggests that critics should have been included.

If this was obvious, why weren't the critics at the table? A more generous interpretation is that the U.S. Department of Education had worked hard for a particular kind of balance on the committee, one that included the expertise and perspectives of many constituencies—teachers, teacher educators, curriculum developers, and the like. A less generous interpretation is that every time the progressives or the traditionalists had an opportunity to take control of a process, one side willfully excluded or marginalized the other. There wasn't a well-known critic on the expert panel. No progressive educator was invited to speak at the Hoover Institution's "What's Gone Wrong in America's Classrooms? (And How to Fix It)" conference.[60] The "sides" tended to talk among themselves, not across groups (I use the term "sides" cautiously, for there was too much diversity within any identifiable group—traditionalist/progressive, mathematician/teacher, for example—to claim that any group was clearly a "side.") This was understandable, in many ways, for the debates were so caustic at this point, and the sides so rigidly formed, that consensus seemed more chimera than reality. Given the contentiousness and rising suspicion on all fronts, this more paranoid interpretation seized the day.

Regrettably, the language of war, accompanied by a rising suspicion of anyone who was not seen as an ally, obscured one important issue. The mathematicians were not arguing for the representation of "critics" in deliberations concerning mathematics education. They were most concerned that no one with deep knowledge of mathematics was present in these discussions. Why should mathematical eyes and ears be present? While some ideas sound or look promising to educators who know what interests and motivates children, those very same ideas can seem strange to mathematicians, who know what mathematics is really like. Consider one idea that gained popularity in the reformed curricula: children should be encouraged to invent their own algorithms, for it is in inventing algorithms that children demonstrate their own mathematical understanding. One mathematician, curious about this claim, polled his fellow mathematicians at Yale, Harvard, UCLA, and Berkeley. None of them had ever invented an algorithm as a child. To them, this claim that children need to invent algorithms is not only curious (for it does not resonate with their experience), it is also potentially un-mathematical.[61]

Now it may be that children can invent mathematically sound algorithms. We do not know much about those possibilities. But claims like these sound foreign to many accomplished mathematicians, and those scholars want more people with robust understanding of mathematics present in deliberations about mathematics education. They do not necessarily want to be the sole arbiters of what curricula are nominated as exemplary or what content is to be taught, for they believe that teachers, too, have the right to participate in those discussions. But only three people on the list of ninety-six participants in the review process for the curricula had published papers in *Mathematical Reviews,* a database that includes almost all peer-reviewed mathematics publications. And while the many teachers and mathematics educators who swelled the ranks of the reviewers might have had varying degrees of mathematical knowledge, the dearth of participants who were highly regarded mathematicians hit a raw nerve, which led to a very public, political act.

The NCTM *Principles and Standards for School Mathematics 2000*

Given the discussion that arose around the original NCTM *1989 Standards,* including letters from critics calling for revisions, the NCTM began organizing a new round of Standards writing. A twenty-six-member writing committee was created, chaired by Joan Ferrini-Mundy, who had a history of working with mathematicians and mathematics educators alike.

While the NCTM *1989 Standards* involved substantial participation by multiple communities (including mathematicians), an even more elaborate review process was established for the NCTM *PSSM 2000*. It included systematic input and review from myriad constituencies, including the AMATYC (American Mathematical Association of Two-Year Colleges); AMS (American Mathematical Society); ASA (American Statistical Association); ASL (Association for Symbolic Logic); ASSM (Association of State Supervisors in Mathematics); AWM (Association for Women in Mathematics); Benjamin Banneker Society; INFORMS (Institute for Operations Research and the Management Sciences); MER (Mathematics Education Reform); MAA (Mathematical Association of America); NCSM (National Council of Supervisors of Mathematics); RUMEC (Research in Undergraduate Mathematics Education Community); SIAM (Society for Industrial and Applied Mathematics); and the Society of Actuaries. Association Research Groups (called ARGs) were formed. The NCTM writing team sent them drafts, as well as particular questions to answer.

Lines of communication were created, sustained, and used. And the process allowed for new discussions to occur. For example, on the AMS ARG, mathematicians with decidedly different stances were included, many of whom had already become vocal (as advocates or critics of particular views), including Hyman Bass, Richard Askey (one of the coauthors of "the letter"), and Wayne Bishop (whom Debra Saunders called the "Ralph Nader" of math curricula). The process allowed for multiple communities to express their opinions and concerns. The AMS ARG, for example, urged the NCTM *PSSM 2000* authors to be more specific, and to emphasize the importance of proofs, as well as algorithms.[62]

A draft of the standards was issued in October 1998, and 30,000 copies were distributed nationwide. The draft was also available on the Internet, and 20,000 copies (or sections) were downloaded during the review. Twenty-five formal reviews were commissioned. The feedback was then analyzed in an eight-stage iterative process. The National Research Council praised the organization for its inclusive process: "The committee finds the process established by NCTM to solicit comments from the field to be commendable and the process established by them to analyze those comments to be exemplary."[63]

After three years of writing and revising, the *PSSM 2000* were unveiled at the association's annual meeting on a windy, cold April day in Chicago. Twenty thousand people attended this meeting, walking around in NCTM tee shirts, draped with leis made with manipulatives instead of flowers. Energy and élan were high; excited anticipation was in the air. The ballroom was packed, the front lined with three projection screens twenty feet tall. Strobe lights circled the room, and a band played. I had never been in a crowd this large in one room. Accustomed to quieter, more modest academic conferences, I was taken aback by this spectacle, which reminded me alternatively of a prom and a revival meeting.

Glenda Lappan, then NCTM president, had spent two years traveling around the country in her role as leader of this organization. It is a full-time job, one that took her away from her university work as professor. She was—by this time—used to crowds. Walking onto the stage, she looked tiny against the backdrop of multiple images of her on the huge screens. A film was shown that summarized the new *PSSM*, including videoclips of many teachers speaking about their importance. The faces of children—in all their diversity of color and ethnicity—were omnipresent. Lappan spoke of her "deep love of things mathematical," and the crowd cheered. She ended her talk by reminding the audience to hold themselves to high standards, to engage students in meaningful mathematics. "Our children deserve nothing less. . . . Go forth and do good."

The press had been there all day. At a morning press conferences, six cameras flashed constantly as Lappan, Ferrini-Mundy, the new NCTM president Lee Stiff, and others answered questions—some inhospitable—from the press. It didn't come as a surprise that reviews were mixed. Articles ran in *USA Today, Education Week,* and the *New York Times.* The *Chicago Tribune* reported that NCTM members had embraced "new new math,"[64] much to the bewilderment of parents everywhere. Vocal critics put a "back to basics" spin on the new standards. The lead for the *New York Times* article called it an "important about face."[65] Bill Evers and Jim Milgram (respectively, the leader of the HOLD group and a Stanford mathematician in the midst of analyzing and revising the NSF-sponsored curriculum) wrote: "We commend the NCTM for acknowledging that its last try at writing national standards had serious flaws. The council has learned from actual teaching experience and has put the interest of students above saving face."[66]

Meanwhile, the *PSSM* authors saw this as a misrepresentation of the document. The 1989 *Standards* had done just what the organization had hoped for: stimulated discussion and debate. Deborah Ball used the image of a maypole, a standard around which crowds rally and talk, to describe NCTM's hopes for their national standards.[67] From this perspective, the earlier standards "worked," and led to revision that was more informed than the previous one. The NCTM insiders had worked hard to create a process that moved the discourse about mathematics education forward. They had not intended, nor had they seen, their process to be one of capitulation.

Consensus: Solution or Problem?

Mathematics education—as just one piece of the larger education landscape—is clearly a busy, porous, and sprawling enterprise. There were the teachers—progressive and traditional—and the mathematicians—progressive and traditional—and the parents, the School Board, the universities, the California Department of Education, the American Educational Research Association, the American Mathematical Society, the National Council for Teachers of Mathematics, the press. Everyone seemed to want to put in his or her two cents.

Part of the problem was the issue of the role of consensus. Bill Honig and his staff, from the start, recognized that broad consensus necessarily waters things down. The very act of trying to serve many masters and satisfy multiple interest groups might have compromised the potential of the original 1985 *Framework* to make a real contribution, for policy making by consensus can lead to weakening the message. This was certainly a concern that one heard from the critics. Debra Saunders had poked fun at consensus early on: "The other side of their [the educrats] Love of Process can be seen in the many committees they assemble. They meet and meet and write drafts and then happily agree—because, they all agree, 'consensus' is all important. . . . These Kremlinesque committees have been stacked with like-minded, consensus-loving, assessment-fearing clones. They were the ideological arm of the educrats' oligarchy. Process-Firsters used their consensus-loving committees to control through and suppress opposition."[68]

Some critics saw consensus as a progressive and liberal tendency that worked against the development of clear, well-articulated high standards. Ann Watkins, a coauthor of one of the nominated exemplary curriculum programs, was quoted as saying, "It's a shame when mathematicians are criticizing other mathematicians."[69] Ze'ev Wurman, one HOLD parent, wrote a letter to the editor: "Maybe Ms. Watkins needs to indulge in some critical thinking, a skill much ballyhooed by many of those 'exemplary' programs. If mathematicians do not criticize others, mathematicians or not, when they think others are wrong, they would be behaving unethically and immorally. It seems that in Ms. Watkins' opinion, consensus is more important than the truth. I hope she does not reflect the teaching community as well."[70]

Dr. Wurman is, of course, right. We should engage in critical discourse; it is our duty. But his letter to the editor takes an oversimplified linguistic turn, casting consensus in opposition to truth. As many scholars have noted, establishing educational goals is a *political* process, one value-laden and, therefore, often contentious. David Labaree writes, educational "goal setting is a political, and not a technical, problem. It is resolved through a process of making choices and not through a process of scientific investigation."[71] Jerome Bruner points to the influence of culture in this political process when he explains that education's "aims are culturally constituted—generated within a culture. 'Educating' someone is drastically different from keeping the person alive or preventing death. There is nothing 'naturally' desirable, for example, about teaching your ladies in antebellum Virginia to speak and read French. It was simply taken as a sign of cultivation among Virginia's gentry."[72]

As a society, we determine what it means to be well educated. Bruner goes on to say that this vision of "well educated" is derived not from "laws of nature but from some cultural consensus, from some canonical pattern that emerged after long, often fitful maturing."[73] Some critics of the earlier reforms in California came to see consensus as an unproductive strategy that thwarted attempts to improve education. This was unfortunate, for while consensus has its negative aspects, it also has tremendous educative potential. Forums dedicated to consensus building often help people with very different perspectives learn to see things in new light.

But deliberative conversations among opponents were not common practice. Instead, the critics, through their networks and the information they collected and read, developed a consensus within their ranks of a good mathematical education. Further, they viewed it as unethical not to argue for the ascendancy of their image.

At the same time, the more progressive educators, who had different views of what it meant to be well educated mathematically and what it takes to help children learn mathematics, had developed their own consensus. They, too, saw it as their moral duty to argue for their position. I am, of course, oversimplifying here, for there were, no doubt, more than two clearly defined positions on what a mathematically well-educated student is. But for the sake of argument, let us consider the problem presented by two, on the assumption that an inspection of the two will generalize to other cases.

In the case of the Commission for the Establishment of Academic Content and Performance Standards, the commission strove for its own version of consensus and constructed a deliberative process to help further that agenda. But the board vetoed that group's standards and had them rewritten, with the help of some mathematicians who were concerned about the mathematics and perceived as allied with the traditionalist view.

In the case of the exemplary curriculum, the progressives' view dominated. The committee was seen as "stacked" with progressive educators. There were no opportunities to bring the two visions together, and the progressive standards won out. The NCTM also aimed for a deliberative process, only to be scolded about the need to "save face."

What to do? Dr. Wurman believes that it is a moral imperative to argue for truth (I am assuming here that by "truth," he means his community's standards), and that consensus is the nemesis of "right." Yet many scholars would argue that our collective image of an educated American is, by definition, a matter of consensus, for consensus is often the route to determining the right thing to do. But in the case of mathematics education there were multiple, perhaps incommensurable, consensuses.

The Clash of Discourse Communities

There were other problems beyond that of consensus. The participants in the debates—ranging from State Board members to mathematicians to parents to teachers to teacher educators and education researchers—came from radically different discourse communities. They lived in different worlds— worlds characterized by different norms for interacting, different assumptions about what counts as true. At the risk of oversimplifying, let us consider a few of these differences between mathematicians and teachers (remember that no group is monolithic, and that there is considerable variation within and across groups).

As I have noted, schools—especially elementary schools (the focus of this inquiry)—are places in which dissension and debate are avoided. Discourse is polite, differences seldom made explicit and discussed in public forums. Teachers who think very differently about the goals of education— or the nature of instruction—avoid confronting their differences. Nonetheless, as we saw with the teacher networks, teachers will find like-minded colleagues as they search out professional development opportunities, attend conferences, and the like. This is not to say that schools are harmonious places: they are not, and the political forces within them can do considerable damage to any attempt at reform.[74] It is simply not part of the school culture to make those disagreements public.

Mathematicians live in a very different world. In their world, debate and refutation are central parts of developing new knowledge. They work alone and together, present their thinking for public review, attend conferences and seminars, engage in sometimes sharp discussions about the validity and quality of one another's work. Teachers do not do this. In part, this might be because teaching is seen as so personal. Unlike a mathematical proof—which must be wrenched from any particular context in order to be valued—teaching remains situated, often idiosyncratic, and deeply personal. Thus, knowledge of teaching does not get subjected to the same critical commentary that mathematics does.

The discourse among the teaching and mathematics communities differs in yet other ways. What counts as knowledge varies considerably. Teachers value experience, and are often suspicious of outsiders who spend a few days or weeks or months in their classrooms and then make claims— based on "research"—about how and when and why instruction does or does not work. In part, this position is rooted in the situated nature of teaching knowledge: no rules hold true always; children and what they bring with them interact with school resources and with teachers' knowledge and skill and administrators' leadership and parental support to create an education that varies from situation to situation. Teachers typically build their knowledge as a lawyer would build knowledge of a case. Lee Shulman argues that teachers use this case knowledge to practice a sort of casuistry; casuistry not in the specious sense of false reasoning, but in applying general ethical principles to resolve moral dilemmas that arise in particular instances.[75]

Mathematicians work within a very different epistemological world. They search for absolute truths about ideal objects. They study exact relationships. Mathematics depends on rigorously defined concepts. "A proven mathematical result has a deeper truth than any other truth because it is the result of step-by-step logic," Simon Singh argues. He continues: "More than any other discipline mathematics is a subject that is not subjective."[76] "Precision," "absolute," "certain"—these are words that matter to mathematicians, and words that guide their inquiries. "Other sciences have hypotheses that are tested against experimental evidence until they fail, and are overtaken by new hypotheses. In math, absolute proof is the goal, and once something is proved, it is proved forever, with no room for change."[77]

These different epistemologies—situated and narrative knowledge versus ideal and propositional—were an important undercurrent in the debates. Understanding the clash among various constituencies, in part, might involve considering what it means to talk about knowledge of teaching mathematics. The more progressive reformers emphasized the *teaching* part of that phrase, and worked to include in their descriptions of mathematics teaching the contexts of teaching—hence the heavy reliance on vignettes (narrative and case-based) that situated teaching mathematics within its school parameters (that students will not be motivated to learn, that teachers need to capture their attention, that teachers need to vary their practices, that students need to be seduced into learning). The mathematicians emphasized the *mathematics* part—the absolutes, the ideals, the relations that every student must know.

Why Are They the Experts?

Each group's expertise seemed relevant. However, the professional standards (the *1985 and 1992 Frameworks,* the NCTM *1989 Standards*) erred on the side of teaching knowledge, and mathematicians had a field day finding mathematical errors in various texts. Finding pedagogical errors was almost impossible, for there exists no authoritative text on the nature of effective mathematics teaching. The fact that teaching knowledge is so "soft" disarmed the teachers, who could not call on any higher authority in objection to the teaching claims the mathematicians made. I've experienced firsthand how frustrating this can be. At my own university, for example, Deborah Ball and Hyman Bass were discussing a videotape of Ball teaching third graders. At one point, a mathematician leapt into the discussion and proclaimed—as if it were a mathematical truth—the one right way to teach odd and even numbers. When pressed, of course, he admitted that his "knowledge" of teaching was based on his own intuitions about what would work (given the mathematics), but his tone and stance suggested that he gave his personal experience a great deal of credence. The mathematician was a sensible man, and his ideas about teaching deserved to be heard. But we have little experience in how to talk about teaching, and even less understanding about the appropriate or valid warrants for making pedagogical claims.

Since there was (and is) no forum in which mathematicians and teachers could begin working out their differences, and no third party to mediate, the debates in California remained contentious. Very few of the participants paused to explain whether they were an expert and what their relevant field of expertise was. The progressives crafted mathematics problems they thought would be interesting to students, but they did not invite a wide array of mathematicians to comment on how worthy those problems were (recall Wu's early analysis of the strengths and weaknesses of some problems). As teachers, they did not often use criteria like "absolute" and "certain" to judge the value of a problem. Just as I was naïve about the education system when I began this study, so, too, the progressives were naïve about the mathematics of some of their problems. Just as my naïveté was sometimes misread as arrogance, so, too, the critics found the progressives arrogant and dismissive of dissent.

The mathematicians who joined the camps of critics, on the other hand, demonstrated a different sort of naïveté/arrogance. They applied the same habits of mind that worked for them in mathematics to their analyses of mathematics teaching. Hyman Bass and Deborah Ball recall their early collaborations, and how swiftly Bass—a world-class mathematician—would presume to know what a child knew simply by what a child said.[78] For example, if a child said, "I get it" on a videotape of a mathematics class that Bass was watching, Bass assumed that the child had a mathematical insight. But any parent or teacher knows that the relationship between what a child says and what he or she means is fragile at best. Students say "I get it" and mean, "I give up" or, "I'll agree with you so that you will stop hounding me here" or, "I'll agree with you because you're trying so hard to teach me, even though I don't understand what you are saying." As Clifford Geertz reminds us, a wink is not a wink is not a wink.[79] Gestures and words are, instead, embedded in complex webs of meaning that make one wink a twitch and another an insider's signal.

The empirical world of classrooms—of words spoken, of hidden intentions, of hard-to-decode behaviors and comments—is very different from a mathematical problem. And good teachers know a great deal about the difference between what is said and meant, what is repeated and what is learned. They also know that the same method will not work across all contexts, for teaching and learning are inevitably shaped by the contexts in which they take place. When they thought of standards for teaching mathematics, the reformers thought in those situated, contextualized ways. For them, the lists of things to know (basic computations and automatized knowledge) left out the contexts that provided meaning for those necessary—but not sufficient—basic skills.

In the later rounds of the California mathematics saga, the experiences of the progressive teachers and teacher-leaders were marginalized. The open letter to the editor that ran in the *Washington Post* was signed primarily by mathematicians and scholars (a few teachers did sign their names), all of whom proudly listed their universities—Harvard, Stanford, Berkeley, UCLA—and any prizes won, Nobel or otherwise. Yet none of them mentioned whether they had received a teaching award, even though universities regularly commend professors for the quality of their teaching. Knowledge of mathematics seemed to be the thing that mattered. (The exception here was Jaime Escalante, the teacher whose life story was told in the book and movie *Stand and Deliver* and whose name was used regularly by the critics as their teacher poster child.)

When a progressive reformer raised questions about the mathematicians' expertise in K–12 *teaching*, he or she was characterized as being "anti-intellectual." This was, like so many other things, too facile a rhetorical spin, one that ignores the fact that there are considerable differences between the skills and knowledge required to teach K–12 students mathematics and the knowledge and skills necessary to win a Nobel Prize. And although teaching in the university might provide one with important teaching experience that is transferable to the K–12 setting, the contexts are different enough to make one pause: students in the university are there voluntarily; students in K–12 settings are not. The university has the privilege of conceptualizing its role as "the last line of defense," even if this means that students fail at alarming rates. My friend Brendan, who majored in mathematics at the University of Michigan, often spoke of the "weeder" classes, low-level courses designed to sort the promising students from the "terminal" ones. Famous mathematicians seldom teach those "weeder" classes. They get the more coveted classes, with the elite students who have "made it."

Public school mathematics teachers don't have the luxury of choosing only high-functioning, interested students. In fact, that scenario flies in the face of their charge: to help every student have access to high-quality mathematics instruction. When a university student fails a course, no mathematician is obliged to go back and help her learn what she did not understand. Mathematicians are not accountable for the number of students who fail their university courses, and don't have to justify the fact that hundreds of students eventually disappear from the roster. Schoolteachers are. If someone doesn't pass, parents, students, administrators all want to know what the teacher did not do to help. The students don't go anywhere, and the teachers are left to help them make it through the curriculum, no matter how hard it is, no matter how irrelevant it might seem to students.

These different realities led some participants to question the sincerity of critics' concerns for disadvantaged students. Almost everyone participating in the discussions remarked on the need to improve achievement for *all* students, regardless of their background. And many of the critics of the earlier reforms were deeply committed to the education of all children. Some progressive educators made stinging accusations that these mathematicians were elitists. No coalition in these debates was above incivility: innuendos were launched from every direction; everyone felt attacked at some point.

Nonetheless, there were legitimate questions to be raised about the commitments and knowledge of various participants. As I have already pointed out, schoolteachers must deal with students who fail their courses, whereas university mathematicians are not always held accountable for the students who do not make it through their introductory courses. The campuses of Stanford and Berkeley are much different from the classrooms of Fresno, Hayward, and Los Angeles. One is a world of privilege, the other is not. Not to be forgotten were the comments made by some parents in Palo Alto about making sure their children were not "held back" by other, less gifted students. The chasm between the worlds of the university and the schools, between communities like Palo Alto and others less fortunate, helped fuel a deep skepticism among some educators about whether critics—be they mathematicians, parents, policy makers, or educators—really cared about or understood issues of equity and what it takes to teach mathematics to all students.

But these questions could not be answered through the processes that were in place, for there were few opportunities for the participants to engage in sustained dialogue so that they might learn about one another's perspective. I return to this point in Chapter 10.

A Story That Has No End

When I first set out to write this book, it was 1994. I intended to tell a story of the slow, consistent, and persistent "triumphs" of progressive teachers and reformers. But then all hell broke loose, and the story changed from one about the reformers to one that included multiple actors and communities. And the story has no end, for the contentious discussions of what kind of mathematics to teach and how continue, both in California and nationally.

One battle took place in Massachusetts when the state developed a new mathematics framework. The battle cries were the same, the concerns familiar: What counts as research? Where are the basics? Should standards include talk of instruction? Mathematicians and mathematics educators from California were pulled into the debate. Critics of the earlier reforms in California consulted with traditionalists in Massachusetts. Teachers consulted with other teachers about how to lobby for a more progressive view of teaching and learning. The name calling, ideological rigidity, righteous anger, and lack of clarity about what anyone meant by "balance" and whether consensus or voting should rule the day walked right through the door, along with the actors.

And articles appeared regularly in high-profile newspapers. *The Christian Science Monitor,* for example, ran an extensive series that aimed, it appeared, for a balanced perspective. The articles reported not only on parents and children who were happy with the new curricula and reforms, but also on students who were "cheated" by them. The series even included a math problem. In one piece, a staff writer made a point often lost in the debate: "U.S. teachers have developed a thick skin against frequent reforms that encourage wild swings or suggest a lost golden age of learning."[80]

In the spring of 2001, a similar crisis hit the New York City public schools. Journalists interviewed progressive and traditionalist teachers, parents, mathematicians. Some of the California players got into the act. Teachers felt betrayed by a misrepresentation of what they said; traditionalists were angry at not being listened to. The rapidity and sad predictability of a querulous, rancorous public discussion was a sign that little progress had been made.

9 Parsnips and Orchids Side by Side:
A View from the Classroom

> Most teachers hedge their bets. Few teach only the facts; fewer still
> devote 100 percent of classroom time to students' constructing
> their own knowledge. Few teachers choose to plant only one kind of
> flower; few risk committing themselves to a distinct, exclusionary
> philosophy. Few teachers maintain a pure worldview of what a
> classroom should be; most put each finger and toe in as many ped-
> agogical universes as they can stretch to. And so tubs of pattern
> blocks sit side by side with skill-drill worksheets. To straddle the
> pedagogical fence—to drill students on math facts and at the same
> time expect them to think and discover and create for themselves—
> may be to plant parsnips and orchids side by side. But perhaps a
> good definition of what it means to be a teacher is to hold two—
> maybe even fourteen—contrary notions in one's belief system at
> the same time.
> —Susan Ohanian

Critics of the earlier reform jumped quickly to a conclusion that the steep
decline in California's National Assessment of Educational Progress rank-
ing—in mathematics and language arts—was due to the frameworks. The
finger of blame was steady and strong. Sweeping, facile generalizations
were made. John Derbyshire confidently proclaimed that the revised NCTM
Principles and Standards for School Mathematics 2000 "revives such practices
as rote memorization of multiplication tables, which math students have
not been able to avail for a number of years."[1]

Unfortunately, most critics had spent little time in schools, and were
relatively naïve about the power of policy to change practice. Such com-

ments reflect little knowledge of how the vast, sprawling education system mediates policy. Policy doesn't travel, like an arrow, directly to its target. Instead, teachers and administrators, students and communities, districts and leaders "mutually adapt." As David Tyack and William Tobin explain, "Reformers believe that their innovations will change schools, but it is important to recognize that schools change reforms. Over and over again teachers have selectively implemented and altered reforms."[2] Or, as Susan Fuhrman and Richard Elmore claim: "Most state and federal policies in the past have engendered a range of local behavior rather than uniform compliance . . . the most typical outcome is some compromise between what high/level policymakers intended and local actors' needs."[3]

This more interactive interpretation of policy and practice mutually shaping each other is quite different from the more unidirectional view of some critics who presumed that questionable policies automatically lead to questionable practices.

In our inquiry into reform in California, we saw no passive acceptance of mandates, no schools or teachers unquestionably accepting the "fads" offered in the frameworks. We saw no panaceas. Although some teachers were actors in this turbulent policy story, most of California's 250,000 teachers were not. For many, these debates seemed unreal and irrelevant, for the dichotomies and dramas owned by the outsiders have made little sense to the insiders. Every school district person we asked in our last round of California interviews chuckled at the inflamed rhetoric of the math and reading "wars." For them and for many teachers, no wars were being waged. Instead, teachers were making quiet accommodations. A brief look inside of classrooms is in order here.

In the late 1980s, Andrew Porter and his colleagues at Michigan State University reported on a large-scale study of mathematics teaching. They found that elementary mathematics classrooms had four significant features. First, teachers spent most of their time emphasizing skills, noting a lack of "balance": "A ubiquitous and pronounced lack of balance exists across concepts, skills, and applications. Teachers spend a large amount of their mathematics time teaching computational skills—approximately 75%. The remaining time is distributed between teaching for conceptual understanding and applications in ways that vary from teacher to teacher."[4] These researchers also found that elementary mathematics teaching entailed touching upon a large number of topics in short periods of time (70 to 80 percent of the topics taught in a school year received less than thirty minutes of instructional time); that students were rarely asked to formulate mathematical problems; and that mathematics received much less instructional attention than did reading and language arts, with most classrooms averaging less than an hour a day.

Nearly twenty years later, researchers participating in the Third International Mathematics and Science Study (TIMSS) reported similar findings. The curriculum in the United States—when compared to that of other countries—seemed watered down, too superficial: "Lessons from the U.S. were characterized by teachers presenting information and directing student activities and exercises. The multiplicity and diversity of both topics and activities was a unique feature of the U.S. lessons. Both teacher and student activity tended to emphasize the basic definitions, procedures, and concepts of the subject matter. . . . The preponderance of the lesson discussion involved information about procedures, exercises and basic facts."[5] While some scholars characterize this as covering too much, it might be more appropriate to note that ideas are seldom rigorously "covered." Rather, for many, ideas are simply mentioned.

Intensive analyses of videotapes that complemented the TIMSS survey methods echoed the results: in the United States, teachers present definitions and model procedures, the curricular content is thin, and students "learn terms and practice procedures."[6] Other research, ranging from field studies of individual classrooms to state and national surveys, revealed even more support for these findings.[7]

It appears that, in response to dramatic calls to improve American education, local schools and districts, administrators and teachers act prudently and conservatively. As one CDE staffer put it: "What keeps us from absolute sea-sickness is that locals don't jump as quickly" onto some new reform bandwagon. This has become increasingly so in this age of heated political debate. Superintendents told us they were looking for ways "not to get burned" by the state, which was increasingly seen as part of the problem ("creating factions and fights") rather than part of the solution. In 2001, when asked "How do you deal with the state-level educational politics?" one superintendent told me: "Now they are telling us that what they told us ten years ago is completely wrong and that now we have to do this. But why—if they were completely wrong ten years ago—should I believe that they are completely right now?"[8]

In the face of conflicting mandates and guidance, the locals—teachers and administrators alike—try to do the right thing. For the most part, this means that they tinker with reform curricula and practices and the status quo persists.

My colleagues and I—Deborah Ball, Penelope Peterson, Robert Floden, David Cohen, Ralph Putnam, and Richard Prawat among them—visited nearly three dozen teachers between the two programs of research that informed this inquiry.[9] To a one, we never saw radical change. Instead, we saw, as David Cohen put it, "something old, something new." Teachers mixed their old practices (memorizing multiplication tables and distributing drill worksheets) with some new practices (using new materials like manipulatives, introducing a "problem of the day" on Fridays for a change of classroom pace). Teaching seemed to remain largely the same. "Old wine in new bottles," as David Cohen wrote in several project memos.

Yet there was change. Most teachers we interviewed added some new practices and problems to their teaching. For some teachers, this felt revolutionary. But what seemed radical to them appeared more incremental to us, as observers crouched in small elementary school chairs. Other teachers more actively resisted the reforms. I visited one teacher who simply took the new textbook his school district had adopted and edited out the pages with problem solving (he neither liked them nor understood them), substituting old worksheets he had accumulated over the years. His was not a unique strategy. Teachers told us repeatedly that, even when they were told to abandon old materials, they did what they thought was best behind the closed doors of their classrooms.[10]

We also conducted a survey of second- through fifth-grade teachers statewide.[11] Teachers' responses suggested that learning algorithms and developing computational speed were still a mainstay in elementary school classrooms. For example, when asked whether students should learn rules for manipulating fractions, respondents, answering on a five-point Likert scale (1 = strongly disagree, 5+ = strongly agree), reinforced the view that conventional teaching had not disappeared (Table 9.1). Only 17 percent of the respondents disagreed or strongly disagreed with the assertion that students needed to learn such rules.[12] Their responses also suggested that many teachers had never abandoned automaticity as a goal (Table 9.2), for over half the respondents agreed or strongly agreed that students needed to develop computational speed.

Overall, the view provided by the survey is one of instruction that includes elements of conventional teaching with some reform-minded commitments. On the one hand, teachers reported that they emphasized the

Table 9.1. Teachers' Responses to Prompt: Learning Rules about Manipulating Fractions

Q12A	Frequency	Percent	Cumulative Frequency	Cumulative Percent
1	46.90	8.0	46.90	8.0
2	53.69	9.1	100.60	17.1
3	173.10	29.4	273.70	46.5
4	195.25	33.2	468.96	79.6
5	119.94	20.4	588.90	100.0

Frequency missing = 6.091786127

learning of procedures for reducing fractions (Table 9.3). On the other, they reported that students needed to understand the concepts behind those procedures (Table 9.4).

Given the diverse perspectives on what counts as good teaching practice, there are those who will be appalled at these survey results, arguing that it is shameful that 17 percent of the respondents disagreed or strongly disagreed with the idea that students ought to learn rules to manipulate fractions, while 28 percent disagreed or strongly disagreed with the idea that children ought to learn procedures for reducing fractions. Surveys, like all research methodologies, are flawed. We do not know whether these percentages mean that 17 percent or 28 percent of teachers (respectively) were not teaching these procedures, for these are simply self-reports of opinions. More important for this analysis is to notice the instructional eclecticism reflected across the items: no ideology dominated teachers' opinions of what children need to learn. Instead, teachers' beliefs included pieces of

Table 9.2. Teachers' Responses to Prompt: Developing Computational Speed with Fractions

Q12C	Frequency	Percent	Cumulative Frequency	Cumulative Percent
1	104.26	17.6	104.26	17.6
2	156.75	26.4	261.01	43.9
3	251.65	42.4	512.67	86.3
4	66.48	11.2	579.16	97.5
5	14.85	2.5	594.01	100.0

Frequency missing = 0.9858801525

Table 9.3. Teachers' Responses to Prompt: Learning Procedures for Reducing Fractions

Q12E	Frequency	Percent	Cumulative Frequency	Cumulative Percent
1	79.3898	13.4	79.3898	13.4
2	90.1070	15.2	169.4969	28.7
3	155.2272	26.3	324.7241	54.9
4	169.1486	28.6	493.8726	83.5
5	97.3031	16.5	591.1758	100.0

Frequency missing = 3.8244665989

conventional or traditional instruction and pieces of more progressive pedagogy. Parsnips and orchids did seem to exist, side by side.

In sum, these survey results support the results from our case studies of individual teachers. Some pieces of the reform were readily and easily picked up and integrated into conventional practice: teachers reported the use of small groups and manipulatives. They reported that students spent time working individually on problems in textbooks and workbooks and regularly practiced or took tests on important mathematical skills.

Less popular were group or individual projects—often referred to as investigations—that took several days, suggesting that teachers were still driven to provide closure each day for their students' mathematical experiences (see Table 9.5).

In our later research, Robert Floden and I found similar results in elementary mathematics teaching: "When asked, every teacher explained that students needed to master basic facts and skills, as well as have plentiful opportunities to solve problems. No one endorsed a narrow conception of

Table 9.4. Teachers' Responses to Prompt: Learning Ideas about Fractions

Q12F	Frequency	Percent	Cumulative Frequency	Cumulative Percent
1	7.6630	1.3	7.6630	1.3
2	9.9531	1.7	17.6162	3.0
3	80.7808	13.6	98.3970	16.6
4	191.5492	32.3	289.9463	48.9
5	303.2363	51.1	593.1825	100.0

Frequency missing = 1.8177124227

Table 9.5. Teachers' Reports of Classroom Practices

	Never	A Few Times a Year	Once or Twice a Month	Once or Twice a Week	Almost Daily
1. Make conjectures and explore possible methods to solve a mathematical problem	1.0	7.4	18.3	42.8	30.4
2. Discuss different ways that they solve particular problems	0.9	5.0	14.6	46.6	32.9
3. Practice or take tests on computational skills	0.6	9.7	33.4	42.6	13.7
4. Work in small groups on mathematics problems	1.2	3.8	20.4	46.4	28.2
5. Work individually on problems from the textbook/workbook	3.0	4.3	9.7	38.1	45.0
6. Work on individual projects that take several days	23.5	36.7	26.5	10.6	2.6
7. Work on group investigations that extend for several days	25.4	36.2	26.1	9.4	2.9
8. Write about how to solve a problem in an assignment or test	11.6	16.9	33.7	28.8	9.0
9. Do problems that have more than one correct solution	8.1	14.1	33.0	32.8	12.0
10. Use manipulative materials or models to solve problems	0.9	5.0	19.7	40.0	34.4
11. Use calculators to solve problems	12.7	20.4	29.1	29.6	8.3
12. Do mathematics in conjunction with other subjects or class projects	1.1	10.1	33.5	36.9	18.3

Source: David K. Cohen and Heather Hill, *Learning Policy: When State Education Works* (New Haven: Yale University Press, 2002), 81.

mathematics teaching—say, a steady diet of memorization—but every teacher explained that basic skills were essential. Without mastery of basics, students could do little else. Teachers at the lower grades reported emphasizing the basics over problem solving, teachers in upper elementary reported more variation, depending on how solid students' basic knowledge was."[13]

Other scholarship and recent research on standards-based and systemic reform echo these results. Larry Cuban, in his historical analysis of teaching, demonstrates clearly the stability of teacher-directed teaching.[14]

William Firestone and his colleagues found, when they investigated the effects of testing in Maine and Maryland, that teachers largely continued to teach in familiar ways: "Rather strong forces in the educational system maintain an approach to teaching that emphasizes practicing on many, small problems and shallow coverage of many topics."[15]

These findings are not surprising, for the route of a policy from a glossy brochure issued by the state department of education to a teacher's classroom is circuitous. As Linda Darling-Hammond and Arthur Wise noted, "Policies can only be implemented if an organization has the capacity to control the political and technical aspects of the work."[16] The California Department of Education did not have that kind of control, even though it worked hard to use other organizations to support its work, including the California Subject Matter Project, Marilyn Burns's network, the California Mathematics Council, and the like. When the critics read the 1985 or 1992 framework or the California Learning Assessment System, they presumed a direct, rational relationship between what was in those texts and the material presented to students in elementary schools. Things were never that simple, a point the insiders to the reforms always knew. But passions flared when test scores dropped, and facile conclusions were made about the relationship between policy and practice.

A Stable Practice

What makes the policy–practice connection so complex? There are at least four potential answers to that question.

First: Views that policies like the California frameworks and associated reforms can swiftly and directly influence practice presume too much rationality in the system. The education system presents, like hospitals, the *illusion* of coherence. Housed in related buildings, these systems encourage outsiders to presume the existence of coordinated action and clear communication. Yet anyone who has spent time in a hospital knows that the doctors don't always talk to one another, that messages get lost or distorted, and that one needs a manager to sort out who should be doing what.

Similarly, the American education system is fragmented, decentralized, and fraught with conflict. Despite the fact that CDE policy makers intentionally and carefully worked to align all their messages and mandates, teachers nonetheless received mixed messages (at least during the early years of the *1985 Framework*), for districts continued—even while implementing the new frameworks—to require basic skills curricula and testing programs.[17] As David Cohen argues, teachers "wander in a great carnival of instructional guidance, deluged with advice": "In such a carnival, students and teachers can make up their own minds about many matters. Though many are aware of different sorts of advice, few are keenly aware of most of it; for few voices can cut clearly through the din of the multitude. But many educators know that most guidance is either weakly supported or contradicted by other advice. That much they can learn from experience. Most also know that much instructional guidance can safely be ignored. The din of diverse, often inconsistent, and generally weak guidance offers considerable latitude to those who work within it."[18]

This was as true in California as in other states. In research that preceded ours, Denise Cantlon, Sharon Rushcamp, and Donald Freeman found one California school district that mandated its own homework assignments and chapter tests, and focused teachers' attention on mastery of basic skills, which was "in many ways at odds with teaching for understanding and thinking as depicted in the state's curriculum framework." "In other words," the authors state, "the district's curriculum guidelines in mathematics represent a straightforward compromise between state and district goals."[19]

Second: Even within that noisy carnival, all teachers did not encounter an unadulterated version of state policies. Although the frameworks were circulated widely, many California teachers never actually saw them, no less read them. In fact, only two of our case study teachers had read the *1985 Framework*. For the rest, it was a yellow blur waved at them at the fall faculty meeting. For most, other policy levers became the messengers of the reform: newly adopted textbooks, new assessments like the CLAS, professional development like that offered through the California Mathematics Project or Marilyn Burns institutes, replacement units, Marcy Cook Math. Teachers trusted that these representations of reform-minded teaching had fidelity. But the messages across those media varied, and, like the game of telephone, individual teachers' enactments of "the Framework" seldom looked to us like close cousins of the original document.

Third: Although both the *1985 Framework* and *1992 Framework* called for "teaching for understanding," it remained unclear what that actually entailed. Although a model curriculum guide was developed, it fell far short of strong and clear guidance about how teachers should teach and what they needed to do to develop their new practices. As David Cohen and Deborah Ball noted during the first round of our data collection: "The leading ideas of this movement do not yet cohere in an integrated conception of mathematics teaching and learning, rooted in a distinctive epistemology and framing a distinctive practice. This quality of the movement's leading ideas also makes it more difficult for followers and bystanders to understand how the new instruction might look if enacted well. Indeed, it increases the likelihood that each teacher will apprehend and enact the ideas in his or her own terms."[20]

And the teachers we met did.

Fourth: Complicating things further was the fact that to enact the vision well, teachers would need a thorough knowledge of mathematics, which many elementary school teachers do not have. Research on the level of knowledge of mathematics teachers demonstrates clearly that many elementary, and a substantial number of secondary, teachers have fair algorithmic and weak conceptual knowledge of mathematics.[21] The earlier frameworks asked teachers to teach a mathematics they did not know, in ways that were unfamiliar. They could not. They did not.

Instead, they taught to their interpretations of the policies, interpretations that were filtered through their knowledge and beliefs. As David Cohen explained in his case study of one teacher: "The teachers and students who try to carry out such change are historical beings. They cannot simply shed their old ideas and practices like a shabby coat, and slip on something new. Their inherited ideas and practices are what teachers and students know, even as they begin to know something else. Indeed, taken together those ideas and practices summarize them as practitioners. As they reach out to embrace or invent a new instruction, they reach with their old professional selves, including all the ideas and practices comprised therein."[22]

Throughout the "math wars," many people expressed concerns about whether teachers could pull off the reforms. Hung-Hsi Wu wrote about how problems could be misused if teachers did not have adequate mathematical knowledge The Stanford mathematician I spoke with was not worried about the Friday the 13th problem; he was concerned with teachers' capacity to use it well. This is the double bind of curriculum reforms: teachers are necessary actors in improving schooling. But teachers' prior knowledge, experience, and beliefs act as powerful filters for how they interpret and what they do with reforms.

Finally: Classrooms are human and social sites, places where teachers and students negotiate instruction. While there is much to be learned from Diane Ravitch's analysis in *Left Back*, she never satisfactorily addresses the issue of classroom realities. Many students don't see why they need to know math. Yet learning math (like learning any challenging content) requires will and stamina. It is hard, takes practice, and mathematical knowledge accumulates slowly. As John Derbyshire has noted: "Lurking beneath all of these considerations is the fundamental, perhaps intractable problem of math education: Math is hard. Probably no large number of people will ever be much good at it, or like it much. Mathematical thinking is, in a sense, deeply unnatural. Mathematical truths are revealed to the human race very, very slowly, after unimaginable intellectual effort and lifetimes of frustration, against all the grain of ordinary human thought and language processes."[23]

Progressive educators believed that the solution was motivational: find ways to help students connect with content in meaningful ways. But what was produced in the name of progressive education—sometimes—was watered-down-beyond-recognition content. Diane Ravitch points the finger of blame at the education establishment and the progressives for this mindless curriculum, especially colleges and schools of education.[24]

There are, of course, large grains of truth in Ravitch's analysis. A lot of nonsense is offered in the name of teacher education and reformed curriculum. But in the busy, buzzing confusion that is school, other factors also shape instruction. Students are involuntary participants in American public education. Teachers need to cajole them into learning. This requires an inspired and robust pedagogy. In good schools of education, new teachers can learn to enact such a curriculum and pedagogy.

Mathematicians do not often have to deal with this particular problem. In my university, for example, over 8,000 seniors graduate every year, and every year fewer than 50 of them are mathematics majors. The more than 100 tenured faculty members of the mathematics department—while they offer many service courses for students across the university—are not accountable to parents or failing students or for their 1:2 major:faculty ratio. They can teach as they see fit, for they have the privilege of "holding their ground."

When a public school student fails algebra, on the other hand, public school teachers have an obligation to respond, to find other ways to help the student learn. That is not simply an issue of standards. It is also an issue of a sound, accomplished pedagogy. Maybe the progressive educators have not gotten it right, but neither have the conventional teachers, for the problem remains: many students do not learn mathematics. One is reminded of this every time one watches a checkout person look for the calculator instead of doing a simple mental math problem involving a 10 percent discount.

The answer to improving schools lies in attending to both high content standards and dazzling teaching. One without the other won't work.

One factor that makes reaching high standards difficult is the mass enterprise of schooling. Teachers need to manage children in groups, and groups of energetic 6-year-olds or adolescents are hard to control. Bargains get struck: we'll all get along as long as school is not too demanding.[25] In part, these compromises are made because of the profound ambivalence toward intellectualism in the United States. One anthem sung by critics of the education establishment is that teachers and colleges of education are "intellectually bankrupt."[26] What they fail to acknowledge is that the United States is intellectually bankrupt. Schoolpeople could hold higher standards, granted. But they work in and come from communities that do not uniformly care about academics. In some cases, these communities have other priorities—for example, keeping children safe or having a championship football team. Even in the best of schools, scholars have documented how students browbeat teachers for credentials, with little interest in the knowledge and skill that the credential is supposed to represent. No one is above this.[27]

These forces are, of course, not necessarily in tension: a school can graduate educated children and have an award-winning swim team. I note these forces, instead, to remind us all that the realities teachers face include the need to convince students (and sometimes their parents, other teachers, and the community) that knowledge matters.

It is amazing how contentious the "math wars" debates were, and how few teachers' voices were heard in the fray. Pulling the discussions out of schools allowed progressives and traditionalists to speak in abstractions. The problem with abstractions is that they rise above the details, and—in the case of teaching—details matter. Teaching and learning sit at the center of a complex historical, social, interpersonal, psychological, sociological world. Standards could affect that world. Teachers shape that reality—no doubt. And they could, standards in hand (with the right capacities and right supports), help students learn more.

But what the supporters and critics of the earlier reforms forgot, and what the triumphant new standards-bearers run the risk of ignoring, is that conventional practice, for teachers, is not a problem. It is the solution to a problem: how to teach mathematics when one is not necessarily well prepared to do so, to students who don't necessarily care about learning it.

10 Toward a Civil, Constructive Discourse

In the long run, a more important matter for the field [is] . . .
whether they can, amid nurtured rancor and piqued honor,
keep the conversation going.
—Clifford Geertz

I am a person with many, and strongly held, opinions. My goal in this book, however, is to make a contribution to the discourse about mathematics education by, first, withholding my opinions and presenting the ideas and actions of progressives and traditionalists, reformers and their critics, parents and policy makers in an empathetic light. Far too many people have quickly jumped to conclusions about elitist mathematicians, process-first educators, the intellectually bankrupt education establishment, and the like. Few people have seemed willing to first try to understand why, to paraphrase Philip Cusick, the actors involved in mathematics reform in California were well-intentioned people whose actions and reactions made sense to them. No one treated the problem as a variegated one. Instead it was oversimplified—us/them, Democrat/Republican, liberal/conservative. It was much simpler to dismiss someone with whom one disagreed as empty-headed or elitist. As an outsider—to California and to mathematics education—I thought a "balanced" perspective was something I might contribute.

But researchers have an obligation to go beyond description to explanations, and pragmatists (among their ranks are many teachers like myself) wish to offer sensible advice about how to make progress. So in this final chapter, I make a case for why and how we might move toward a more constructive and civil discourse about mathematics education.

My story documents what typically happens. In the United States, everyone wants a say in what their children—and, by association, other children—learn. This inevitably results in curricula and standards (or, more accurately, a confusing panoply of multiple curricula and many standards) that, in trying to serve various masters, aim to do everything simultaneously and continuously. William Schmidt's argument, based on his immersion in the international comparisons of the Third International Mathematics and Science Study, is that an unhealthy and distracting curricular diffusion results from this democratic decision making. We have a mathematics curriculum that aims to do everything and produces nothing.[1] Schmidt takes the argument further: in the midst of this diffusion, socioeconomic status (SES) rises like a phoenix and becomes the critical factor in whether or not students learn mathematics. In the absence of an intelligible, focused, cumulative curriculum that could act as a powerful educative "treatment" for all children, SES, already proven to be a powerful (indeed, perhaps the single most powerful force) in a child's future, steps in and claims the day.

And so history repeats itself: mathematics is taught conventionally, and children are exposed to limited, often overly algorithmic, aspects of mathematics. Some of those students, in turn, go on to become teachers, who are wary of mathematics and unprepared to teach it in all its rich complexity and depth.[2] The students who manage to succeed tend to be the ones from more advantaged backgrounds. Each generation bemoans the sorry state of mathematics education, and the story never ends.

Where to Go?

What would it take to make history, rather than repeat it? I cannot offer a proof, for mathematics teaching and learning exist not in a mathematical world of absolutes but in the human world of contingencies. We can begin, however, with a handful of axioms, observations I hold to be true based on this analysis:

- In the end, teachers will enact and mediate any effort to improve mathematics education.
- Historically and currently, discourse about mathematics education is contentious and unstable, easily inflamed, not so easily resolved.
- All sides can be uncivil.
- Neither progressive nor traditional education has been implemented well on a large scale in the United States.
- Most American children experience the "conventional" teaching that both the reformers and the critics worried about.

So, we have an unstable discourse and a stable classroom experience, neither of which satisfies *any* reformer or participant in this story, no matter their perspective. Further, we are dependent on teachers—they are necessary agents of reform, while also, in this case, being targets of the reform.[3] Given the fact that a large-scale implementation of high-quality traditional *or* progressive mathematics education has never occurred, we know little about the relative educative merit of those paradigms. What we need, then, is to stabilize the discourse—making it deliberative and sustained—while destabilizing practice, pushing it to be more mathematically rigorous *and* more accessible to more children.

Problem Parameters

How can this be done? Let us first consider three of the problem's parameters. First, everyone wants a say. There are the mathematicians and the teachers, each group (with considerable variation within and across) with relevant experience and some expertise (albeit contested). There are also the parents and other concerned citizens, professional associations, higher education professionals, curricular framework authors, the textbook industry, the National Science Foundation, the National Research Council, leaders in education policy in the legislature, state and local boards of education, teacher preparation professionals, interest groups, and the Office of Educational Research and Improvement.[4] As Michael Kirst and Gail Meister note, "Curriculum planning belongs to professionals, parents and officials together."[5]

While curriculum planning might be the bailiwick of all those groups in the United States, all groups are not equally qualified. Parents, for instance, might be experts about their own children; they are not necessarily experts about mathematics. In the math wars that have erupted recently in Manhattan, for example, a parent was quoted as deriding the new math curriculum in his child's school, using as an example a problem that involved flipping marshmallows, explaining to a reporter that this problem was a perfect example of the idiocy of the reforms. A mathematician was appalled when he read the article, for, being the internationally renowned geometer that he was, he thought the problem was an excellent one for investigating important mathematical ideas. The mathematician could see things mathematical in the problem that the parent, knowing only the mathematics he had been taught, could not. The parent saw a sweet, the mathematician, geometry. Yet the press treated the parent as an authority. The mathematician saw the parent as proof positive that the education system does not work, for the parent confidently believed he had adequate mathematical understanding but did not.

So we have a democratic system that opens itself to participation from multiple communities—communities with disparate levels of expertise and experience. Everyone assumes they have the right to opine about mathematics teaching, even when they do not have obvious expertise. This assumption is encouraged by the fact that these debates concern teaching, for everyone thinks they know how to teach. We're caught in a double bind: decisions concerning education are democratic ones in the United States. But our democracy is not uniformly mathematically or pedagogically literate. "Democratic governance," as it turns out, "is no panacea for the problems of the educational system."[6]

A second problem parameter concerns the clash between the assumptions of standards-based reform and the realities of schools.[7] Standards-based reforms presume rationality: set standards, line them up with assessments, hold schools accountable. If the standards are clear and the tests have authority, students will learn more meaningful mathematics.

But schools and classrooms are not coolly rational places. Students are not in schools as a matter of free will, and much as we would wish otherwise, we cannot mandate learning. Students come from a society deeply ambivalent about intellectual life. Many of them currently fear or loathe mathematics, many see no reason to learn math. (In the best of all possible worlds, this would not be true. But we live in this world, not another.) Teachers know this, and they know they have to cajole and encourage, seduce and support students. Teachers can hold high standards, but without the willing participation of students, no learning can take place. This is why we need to talk about instruction *and* content.

This explains the two sets of standards: one set—the public, *Academic Content Standards* of the commission—listed the content, the mathematics all students should know. Another set—the NCTM *1989 Standards,* as well as California's mathematics frameworks—embedded that content in the contexts in which teachers work.[8] Teachers need several forms of guidance, including guidance about the mathematics to be taught *and* guidance about the various ways one might effectively present mathematics to students who are not always eager collaborators in instruction. The first set of standards reasonably drew on the knowledge of expert mathematicians; the second set just as reasonably drew on the knowledge of experienced teachers who understand the situated nature of teaching and learning, as well as the particular problems associated with teaching mathematics. Moving forward, rather than repeating history, will require the participation of both communities, accompanied by a genuine, mutual respect for their varied and quite different experience and expertise.

A third parameter involves considering the question, "What is this debate about?" While on the surface it was called "the math wars," a close examination reveals that the disagreements were not always about mathematics. This is not surprising. As Murray Edelman points out, "There is a diversity of meanings in every social problem, stemming from the range of concerns of different groups, each eager to pursue courses of action and call them solutions."[9]

For some participants, this debate was about mathematics, plain and simple. For others it was about equity, for others about excellence, for others about identity. In working out what mathematics we want all children to know, the actors were also working out larger social issues about the role of intellectual life in the United States, equality and equity, the rights of the individual versus the common needs of the nation. As David Cohen notes, "Policymaking ought not be understood only in terms of its effects. For policymaking is not simply an instrumental effort in which political ends are defined, and suitable means selected. Policymaking also is part of larger and more diffuse conversations in which a society tries to get its bearings— to sort out what it is, where it is, where it is going, and why."[10]

But in California (and elsewhere), no sustained attention was paid to the fact that these "wars" were not simply about mathematics. They were also about our national identity; about what individual parents hoped for their children; about what some scholars and teachers hoped for the improvement of American society; about a deep suspicion of the education establishment, and an equally deep suspicion of elite mathematicians and intellectuals. They were about the warrants for making curricular decisions: many people called for "research-based" decisions, while reasoning by anecdote. Under the surface also ran concerns about knowledge, efforts to professionalize teaching, questions about whether there is any specialized expertise in matters of education, and questions of who has the right to determine curriculum in the United States.

While other parameters exist, these three capture much of what we need to attend to. We have a system that allows for diverse, democratic participation, yet through that egalitarian door walk participants with uneven, sometimes questionable expertise. We have a problem that requires the expertise and wisdom of both mathematicians and mathematics teachers, but recent history leaves many of those people wary of everyone save their closest allies and colleagues. And we are not all always talking about mathematics; these discussions of mathematics education are also debates about our individual and collective identities. No one has made this explicit.

Deliberative Discourse

In his book *Bowling Alone: The Collapse and Revival of American Community*, Robert Putnam joins the ranks of other scholars who argue that the health of our American democracy depends on our capacity to create a deliberative discourse, one characterized by sustained, active participation by many groups.[11] The argument goes something like this: traditional democracy has not worked as well as it might. The public has difficulty accepting tough solutions to intractable problems; powerful interest groups end up dominating debates, while other citizens complain of being dismissed and marginalized; and those debates are often uninformed by research and knowledge. Decisions are made by the numbers—which side has the most votes—rather than through reasoning informed by knowledge.

Deliberative democracy, on the other hand, involves all interested parties in the decision making process. Public opinion is replaced by public judgment, a judgment grounded in a sustained and thoughtful deliberation. A diverse group of participants explore the complexities of situations, confronting the necessary costs and benefits of particular decisions. This reasoned, sustained deliberation greases democracy's wheels. As Lorraine McDonnell and Stephen Weatherford explain: "Discussion in face-to-face meetings, in a context in which the group comes together repeatedly to deal with common problems, is central to the promise of deliberation, because personal interaction helps to break down the perception of competition and to undermine the idea that individual behavior must be based on self-interest. When people interact repeatedly, cooperation often evolves out of an initially competitive situation; face-to-face interaction and discussion can further strengthen cooperation by providing grounds for trust among the members of a group and by fostering a sense of identification with the good of the community as a whole."[12]

In his argument of how deliberative democracy helps, Putnam uses the central concept of social capital, the idea that our connectedness to others in networks and communities is a resource that can improve both individual and collective experience. Just as money (financial capital) or strong muscles (physical capital) or a good education (human capital) can improve democracy, so too can collective enterprises: bowling teams, 4H clubs, the Elks, the Girl Scouts.[13]

Putnam goes on: High social capital, focused in positive directions, has widespread effects on education, economics, child welfare. Synthesizing the scholarship of researchers like James Comer and Anthony Bryk and his colleagues, Putnam argues that, "at Harvard as well as in Harlem, social connectedness boosts educational attainment. One of the areas in which America's diminished stock of social capital is likely to have the most damaging consequences is the quality of education (both in school and outside) that our children receive."[14]

Critical to acquiring more social capital is the idea of increasing public participation in social networks, formal and informal. Putnam's argument is a simple one: the health of our democracy, and the quality of our individual and collective lives, depends, in large part, on how often we interact with myriad others. "We Americans," he argues, "need to reconnect with one another."[15]

California Dreaming Revisited

Reviewers of early drafts of my inquiry often remarked on the title, noting that, for many, it was a misnomer, as the "California dreaming" of the early reformers had turned into a collective nightmare for all. As an outsider, protected from the biting sarcasm of the debate, I saw things differently. With the protected privilege that distance offers (I never experienced the personal sense of character assassination that many insiders reported), my story remains one of hope—and dreams.

Dreaming, of course, has multiple meanings, ranging from a deep, admirable aspiration to a wild, naïve fancy. Both apply here, to all parties. The early reformers dreamed of classrooms in which students loved mathematics, and felt entitled and motivated to learn it. It was their heartfelt, serious aspiration to bring mathematics, good mathematics, to all students. They imagined schools in which students would be so intrigued with authentic problems that they would voluntarily submit themselves to the training it takes to master mathematical basics. Their vision was also naïve, for even though they knew that reform was complex, they did not consistently confront those complexities. Nor did they consider the uneven mathematical knowledge within their own ranks. They learned much along the way about how curricula would be misused and misinterpreted, and about the political nature of educational decision making.

The critics, and participants in later reforms, also had dreams. Dreams of rigorous mathematics delivered to all schoolchildren, dreams of an American citizenry that would know, in powerful ways, how to think mathematically. They too were naïve, for they dismissed the need to work with the education establishment. Reforms will not work if teachers and mathematicians—all sorts of teachers and all sorts of mathematicians—work together. They emphasized the mathematics and paid fleeting attention to teaching. They did not always attend to important differences in discourse and status.

While recognizing various actors' naïveté, I was most taken with their hopefulness, and the collective, seemingly boundless energy (not always targeted in constructive ways) devoted to the cause. The participants are all busy people: teachers and parents and mathematicians and research scientists. Most of the time they devoted to these debates was time they could have used for other personal and professional endeavors. The much-maligned state School Board members, for example, worked eighty-hour weeks for no pay. And so I also have hope, a hope inspired by and grounded in the enthusiasm, expertise, and commitment of many actors in this complicated story. Progressives and traditionalists, early reformers and later ones, journalists and researchers poured time and energy into these discussions. The investment of this human capital—on all sides—was impressive.[16]

Granted, many participants appear to be adversaries. My hunch is that this is more fiction than fact—a fiction created by a culture that embraces stereotypes and rejects complexity, a discourse that tends to inflame rather than deliberate, pressed into actions taken too quickly for political reasons and rooted in a history of curricular pendulum swings that colored everyone's view. There were zealots on all sides, believers with opinions firmly held, blinded by their righteousness. But most people were not like that. They were not on a mission to "destroy" a person, a curriculum, a reform. They had strong feelings and critical opinions, but the core group of participants were learners, open to seeing things in a new light.

Nonetheless, it is also clear from my analysis that there exist serious differences to be reckoned with. That is a given, for the differences run to themes much larger than what kind of mathematics children should learn. But the deep reserves of pedagogical and mathematical expertise, combined with the clear commitment to bettering education, seem overripe with promise for changing the wearily redundant history of mathematics education. Putnam's analysis suggests one answer: the networks.

"Factions of Mischief"

James Madison was suspicious of interest groups, or "factions of mischief," as he referred to them in *The Federalist Papers*.[17] Yet an examination of the early networks that emerged—I focused here on the California Mathematics Council (and its national affiliate, the National Council for Teachers of Mathematics), as well as the California Mathematics Project—suggests that they were rich in social capital. Within them there was enormous trust, good will, and élan; teachers and teacher-leaders shared their experiences, learned from one another, grew professionally and personally. Communication channels were open, used frequently, often aided by the Internet.

But, as Putnam explains, "Social capital is often most easily created *in opposition* to something or someone else,"[18] and so it is not surprising that an opposition to the education establishment and progressive networks led to the creation of yet more social capital, in networks like HOLD and Mathematically Correct. These networks, too, were rich in social capital, and participants built internal trust, shared commitment, communicated frequently, and supported one another's efforts.

Also important was the fact that both sets of networks became "schools for democracy": teachers and mathematicians, parents and policy makers learned to speak in public, debate issues, write letters.[19] In this way, the networks added to civic participation and, accordingly, enhanced American democracy. Ironically, then, polarization helped our democracy, since it led to increased civic participation. However, the polarization also meant that these networks were "bonding communities," associations that look inward and tend to be homogeneous. Such communities are good for mobilizing solidarity; Putnam calls them a "kind of sociological superglue."[20] However, "By creating strong in-group loyalty, [they] may also create strong out-group antagonism."[21] The antagonism may now have stalled any hope of real reform.

If we aim for a sustained and deliberative discourse, then, we will also need what Putnam calls "bridging communities," networks more inclusive and that aim for a broader collective identity. Taking a step toward progress, in California, will require the development of such communities, formal and informal, in which seeming antagonists deliberate over the knotty problem of how to improve mathematics education for all children. Setting high standards is not enough. If the history of curriculum reform tells us anything at all, it is that we lack the knowledge necessary to help teachers and students, schools and communities meet those high standards for all students. There were no good old days, when children from diverse backgrounds learned high-quality content. If we want all American children to have access to significant academic knowledge, we have much work to do. And that work will require coalitions built across the heretofore separate communities.

Are such networks possible? I think so, although the evidence is sketchy. The U.S. Department of Education sponsored a panel of concerned participants to deliberate over a research agenda for mathematics education. The effort was not without its trials, but the commitment to sustained deliberation paid off. The National Research Council sponsored a Mathematics Learning Study Committee, which included teacher educators, teachers, and mathematicians. Its report, *Adding It Up: Helping Children Learn Mathematics,* is the most balanced portrait of mathematics education the community has ever seen.[22] Further, Hung-Hsi Wu, one of the most vocal mathematician-critics of the earlier reforms, is currently working with Elizabeth Stage, the wordsmith for the 1985 *Framework,* to create professional development experiences through the California Professional Development Institutes that are both pedagogically rich and mathematically rigorous. This seems an act of commitment and faith, for finding ways to help teachers learn mathematics in ways that will help them teach students is, in the end, the most important thing we can all do. All the arguing in the world about the wording of policies will not bring us closer to reformed teaching. Working with teachers and mathematicians, respectfully and over time, might.

From Bonding to Bridging

Most heartening, too, was a story from a very prominent teacher-leader. Over dinner, she told a group (of which I was a member) that she had been at a meeting where she was presenting her ideas about mathematics teaching. After the session, a mathematician—one of the most vocal and critical—approached her to debate several of the points she had made in her presentation. She was taken aback and wary (his previous writing had struck her as unnecessarily caustic), but nonetheless she talked with him. Time ran out and as they parted, he invited her to his home the next day to continue the conversation. Other obligations prevented her from going. This seemingly unremarkable encounter is significant to those who have participated in the fray over mathematics education. Ordinarily, people do not invite adversaries into their homes; we tend to open our homes for positive, intimate, and personal occasions. Homes are places where we break bread, drink wine, relax, and talk. We unwind, open up, feel safe. Making progress on the mathematics education front will require the breaking of bread, as well as more formal deliberation—something both the parties in this case seemed interested in doing.

While it is unlikely that the protagonists in this story will all join the same bowling team, it is possible that they will begin listening to one another before reacting, whether they share meals or committee membership in teacher education programs or staff positions in K–12 schools. Critical will be a commitment to shared work and responsibility, for nothing will change if one group asserts itself as an expert and refuses to listen to another.

Developing these new, bridging networks will not be easy. Disentangling the themes of the conversation—what kind of mathematics ought to be learned, what research tells us, whose research counts, our diverse goals for our children, our different views on the goals of a public education, what we mean by "balance"—will take considerable time and careful analysis. Managing the tension between the participation of people with relevant expertise and experience and the participation of ordinary citizens will require artful and skillful direction. Allowing the zealots and ideologues to participate is essential, but finding ways to control their impact will take equal doses of courage and will. Teachers have to deal with reticent students every day; so, too, must reformers face doctrinaire colleagues who are eager to hold firmly onto their beliefs rather than change their minds. Creating forums in which sustained deliberation can occur will require protecting those forums from the political winds that threaten to turn deliberative democracy into traditional democracy. Education takes time.

Perhaps most important will be the replenishing of trust. The past five years or so of the "math wars" has left California with a legacy of distrust, fueled by unintentional and intentional disrespect for the rights of everyone to participate in these deliberations, not to mention the premature dismissal of different participants who could bring varied expertise to the table. The critics' wariness of consensus will make the development of trust hard, for building trust sometimes looks suspiciously like building consensus. But a democratic deliberation leads to informed judgment, not unanimous agreement. Trust is crucial.[23]

While trust is hard to rebuild, it is nearly impossible when extremists are given free rein. When extremist progressives summarily dismiss all critics and refuse to invite any critic into deliberations about state policy, alternative assessments, or new curricula, that dismissal invites the wrath of all critics. When an extremist critic "goes after" a curriculum, professional development, or assessment project, that active attempt to sabotage invites retrenchment from all critics. By provoking wrath and retrenchment, the extremists help sustain the illusion of sides.

A crucial step in moving away from the "wars" will necessarily involve progressives and traditionalists alike publicly and proactively working to avoid the damage that extremists can do. Bridging communities would help. I have some colleagues who lead an innovative assessment and professional development project for mathematics teachers. They are now "under attack" by several extremists who want to derail their efforts. Left to their own devices, my colleagues—feeling embattled—reach out to their networks for advice and help. If bridging communities existed, then those networks would include traditionalists and progressives, mathematicians and teachers, K–12 schoolteachers and higher education faculty who could help them develop a response to this attack that would look more like engagement than retrenchment. A few actors are nurturing such coalitions, but these fledgling networks are not fully developed and have not yet begun to reach all concerned actors. So my colleagues can only consult their extant networks—their bonding communities—rather than the bridging communities that would be essential to making progress. The same is true of the critics who, when attacked at a meeting, turn to other critics rather than a wider spectrum of participants.

The fact that most of these networks communicate primarily by email complicates matters further. If individual actors do wish to share their hurt, anger, or fear with someone outside their immediate circle, they cannot do this via the Internet, for there is no control over what gets forwarded to whom. Hence the need for trust and well-designed trust building activities. These activities will require face-to-face deliberations, over time, among the widest array of actors, as well as strong leaders who will allow everyone to be heard and no one member to undermine those efforts.

Although my story suggests that making progress will be challenging, my stance is nonetheless a hopeful one. Some might ask: How is that possible? Because every person I spoke with for nearly a dozen years was kind and generous, reasonable and concerned. Sometimes they spoke harshly, but the various actors in the discussions come from very different discourse communities. Teachers can learn to look beyond the brusqueness of some critics' comments. Critics can look beyond the attention to teaching, and hear the concerns for mathematics that lie within good teachers' comments. I know that some participants were not being civil and reasonable, but I did not meet them. I remain convinced that the tide can turn again, not back toward the original vision of the early reformers, but toward a new vision, a product of sustained, critical, civil discourse. That was, after all, what the NCTM had in mind. Progress will require sustaining and continuing those conversations. As David Tyack and William Tobin note:

> Cultural constructions of schooling have changed over time and can change again. To do this deliberately would require intense and continual public dialogue about the ends and means of schooling, including reexamination of cultural assumptions about what a 'real school' is and what sort of improved schooling could realize new aspirations. Shared beliefs could energize a broad social movement to remake the schools. To do so would require reaching beyond a cadre of committed reformers to involve the public in a broad commitment to change. This would require not only questioning what is taken for granted but also preserving what is valuable in existing practice. The cultural construction of schooling need not be a block to reform. It can be an engine of change if public discourse about education becomes searching inquiry resulting in commitment to a new sense of the common good.[24]

But why would anyone agree to a long, complicated process?

The NCTM's past president Glenda Lappan and I live in the same town, and sometimes we accidentally meet in a coffee shop. Years ago, I ran into her waiting in line for a latté; she looked tired and drawn. I asked her when she would take a break. She said she couldn't, for there was so much to do for the children. The first time I wrote to Dick Askey and asked him "Why the vehemence?" he responded: "Because of the children."

I tend to be slightly cynical, and so I found both comments—at first blush—a touch melodramatic. But after telling this California story, I see their responses in a new light. Across an apparent divide—Glenda is a progressive mathematics educator, Dick a critical and concerned mathematician—they were saying the same thing. I believe them both. Only passionate commitment can explain the energy and perseverance, the vitality and vigor (and even the incivility) that everyone puts into these efforts. If only these dedicated people would stop oversimplifying differences, caricaturing others, and dismissing critical questions and use their considerable intelligence, experience, and enthusiasm to deliberate rather than debate, we might begin to do the hard work of reforming mathematics education in the United States. For what purpose? At the risk of sounding melodramatic: for the children.

Methodological Appendix:
"This Frightful Toil"

This is unmediated actuality, in all its multiplicity, randomness, in-
consistency, redundancy, *authenticity*. . . . Each person who sits
down to write faces not a blank page but his own vastly overfilled
mind. The problem is to clear out most of what is in it, to fill huge
plastic bags with the confused jumble of things that have accreted
there over the days, months, years of being alive and taking things
in through the eyes and ears and heart. The goal is to make a space
where a few ideas and images and feelings may be so arranged
that a reader will want to linger awhile among them, rather than to
flee. . . . But this task of housecleaning (of narrating) is not merely
arduous; it is dangerous. There is the danger of throwing the wrong
things out and keeping the wrong things in; there is the danger of
throwing too much out and being left with too bare a house.
—Janet Malcolm, *The Silent Woman* (1993)

Probably indeed the largest labour of an author in composing his
work is critical labour; the labour of sifting, combining, constructing, expunging, correcting, testing: this frightful toil is as much critical as creative.
—T. S. Eliot, "The Function of Criticism" (1932)

There are two distinct genres of methodological appendix. In one, the author explains what she did—who she interviewed and observed, how data
were analyzed and interpretations were checked. In the other, the author ex-
plores themes and central issues—relationships, problems encountered,
insights achieved. These genres make sense, for as Fred Erickson reminds

us, one's research method is more than technique: it is a way of reasoning and making sense, of acting and interacting with others.[1] Research method, from this perspective, embraces both the *tools* of research (interview strategies, observation protocols, coding techniques) and its *logic,* how one reasons, establishes relationships, makes sense, and carefully applies tools in particular instances.

Tools are a necessary condition of method, just as basic facts are a necessary condition of mathematical competence. John Dewey argues that the "methods of artists in every branch depend upon thorough acquaintance with materials and tools; the painter must know the canvas, pigments, brushes, and the technique of manipulation of all his appliances. Attainment of this knowledge requires persistent and concentrated attention to objective materials. The artist studies the progress of his own attempts to see what succeeds and what fails. The assumption that there are no alternatives between following ready-made rules and trusting to native gifts, the inspiration of the moment and undirected 'hard work,' is contradicted by the procedures of every art."[2]

But tools alone do not constitute a method, for Dewey is right: there is a middle ground between the caricatures of research (or mathematics) as a robotic march through a series of prescribed steps and research as divine inspiration. Hence, the two genres of methodology: one focuses on the technical questions, the other on underlying substantive issues—be they theoretical, analytical, political, or ethical.

In this story, one in which research—whose research, what research—was both a persistent question and a bone of contention, it behooves me to explain in some detail the tools and design we used to gather data, as well as my own analysis methods (in that second and more capacious sense of research as reasoning). Making one's reasoning public, after all, is a hallmark of any disciplined inquiry. I begin by discussing the technical aspects of research before moving to a discussion of my reasoning.

Design and Tools
Traditionally, policy research has kept it simple: interview policy makers, understand their intentions, collect demographic data, conduct surveys, analyze critical documents. The research projects upon which this book is based took a different route: investigate the "system" in systemic reform, up and down. Interview and observe teachers, principals, school district

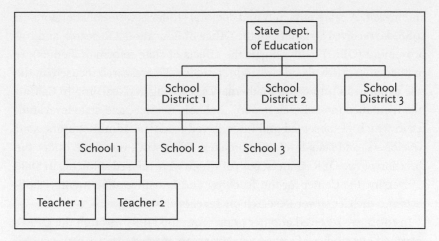

Figure 1. Nested Contexts of Research

staff, local school board members, state department staff, policy makers. All research requires a narrowing of focus. Ours focused, in one study, on the California Department of Education to the classroom and, in a follow-up study, From Congress to the Classroom. We took a robust (but not comprehensive) "slice" through that system (for instance, we interviewed state department staff but not teacher educators, even though we knew teacher preparation was part of the full system). We were interested in how policy shaped and was shaped by multiple actors in nested contexts (Figure 1).

This design is one used often by researchers associated with the Consortium for Policy Research in Education (CPRE), and we modeled the research on that tradition (this allowed us to also link our data to previous studies).[3]

Two programs—the Educational Policy and Practice Study (EPPS) and the Policy and Practice Study in Education (PPSE)—constituted the major research that contributed to this inquiry.[4] These studies were collaborative efforts of multidisciplinary teams of researchers. Each study used a multimethod, multisite design, and included the collection of data both qualitative and quantitative. Both studies aimed to understand the relationships between state-level curriculum policies and teachers' practices.

The first study—the EPPS—was actually a collection of iteratively developed research projects funded by multiple partners. The principal investigators were Deborah Loewenberg Ball, David Cohen, Penelope Peterson, and myself. A cadre of faculty and doctoral students were collaborators. In 1988, we received a grant from the Office of Educational Research and Improvement (OERI) to investigate the effects of state reform of elementary mathematics curricula on classroom practice. The research focused on the role of policy in improving mathematics teaching and learning in California. It entailed intensive classroom-, school-, district-, and state-level studies in which we observed and interviewed teachers, administrators, staff developers, and state-level policy makers. This work was done under the direction of two OERI centers, both of which were housed at Michigan State University: the Center for the Teaching and Learning of Elementary Subjects and the Center for Research on Teacher Education.

In 1990, we received another grant from the OERI through the CPRE, to extend our studies of reform in elementary teaching in two ways: across subject matter (to language arts), and across states (to Michigan). The research issues were the same, but the extension into another subject matter and state allowed for contrasts both political (e.g., local control) and epistemological (e.g., what it means to be proficient in reading as opposed to mathematics).

Then, in 1992, we received funding from the National Science Foundation, the Carnegie Corporation of New York, and Pew Charitable Trusts to extend the study in several other ways: we added a survey of California mathematics teachers, and a third state (South Carolina), and we investigated other parts of the education system. In our earlier designs, we had made the same mistake systemic reformers did—and presumed that the education system was isomorphic with its bureaucracy. But the system, as our study shows, is vast, porous, amorphous, and much larger than the formal bureaucracy. These later studies involved reaching into other corners of the system.

Thus, we ended up with a three-state study of policy and practice at multiple levels of the system (classroom, school, district, state), and sought to understand the factors that influenced the extent and nature of changes in mathematics and reading instruction.[5] Our inquiry was multimethod, including case studies and surveys of teachers, as well as studies of teachers' opportunities for learning, observations of professional development, and interviews with principals and district staff. We also interviewed state-level policy makers, and examined documents and policies crafted at the state, district, and school levels. A brief word on the major components.[6]

Case Studies of Teachers

We followed a set of teachers for between three and six years. Studies of teacher learning make clear that teacher change takes time, that significant change in practice is rarely quick.[7] One element of the study focused on approximately seventy-five elementary school teachers who worked in California, Michigan, and South Carolina.[8] We interviewed and observed those teachers, investigating what—as well as how and why—they learned from the reform documents, texts, tests, and professional development. We examined the relationships between their teaching and the reforms. For the same group of teachers, we also examined the influence of school and district contexts.

Although the study design evolved over time, classroom data collection generally focused on whether and how teachers' knowledge, thinking, and practice changed as a result of learning from the reforms. We visited the focal teachers twice each year from 1988 through 1994 (although the sample shifted as we expanded the subject matter focus and added Michigan and South Carolina). During each site visit, we observed each teacher teaching mathematics and/or language arts for one day. We conducted pre- and post-observation semistructured interviews. These methods were adapted from observation procedures and pre- and post-observation interview procedures developed by the National Center for Research on Teacher Learning.[9] Data collection centered on the following four areas: teachers' understanding of mathematics and language arts; teachers' ideas about learners' knowledge and thinking; classroom pedagogy; and teacher learning and change.

This book is one piece of a larger collection of products of this research—products that span dissertations, other books, special issues of journals, and many peer-reviewed articles. A full bibliography of those products is available on my website (*swilson.educ.msu.edu*). Many of the study investigators have reported the case study data. Two special issues of education journals—*Educational Evaluation and Policy Analysis* and the *Elementary School Journal*—were devoted to a first round of case studies. Those journals and other publications include alternative descriptions of our study methods.[10]

Survey of Second- and Fifth-Grade Teachers

The senior investigators on the project were all trained to use multiple methods: micro and macro, case study and survey, narrative and numeric.

Our disciplinary backgrounds were largely historical, ethnographic, and psychological; our interests both emic and etic.[11] To situate the case study teachers within the larger context of teaching and teacher learning, we conducted a mail and telephone survey of a representative sample of elementary teachers in California (we targeted second- through fifth-grade teachers). The survey, administered by Joan Talbert and her colleagues at Stanford University in 1994–95, used a stratified sample of 151 school districts drawn from the 1991–92 Common Core of Data (CCD) agency database from a population of 898 school districts in California. Five strata of school districts were identified, and schools were randomly selected within each of the sampled districts in each stratum. This survey is the basis of David Cohen and Heather Hill's analysis, in which they explain the survey in depth.[12]

The survey was an important element in our research, for it allowed us to place the case study teachers in the context of a larger representative sample of California teachers. More important, the survey shed light on: (1) the extent to which reform *ideas* spread among elementary school teachers; (2) the extent to which reform *practices* influenced elementary school teaching; (3) teachers' knowledge and beliefs about mathematics and teaching, and the relationships between those beliefs and teachers' responses to education reform; and (4) the extent to which professional development played a role in teachers' responses to and interpretations of the reforms.

Occasions for Teacher Learning

Traditionally, inservice programs or staff development workshops have been considered the main venues for practicing teachers to learn new things. However, teachers may also learn from using innovative curriculum materials, from helping to construct or using new assessments for students, from participating in study groups with other teachers, from taking on leadership roles, and from other less standard experiences.[13] There has been little systematic inquiry into what teachers actually learn on official or less official "professional development" occasions.[14] Most studies fail to describe in any detail what program leaders and teachers did over the course of the actual meetings. Studies often document the extent to which teachers found a particular project to be useful or interesting, but they rarely report whether and how the program's experiences factored into teachers' ideas and practices over time. As a result, much of our knowledge about professional development is drawn from a mélange of practical wisdom and unsubstantiated assumptions about teaching and teacher learning. We know what teachers want and what they don't like; we know much less about what they learn.

Our inquiries in this area complemented the individual teacher case studies. In our teacher case studies, we learned about the kinds of experiences and people that influenced teachers' practices and ideas. We thought of this strategy as "backward mapping"—from what we saw them doing and heard them tell us back to the people, events, and organizations to which they attributed their learning.[15] For this component of our study, we selected particular opportunities for teacher learning, and investigated their purposes, character, and rationale. This is what led us to the California Mathematics Project summer experiences, as well as Marilyn Burns's Math Solutions and gatherings of the California Mathematics Council. We examined what participating teachers learned. We documented teachers' actual experiences with these programs, as well as their interactions with new texts and tests (which we considered alternative opportunities to learn, even though they were not conceptualized as formal professional development). We also attempted to track, both over time and across occasions, changes in their professional knowledge and skills.[16]

Again, we adapted program data collection instruments developed by the National Center for Research on Teacher Education (NCRTE). We observed workshops, took field notes, occasionally audiotaped sessions (with the participants' permission). We conducted semistructured interviews with participants and with professional development leaders. We gathered contextual information about each program—its origin and support, how teachers were selected for participation, the constraints and resources that shaped the program's work. The NCRTE program director interviews provided a model for these interviews. Analyses based on these data include a special section in *Phi Delta Kappan,* as well as the Cohen and Hill analyses.[17]

Innovative Assessments
We also gathered data on teachers' participation in the development of innovative assessments like CLAS. Because the format of these development efforts varied, we developed data collection procedures suitable to the sites. We also analyzed the new assessment materials and reporting arrangements, examining them as opportunities for teacher learning. For our analyses of assessment instruments themselves and curriculum materials, we drew on the curricular analyses conducted by the Center for Teaching and

Learning Elementary Subjects.[18] These analyses were central in the Cohen and Hill analysis of what teachers learned from participating in the CLAS.

Texts

We analyzed the opportunities for teacher learning represented in new texts and curriculum materials. These investigations centered on the following issues: (1) To what extent were explanations or other information or orientation provided for teachers about (a) mathematics or reading/writing; (b) learners and learning; (c) pedagogical approaches? (2) How did the textbooks and the accompanying teacher materials fit with the ideas of the mathematics and literacy reforms? How did the ideas and terminology compare with those of the policy documents? (3) How is information presented for teachers? What assumptions seem to hold about teaching and what teachers need in order to teach mathematics and literacy? We also collected data on teachers' introduction to, acquaintance with, and use of the texts or curriculum materials.[19]

District- and State-Level Policy Making

In order to understand the policies, their impact, and their multiple interpretations by various critical actors, we also interviewed individuals who initiated and oversaw policy development and revision. At one level, we focused on school and district administrators who shaped, translated, disseminated, and facilitated the policies. We interviewed and observed individuals responsible for communicating ideas about reforms, and facilitating their adoption within schools and school districts. These individuals included school principals and school-based mentors, district curriculum specialists and intermediate school district staff developers.

We interviewed district-level supervisors and administrators to learn how they interpreted and communicated state-level instructional policies. We spoke with directors of curriculum and instruction, professional development staff, Title I personnel. As with state-level policy leaders, we were interested in these individuals' interpretations of the ideas underlying the reforms. We also investigated local plans for communicating with and supporting teachers. We interviewed staff involved in textbook adoptions and assessments. Much of this district-level work is reported by James Spillane in his studies of the district impact on the policy-practice connection, as well as that of Carol Barnes and Sue Poppink.[20]

We also interviewed state-level policy makers. These interviews focused on their ideas about the reform agenda, their notions of implementation, and their plans for helping to accomplish the aims represented in the policy documents. We interviewed those involved in crafting the policy statements themselves, seeking to learn how the documents were written, what the motivations and intentions were, and what kinds of conflicts were encountered. We wanted to learn about individuals' interpretations of the reform documents—what they thought the ideas represented and what they thought reformed practice looked like. We aimed to learn what or who influenced their thinking, and why they were persuaded of the importance and worth of this agenda. We also interviewed those centrally responsible for developing programs to introduce teachers to the policy and to support implementation efforts.

In addition to interviews with state and local policy leaders, we analyzed the policy documents themselves, comparing one state's with another's, and comparing these statements with earlier policy documents. We examined the language and rhetoric of each document, the central aims and images of instruction in mathematics and literacy and the notions about students and about learning embedded in the texts. We attempted to learn the intended and actual audiences for these documents, and how they were distributed. Data collection for the EPPS ended in 1994–95 (there was some follow-up, but nothing extensive).[21]

The second major study, the Policy and Practice Study in Education, was another collaborative effort, this time with Robert Floden and myself at Michigan State, and Diane Massell and Margaret Goertz at the CPRE at University of Pennsylvania.[22] In the larger "umbrella" three-year study—From Congress to the Classroom—researchers tracked standards-based reforms in twenty-three school districts in eight states.[23] In the first year of the study, we interviewed key state-level policy makers and completed policy inventories in each state. For all three years of the study, we interviewed teachers, principals, and district staff as they responded to local, state, and national pressures to reform teaching and learning. We did not observe policy development occasions as we had in the EPPS, nor professional development workshops or other opportunities for teachers to learn.

In each state, researchers selected three districts for study, at least two having substantial concentrations of poverty. With that criterion in mind, the investigators selected districts with a reputation for reform activity in the focal subject areas. In four of the states (Colorado, Florida, Minnesota, and Texas), data collection stopped at the district level. For each district in the four other states (California, Kentucky, Maryland, and Michigan), however, three schools were selected, at least one of which was a Title I school-wide project school. At those schools, the study design called for a first round of observations with five teachers focusing on grades 2–5—teaching math and language arts. Follow-up interviews were conducted with the teachers. In the second round, a year later, the design called for three teachers from the first round who were still teaching grades 2–5 in the school to be observed and interviewed again. As the policy environment in California became increasingly charged, access became more difficult, and we ended up studying two school districts.[24]

In the study's third year, we surveyed all the second- through fifth-grade teachers in the schools we studied. We asked teachers about instruction, their opportunities to learn, and accountability. Schools that agreed to participate were given books for their school libraries, with the number of books dependent on the response rate. For the participating schools, surveys were distributed to all the second-, third-, fourth-, and fifth-grade teachers, with envelopes for the teachers to mail in the surveys. Teachers in 55 schools returned the surveys, but the response rates in many schools were below 60 percent, making the results difficult to interpret. Analyses were based on responses from 334 teachers in 34 schools spread across 6 states. No surveys were distributed in Minnesota, and no schools in California had a response rate above 60 percent.

Largely, across the PPSE study, we used a logic for interview and observation design that was similar to that of the EPPS project: We borrowed items from previously developed instruments; EPPS, NCRTE, and NCRTL instruments were particularly helpful. We asked similar questions: about teacher knowledge and beliefs, teachers' opportunities to learn, and interpretations of and reactions to curriculum and assessment policies. We investigated the nested contexts of classrooms in schools in districts in states, and made within school, district, and state comparisons, as well as comparisons across the states. Our subject matter foci were again mathematics and language arts instruction in elementary schools. Data collection ended in 1999. The results of this research have been reported in several CPRE publications, as well as several book chapters.[25]

Given the narrower focus of the second study, it was impossible to interview and observe the larger system that had become so apparent and captivating in the EPPS study. This meant that, independent of the PPSE study, I began to collect other literature that would help me track the mathematics saga. I was in luck, for my undergraduate training had been in history, and as an avid reader of history and philosophy of history, I had some knowledge of how to do analyses based on paper trails alone.

Several kinds of resources became crucial. First, there was the Internet, with resources ranging from newsletters from parent groups to data presented on the California Department of Education's website. One can find a speech to the State Board as readily as National Assessment of Educational Progress scores from 1994; one can search newspaper archives by columnist, date, and topic; one can sign up for updates and newsletters from various associations. I've read the *New York Times* almost every day of my adult life, and to that I added a cursory weekly glance at the *Sacramento Bee*, the *Los Angeles Times*, and the *San Francisco Chronicle*. Similarly, newsletters of education-related organizations helped, including *EdCal* (the newsletter of the Association of California School Administrators) and the *ComMuniCator* (the journal of the California Mathematics Council). I signed up for every newsletter I could find. Friends and colleagues sent me clippings and frequently forwarded electronic articles that reminded them of my story.

California also deserves its reputation for high-quality intellectual work, for research reports and briefs from a number of California-specific organizations also provided critical secondary sources, most notably the Public Policy Institute of California, the National Center for Research on Evaluation, Standards, and Student Testing (CRESST) (which, although it is national in focus, includes much California-targeted research), and Policy Analysis for California Education (PACE). In addition, as the "wars" gained national attention, a growing number of articles were published on the subject, several of which were helpful.[26]

Finally, the national networks of teachers and scholars interested in and concerned about mathematics education and reform involved busy listservs. I do not belong to any listservs (it is a matter of both principle and pragmatism—I find the discourse often distracting, and sometimes depressing, and I can't handle more email than I already get). Colleagues who knew about this book, however, forwarded emails by the dozens. I used them to track the story, but not as "data," for I remain unclear about the ethical issues associated with the new information age and the ways in which letters meant for one person can quickly become letters seen by all. I shudder to think of how quickly one's mail gets wrenched from its conversational context and laid bare for the world to see. That the networks kept their mail private, for the most part, is a sign of the high degree of trust that had developed within those groups. Nonetheless, the combination of asynchronous interaction, easy anonymity and misrepresentation of identity, as well as the lack of all face-to-face cues kept me away from using those emails, or referring to them in any way. The buzzing rumor mills that those listservs became kept me simultaneously dizzy, overwhelmed, and intrigued.

Twelve years of data: interviews and observations with teachers, documents from the CDE and school districts, field notes from professional development and policy seminars, sample curricular materials (both progressive and more traditional), newspaper articles, notes from phone calls, emails. Filing and storing the information was impossible; analyzing it seemed overwhelming.

Because so many of the analyses were conducted by individual researchers and are explained in separate dissertations, books, and papers, I will not attempt to summarize the efforts here. I could—as data analysts with qualitative data often do—invoke Barney Glaser and Anselm Strauss's "grounded theory" or report on coding schemes we developed and used with NUD*IST software.[27] But such descriptions have always struck me as a scholar's version of smoke and mirrors, so instead I will describe my methods and the guiding principles I used in my own analyses.

These methods move beyond straightforward descriptions of tools, so I now turn to the second part of the appendix, focusing on the issues that one deals with when confronted with cupboards packed with transcripts and audiotapes (each duplicated for backups), and yellowing, brittle newspaper articles amassing for twelve years. These principles guided my work as I "cleaned house," as Janet Malcolm describes it, searching for a way to impose a narrative order on an "unmediated actuality."[28]

Principled Analysis

The principles should not be applied rigidly or in a peevish spirit; they are not logically or mathematically certain; and it is better to violate any principle than to place graceless and inelegant marks on paper. Most principles of design should be greeted with some skepticism, for word authority can dominate our vision, and we may come to see only through the lenses of word authority than with our own eyes.[29]

I have always envied good writers. I cut my teeth as a shy teenager and young adult on Tolstoy and Dickens, on essays in the *New Yorker,* book reviews in the *New York Times.* But it is amazingly difficult to learn to write. The advice tends to be relatively vague: read good books, write a lot, get feedback. My students react to such advice alternately with frustration and perplexity. "Now that's really helpful," I can hear them mumble as they leave my office unsure of what to do next. Of course there are how-to manuals, and writing process scripts, attempts to impose some logic, some order on the mystical things that can happen if you, indeed, read good books, try your hand at writing, and get lots of critical feedback. But I've never been much one for how-to's. The lockstep approach to writing research papers never impressed me. Recipes and rules are meant to be broken.

But I am an all-but-indiscriminate consumer of another kind of writing about writing: those books in which authors talk about what they do (how-to manuals, of course), but in ways that help me understand the whys, the reasoning behind the rules and rituals that characterize writers' lives. Stephen King's *On Writing: A Memoir of a Craft,* William Zinsser's *On Writing Well: An Informal Guide to Writing Nonfiction,* Annie Dillard's *The Writing Life,* Anne Lamott's *Bird by Bird: Some Instructions on Writing and Life,* Natalie Goldberg's *Wild Mind: Living the Writer's Life.* I gobble these books up.[30]

If one considers qualitative data analysis a form of writing (often, I think it is), it is amazing how few such books exist that help us reason through data analysis in a practical and principled way. There are only a few, such as Wayne Booth and his colleagues' *The Craft of Research,* Howard Becker's *Tricks of the Trade,* Miles and Huberman's *Qualitative Data Analysis.*[31] This dearth seems surprising in many ways, for disciplines with traditions of narrative analysis—anthropology, history, psychoanalysis—teach new scholars such methods. Indeed, libraries are full of texts on how to interview, how to code, how to be a participant observer. But few books explore what it means to think like an interviewer, and reason like an observer or analyst. My solution has been to read methodological appendixes of the second type I described earlier, in which researchers tell stories of their experiences or explore the dilemmas they faced, the challenges they negotiated, the worries that plagued them.[32] These researchers' actions are principled, and I work to unearth the principles underlying their actions. Alternatively, I use essays written by scholars like Clifford Geertz and Ruth Behar, who identify and then wrestle with critical issues in qualitative research.[33]

But this writing, insightful as it is, does not help students know what to actually *do*. I confront this problem every time I teach research methods to doctoral students who are eager to do analyses but are unsure of what that means. I tell them to read and write, look for patterns, and then read and write some more. This is as unsatisfying as my advice to fledgling writers. As I finish this book, I am in the midst of one such class. All I can think to do in this class is to make my analyses in this book public, to show them through my actions how to think like a researcher. Here, I offer a description of three principles I have told them are central to my analyses.

Principle 1:   My very best teacher ever (with the exception of Lee Shulman), Lincoln Moses, a giant who drove a Dodge Dart convertible, occasionally carried a paper parasol, and taught lots of my classes, once said: *display the data*.[34] With numbers, we know what that means: scatterplots, box and whisker plots, time series plots, narrative graphics. Edward Tufte's work on envisioning and displaying information, launched by the need for more robust statistics, pushes this even further—maps, pictures, data graphical design—and the concomitant considerations of data density, accessibility, and aesthetics.[35] Philip Morrison, Tufte claims, once called the generation of these alternative representations a "cognitive art," and in a series of beautiful books I stare at regularly for inspiration, Tufte demonstrates how we might display numbers, nouns, and verbs.

Display the data. What does that mean with words and newspaper articles and transcripts and field notes? It means coding them, sorting them, reading them, looking for themes and patterns, going through every datum and finding relevant actions and statements. (An important corollary to this principle is: start displaying the data immediately, any way you can.) Once "balance" emerged as a theme in my story, for instance, I culled through everything I had, cutting and pasting every mention of "balance" into one electronic file. I made a chronology of when balance was mentioned, a list of who said what, a frequency distribution. Eventually these alternative displays of data led me to other analyses. I sorted the comments, found differences in what actors implied when they spoke of balance. One display led to another led to another, eventually to a set of metaphors—parity, canceling out, equal representation, symmetry—that helped me characterize the range of meanings that balance had in the discourse surrounding mathematics education.

I displayed the data in multiple ways. We developed NUD*IST codes on the PPSE project, combed interviews and sorted observations, looked for trends. On the EPPS project, we coded every single instance of mathematics in the professional development seminars we attended as we tried to answer the question, "Where's the math?" We identified themes that emerged and seemed important for a while, then tested them out against the data. For example, early on, the metaphor of "old wine in new bottles" was compelling, for the teachers we visited seemed only to be repackaging their old practices—no radical transformations there. In response to this observation, David Cohen wrote a memo about that theme, and the rest of us chimed in. We summarized our understanding of individual teachers by writing descriptive case studies—another display of condensed data.

As I got further into the project, the displays became more layered: the earlier descriptive displays (frequencies, for example) got folded into interpretive displays. (A good student of Geertz, I understand of course that all description involves some interpretation. We are talking about shades of gray here, not black and white, description and analysis.) Analytic memos grew longer, more synthetic, merging data and theory, concepts and scholarship with observations and themes. Those analyses eventually turned into conference presentations and other papers. Those paper-length analyses then led to this longer narrative.

Principle 2: Create an intellectual space in which empiricism and theory, experience and application interact with and mutually inform one another. I was a history major who then moved on to statistics and psychology. My liberal arts undergraduate major and love of literature and history spoiled me. No dustbowl empiricism for me. Research without theory seems boring and useless. When I first realized this, I would tell students that they needed to think of any research enterprise as having two poles, one involving empirical data collected in careful research, the other involving conceptual and theoretical reading. Looking at data with no theory could be endlessly frustrating; theory grounded by nothing empirical could seem worthless, a downright waste of time. The trick, I would tell them, is that they needed to go back and forth. Read the data, browse theories, return to the data with a new and refreshed "vision," one informed by a potentially helpful theory. I was, for example, reading Fukuyama's *Trust* for pleasure when it dawned on me that the analyses therein might help me understand the debates in mathematics education. The social life of information helped me "see" the networks, as did social capital theory and Robert Putnam's work on democracies.[36]

But since then, my understanding of what I mean by creating an intellectual space has expanded. Now I see multiple sources of important experiences and ideas. Analysis requires a sort of peripheral vision—a disposition to see something relevant in almost every activity one engages in. One reads a great methodological appendix and suddenly one sees one's self in new light. Read an essay in the *New Yorker* or the *New York Review of Books*, and hit on a new idea that sends you back to your data to look at them anew. Read theory and how-to manuals, fictions and histories. Read widely and often (aiming most of the time to read only good writing).

Teaching serves a function quite similar to writing, for students' questions and class discussions shed new light on familiar topics. David Cohen and I taught a proseminar for new doctoral students together for several years while we were working on the EPPS project; Michael Sedlak and I taught another, related course repeatedly while Bob Floden and I were working on the PPSE project. This allowed me to work on ideas concerning teaching, policy, the pedagogy of policy, and teachers' knowledge across my research and teaching. The synergy created by that interaction helped me become a better teacher and see my data in new ways.

Consider an example. One of the challenges of teaching the introductory course to all entering doctoral students in our department is that they come with extensive school experiences, and deeply rooted beliefs about "what is wrong" with education: teachers aren't given enough power; policy makers don't know much; children need to be taught using progressive pedagogies. We don't disrespect their positions, but we feel it is our obligation to help them develop more generous ways of hearing and understanding the perspectives of other participants in the education system. Philip Cusick concludes his introduction to *The Educational System* by claiming, "There is one important assumption—that the participants described are reasonable men and women, an honest, hard-working, and well-intentioned lot who do what they do for good reasons. On their own terms, their actions make sense. The goal is to understand the educational world as they understand it, their roles as they play them, and the system as their combined efforts create it."[37]

Watching the battles over mathematics curricula unfold in California, the single most disturbing thing I saw was that few participants—not reformers, not critics—gave one another credence. Reform-minded teachers belittled the concerns of critics; critics called reformers "fuzzy-headed." Not only was this discourse distasteful, it also seemed to be an obstacle toward progress. Not attending to the "other" almost guarantees pendulum swings: one group dominates for a while, until another group gets so angry that they dominate. No one listens to the other. Little sense is made of their differences, nor are those differences used to advance public discourse about the purposes and practices of education in the United States. This became a central thesis in my book. Teaching about it enhanced my analyses.

In my class with Michael Sedlak, we aimed to help students move beyond the tendency to oversimplify the positions of their critics and dismiss them, for we think that an open, more generous disposition toward listening to and understanding critics and collaborators alike is critical to good teaching and good scholarship. The course was designed with this in mind, and we used several devices to enable the work. First, we switched between insider and outsider accounts of schools: students saw school through the eyes of Bart Simpson (the cartoon character), and Rita, her husband, and her teacher (in the movie *Educating Rita*). Our students viewed schools through the critical lens of scholars like Labaree, Cohen, Bowles and Gintis, DuBois. Second, we switched from progressive education ideas to more conservative ones—they read Dewey *and* Hirsch—and we urged them to treat each as a scholar with important ideas. The final assignment required that they find contemporary issues around which there is much debate, and then we asked them to describe multiple views of the topic. Charter and choice, whole language and phonics are popular topics among the students. Once they described the range of views, we asked them to explain them: Why would the views of so many well-intentioned people differ so dramatically? Considering these questions in class sent me back refreshed to think about my analysis.

People have said these things before—teach so that you can learn, read so that you might write. The one new insight for me was that participating in the making of policy might help me see the California story of policy in a new way. During this study, I was asked to chair a group of teachers and scholars charged with crafting standards for beginning history and social studies teachers for the Chief State School Officers. My studies of mathematics curriculum reform led me to studies of the "culture wars" that Robert Hughes and Todd Gitlin wrote about.[38] I was convinced that we cannot make curricular progress without learning how to talk about our differences, and about how those differences are rooted in issues of value and identity. I agreed to chair the social studies committee to test my own ability to shape and nurture the "civil discourse" that Secretary of Education Richard Riley asked of mathematicians in his address to the joint annual meeting of the American Mathematical Society and Mathematical Association of America. Thus, I tested out my theories of curricular reform and civil discourse by trying to manage a group of people who disagreed with one another profoundly about the content, purposes, and nature of history and social studies education.

I understood something of these disagreements from earlier stages in my career, both as a history teacher and also as someone who did research on history teaching. The differences are as startling and dramatic as those in mathematics, something that the entire country witnessed when Congress threw out the proposed national standards for history teaching.[39] When I chaired the committee, I drew lessons from the California story: I made sure representatives from all the relevant groups (multiculturalists, social studies teachers, history teachers, historians, and members of other disciplines) were involved. I made it a rule that people could not send replacements (this tendency turns people into positions rather than individuals, and makes it harder to engage in ongoing deliberation and learning). I worked to create a deliberative context, in which we could move away from ideology toward pragmatism: What can we do, right now, that would be an improvement? What steps could we take?

Of course, I failed in many ways. Policy making is, after all, a lot like teaching—impossible work. (And moderating deliberative discussions is a skill that one must acquire over time.) My experiences in that committee, however—seeing policy making and discord from the inside out—helped me understand adamantine sides, the complex forces at play, and the passionate commitment that drives these disagreements. Feeling alternately powerless and appalled at the drama unfolding in front of my eyes, I understood more about how the insiders experienced the California mathematics debates. I was reminded of how hard it is for people to listen to others, how quickly our preconceptions filter out what we can and will not hear, and how various people—for moral or principled or political or epistemological reasons—simply will not deliberate, and are at the table only to get their way. Again, the experiences of practice (the practice of policy making turns out not to be so much different from the practice of teaching) sent me back to my data with new eyes.

Teaching, reading, researching, policy making: What to do in such a noisy, potentially confusing space? How to keep track of insights from teaching and reading and policy making and data display? I tell my students to keep a kind of "commonplace book." During the Renaissance, "early modern Englishmen read in fits and starts and jumped from book to book. They broke texts into fragments and assembled them in new patterns by transcribing them in different sections of their notebooks. They then reread the copies and rearranged the patterns while adding new excerpts. Reading and writing were therefore inseparable activities. They belonged to a continuous effort to make sense of things, for the world was full of signs: you could read your way through it; and by keeping an account of your readings, you made a book of your own, stamped with your own personality."[40]

In a similar way, data analysis is not simply a set of techniques by which one reads, identifies patterns, codes, and writes analytical memos. Data analysis is a "continuous effort" of sense-making and rewriting. Researchers, like the keepers of Renaissance commonplace books, "read their way through life, picking up fragments of experience and fitting them into patterns."[41] I tell my students to do the same, to create contemporary commonplace books. I show them my own, a shelf full of notes I referenced repeatedly each time a new interpretation presented itself and I needed to reconsider the California data.

Principle 3: There is no escaping it—research and analyses are messy enterprises when one steps outside the limited but well-tested traditional quantitative, experimental paradigms. So these principles, for me, are another set of tools; they give me something to do that might lead to a productive end. Just like one might run a t-test, I display data, read theory, test ideas out with students. Once I think I have a thesis, once my data displays begin to cohere and I begin to see patterns or categories, themes, or structures, I go through the data to look for *confirming evidence.*

But that's not enough, for other good teachers—like Lee Cronbach and Ed Haertel—taught me the importance of other, equally methodical passes through the data and all the displays for *disconfirming evidence.*[42] Sometimes the exercise helps one focus with more clarity on what the thesis is and where its limits are. Sometimes—if one is lucky—the process of disconfirming evidence means you have to throw out your thesis and start again. This, of course, is frustrating (all that time wasted!), for no one ever tells you about the tangents and dead ends entailed in scholarship.

But you can't rely on your own data and a private process of disconfirmation. Once you have gone through the data and your argument, "critically testing" it against disconfirming evidence, examining the argument's logic, you need to start testing the thesis in other settings. For me, this meant asking insiders and outsiders to read my interpretations and react to them. Truth be told, I don't really relish this part of data analysis, for it makes one feel vulnerable. What if I am completely off base? What if they discover how uninformed I am? What if I alienate an informant by putting a spin on an event that she finds offensive?

But those are egocentric fears. There are others as well. Robert Coles talks of how James Agee and William Carlos Williams both felt daunted by the task before them, not up to doing it "right," to telling a complicated enough story, of missing the point, or oversimplifying or misrepresenting.[43] The people who let me interview them year after year, who sent me emails, promptly returned my phone calls, let me watch them as they changed their minds, made sense of their missteps, these people were gracious and open and kind—all of them, early progressive reformers and later critical, more traditional ones. Walter Denham let me witness his triumphs and losses. Joan Akers, Elizabeth Stage, Judy Mumme told me their histories, opening their pasts and presents graciously. Richard Askey and Hung-Hsi Wu, who knew nothing of who I was and what I might do with their comments, rapidly responded to email with answers and insights. Every one of my informants struck me—repeatedly—as thoughtful, insightful, caring, vulnerable people who got caught in a maelstrom of issues and passions they had not expected.

One has an *obligation* to these individuals, and with every thesis—every attempt to impose order on the chaos that is human life, on the sprawling, amorphous landscape that involves education in the United States—one takes the potentially dangerous step of, as Janet Malcolm writes, "throwing the wrong things out and keeping the wrong things."[44] Of doing an injustice to particular people as one tries to understand a social event.[45] The fear of betrayal, of misrepresentation or oversimplification, trumps my fear of embarrassment every time. And so I ask peers to review my analysis, and I often asked insiders to this story to read parts of my interpretation. I posed questions to critics—not unlike the process the National Council for Teach-

ers of Mathematics used in order to elicit critical feedback from various constituencies. I asked mathematicians, teachers, and teacher-leaders to read
drafts. I did not do this so that they could tell me what to change, but rather
to get their critical appraisal of whether the story made sense.

Sometimes their feedback sent me back to the drawing board, looking for
a new explanation. For example, early on in one analysis, I had an oversimplified view of the "sides." I had fallen into the trap that E. D. Hirsch
warns us of: believing the misapplied labels. One of the criticisms of some
progressive educators is that they are too child-centered, that they actually
missed Dewey's point: that subject matter and child are not in tension at all.
So, since the reformers were progressives, and since they kept talking about
the fact that they cared about the children, and since scholars (including
Dewey) had argued that some progressives were narrowly focused on the
children, I began hypothesizing that the differences were characterized as
follows: critics worried about subject matter, and the early reformers worried about children and equity. (I know, I know, this seems so naïve and narrow in the glare of hindsight.)

I had a hunch that my analysis was oversimplified and incorrect, and I
knew I needed critical feedback to help me move that analysis forward. So
I wrote to several people, among them Richard Askey, who I did not know
personally but whose name had popped up repeatedly as a concerned mathematician (I was especially intrigued by an early article entitled, "Who Is
Dick Askey and What Is He So Mad About?").[46] I asked him a question
vaguely related to my hunch, "Why are the debates so inflamed?" I tested
my theory and looked for disconfirming evidence. I got it when he responded: "The reason is very simple in many cases. It is parents whose
children are *not* getting the education their parents think they should have.
You are making a mistake if you think this has anything to do with conservatives versus liberals. There is some truth to the statement that a conservative is a liberal who has been mugged, but education of one's children
cuts across lines like liberal and conservative. I can give you names of very
good teachers who have felt attacked, but attacked by NCTM, and they are
very angry. . . . Here it was not their own children, for in both cases their
children are grown and they do not have grandchildren yet, but the students
they teach and their sense of what they feel they should do."

Occasions like this reminded me of the critical need to look for—not cautiously, but with zest—disconfirmation. Critical commentary pushes schol-

arship forward. Dr. Askey's comments, and many others I received along the way—most invited, some serendipitous—led me deeper into the puzzles of the "math wars."

Researching with Understanding

These principles of analysis are not the only ones I used, but they were critical. Of course, they are also limited, for they just touch the surface of the complex terrain of research method. Under that surface is a world of other, more profound issues related to the research, including issues of power (whose knowledge, whose story) and issues of equity (is there some way we can actually "know" whether everyone really does care about equity when they say they do?).

Questions of equity, voice, power, and privilege need to be addressed. My ideas on such topics are not fully formed yet, and so I look to colleagues who have thought about those issues more deeply. I do know that just as students who can use the algorithms but do not understand them have trouble when presented with unfamiliar problems, so too researchers with technical knowledge are unprepared for the vagaries and complexities— technical and moral—of research. And I end this inquiry with a deeper appreciation of the tangle of conceptual, moral, historical, political, and relational issues that one encounters when doing research. I conclude this appendix with a brief reflection on two lessons I learned about doing research during this project.

The first lesson involves relations and the role of research. I learned how hard it is to do respectable research without the cooperation of insiders, and how equally difficult it is to sustain relationships with those insiders when you are writing about their efforts. Publishing work about easily identified policy makers puts them under the microscope of academic analysis; it makes their learning, their mistakes, their earliest ideas public. For example, we published cases of teachers who were responding to the 1985 *Framework*. All our cases raised critical questions about the policy, its implementation, and teachers' practice. Meanwhile, we continued calling the CDE staff, eager to hear their latest thoughts. Understandably, they felt betrayed by the published cases, which focused on the teachers more than on the policy, and which they had not seen. We had talked extensively about whether and when we would share the cases with the teachers; it had not dawned on us to do the same with the policy makers. Learning how to work with our informants, to act respectfully while maintaining a critical distance was arduous, bumpy, fraught with difficulty. The fact that they continued to speak with us, despite our ham-handedness, is proof positive that they were more interested in improved teaching than in looking good.

Eventually, we found a position, one that allowed us not only to be critical and stand apart from the early reforms but also to establish productive relationships with the actors. In fact, three years into the study, one informant asked us to look critically at the California Mathematics Projects. As a longtime teacher-leader who had much invested in those projects, she thought our critical eye and distance might provide new insights that could improve the summer workshops. Specifically, she was worried about how and when teachers learned mathematics during the summer, and so we did an analysis of where and what kind of mathematics appeared across the CMPs. We went on to write a relatively critical paper about the lack of mathematical depth. After we had established relationships and negotiated the earlier bumps, such critical feedback was not simply tolerated, but encouraged—another sign that the reformers were, for all their political naïveté, learners.

A second lesson I learned concerned alienation—my own. Not only am I a member of the education establishment, I am a progressive educator. I believe in classrooms that are rich with ideas and intellectual adventures, where children learn the canon and are empowered to be critical of it. I, like Diane Ravitch, envy the education her children received at their progressive school.[47] I admire Dewey's vision, while also understanding how hard it would be to enact, especially on a large scale.

When we started this research, I did not know it would require that I examine my commitments and affiliations in a harsh and full light. But it did. As I read the words of the critics, their insights helped me see and hear myself and my colleagues—in teacher education, in educational research, in higher education—in new and unflattering ways. Robert Coles describes the fierce alienation and rage that James Agee felt as he began to understand his subjects in the South.[48] George Orwell experienced a similar alienation as he documented Wigan Pier, and Bill Buford as he hung out "among the thugs," and found himself guilty by association.[49] Helen Garner felt the same sense of alienation as she tried to understand why her feminist colleagues became so dogmatic and unyielding in a confusing case of sexual harassment.[50] I had read all these texts while conducting this research, but it never occurred to me to see myself in those stories. But I was.

My alienation fed itself. I realized that faculty in colleges of education often speak of constructivism or progressive pedagogy in uncritical terms. I witnessed occasions when colleagues jumped to facile conclusions about what critics like E. D. Hirsch or Diane Ravitch actually are saying. I found myself wishing for the critical voice in our deliberations as faculty, and so I would step forward, leading with apologia, "Now this is not necessarily the only thing I care about, but might we not think about the role of factual knowledge?" "Can't we consider teaching people to give good lectures?" Alienation deepened when some colleagues then began to suspect me of being a turncoat.

I overdramatize here. Many of my colleagues did not react this way, for I am fortunate to work in a college that strives for diversity of perspective and is an existence proof that the caricatures of process-firsters and fuzzy thinkers hurled at the education establishment are dangerous oversimplifications. But when some did react as though I were changing my stripes, I felt an alienation from my community that, ironically, helped me intellectually while making me uncomfortable personally.

This research pushed me to new levels of understanding about relationships and alienation. It will take me much more research and many more mistakes to understand those issues in any meaningful depth. Doing anything with understanding requires a balanced view, one that pays equal attention to facts and theory, to skills and principles, to one's immediate colleagues and the larger public, to practice and reflection. The original "teaching for understanding" reform that led to this inquiry asked teachers to attend to two distinct definitions of "understanding": understanding the content (the mathematics) and understanding people (teachers and students, and how they interact with, learn from, and work with one another). So, too, should researchers.

Timeline

	National	California
1942		California Mathematics Council established
1957	*Sputnik* launched; concerns raised about the mathematics and science education of American youth	
1962		CDE issues *Strands Report*
1967–68		CDE issues *Second Strands Report* CA legislature passes Mathematics Improvement Program (Miller Math)
1971		Miller Math defunded
1973		Bay Area Writing Project created
1974		CDE issues *1974 Mathematics Framework*
1982		California Mathematics Project created
1983	NCEE publishes *A Nation at Risk*	Bill Honig elected state superintendent of instruction CA legislature passes Hughes-Hart Educational Reform Act (SB 813)

1984		Marilyn Burns incorporates
1985		*1985 Mathematics Framework* published
1986		All K–8 mathematics textbooks adopsubmitted for statewide adoption rejected
1987		*K–8 Mathematics Model Curriculum Guide* published
1989	*NCTM Curriculum Standards* published National Research Council issues *Everybody Counts: A Report to the Nation on the Future of Mathematics Education*	California legislature creates statewide system of professional development called the California Subject Matter Projects, which includes the California Mathematics Project (SB 1882)
1991	*NCTM Professional Teaching Standards* published National Research Council issues *Moving Beyond Myths: Revitalizing Undergraduate Mathematics*	CDE launches replacement unit strategy
1992		CA legislature passes SB 662 California Alliance for Mathematics and Science (CAMS) established with NSF-SSI funding CDE issues *1992 Mathematics framework*
1993		CLAS implemented in mathematics and language arts Honig resigns after being convicted of misuse of public funds
1994		CLAS administered in mathematics, language arts, science, and social studies CLAS results released: 89% of 5th graders scored below proficient in science; 72% of 4th graders below proficient in mathematics September, Governor Wilson vetoes CLAS reauthorization

1995	1994 NAEP scores released; California children rank next to last in U.S. in reading	Delaine Eastin becomes state superintendent of schools
	NCTM issues its Assessment Standards	Eastin calls together task forces to examine language arts and mathematics frameworks
		Assembly bill 170 passed, requiring instructional materials and frameworks be based on fundamental skills, including basics
		Assembly bill 265 passed, calling for a commission to develop rigorous content and performance standards in all grade levels for all subjects, and statewide pupil assessment system
		Parents in Palo Alto create HOLD (Honest Open Logical Debate) and put materials on website
1996		CDE issues *Mathematics Program Advisory*
		California Commission for the Establishment of Academic and Performance Standards appointed
1997	4th- and 8th-grade TIMSS results released	New mathematics framework drafted for review
	Clinton proposes voluntary 8th-grade test in mathematics	School Board selects SAT-9 for statewide testing
1998	12th-grade TIMSS results released	State Board commissions review of experimental research on mathematics education (the "Dixon Report")
	President Clinton announces federally sponsored Mathematics initiative	State Board rewrites and approves new set of mathematics standards based on work of Commission for the Establishment of Academic
	NCTM creates process for development of revised *NCTM Standards*	

		Content and Performance Standards, the *Academic Content Standards* All CA schoolchildren take SAT-9
1999	U.S. Department of Education issues report on Exemplary programs Mathematicians and their colleagues post letter to Richard Riley, Secretary of Education	New *1999 Framework* published by CDE
2000	*NCTM PSSM 2000* unveiled	

Notes

PREFACE

Epigraph: John Steinbeck, *Cannery Row* (New York: Bantam Books, 1945), 1.

1. E. D. Hirsch, *The Schools We Deserve and Why We Don't Have Them* (New York: Doubleday, 1996), 6.

2. Robert Hughes, *Culture of Complaint: A Passionate Look at the Ailing Heart of America* (New York: Warner Books, 1993).

CHAPTER 1. CURRICULUM WARS

Epigraph: Richard White, "Money Changes Everything: What California Taught America," *The New Republic,* December 1, 1997, 38.

1. David K. Cohen and Barbara Neufeld, "The Failure of High Schools and the Progress of Education," *Daedalus* 110 (Summer 1981): 69–89, quotation at 88.

2. Lawrence W. Levine, *The Opening of the American Mind: Canons, Culture, and History* (Boston: Beacon, 1996), 43.

3. See, for example, Lynne V. Cheney, "EXAM SCAM. The Latest Education Disaster: Whole Math," *The Weekly Standard,* August 4, 1997 (also at www.mathematically correct.com/cheney2.htm), and "Whole Hog for Whole Math," *Wall Street Journal,* February 3, 1998 (also at www.junkscience.com/news/wholemat.htm). For analyses of this inflamed public discourse see, for example, Todd Gitlin, *The Twilight of Common Dreams: Why America Is Wracked by Culture Wars* (New York: Henry Holt, 1995); Robert Hughes, *Culture of Complaint: A Passionate Look into the Ailing Heart of America* (New York: Warner, 1993); and Richard Bernstein, *Dictatorship of Virtue: How the Battle Over Multiculturalism Is Reshaping Our Schools, Our Country, Our Lives* (New York: Vintage, 1995).

4. See Nicholas Lemann, "The Reading Wars," *Atlantic Monthly* (November 1997):

128–134; Catherine Cornbleth and Dexter Waugh, *The Great Speckled Bird: Multicultural Politics and Education Policymaking* (New York: St. Martin's Press, 1995); and Gary B. Nash, Charlotte A. Crabtree, and Ross E. Dunn, *History on Trial: Culture Wars and the Teaching of the Past* (New York: Knopf, 1997).

5. Editorial, *Wall Street Journal,* January 4, 2000.

6. Richard Riley, "The State of Mathematics Education: Building a Strong Foundation for the 21st Century" (remarks to the Joint Conference of American Mathematical Society and Mathematical Association of America, Washington, D.C., January 1998).

7. The letter appeared as an advertisement in the *Washington Post* on November 18, 1999, A5. See Debra Viadero, "Academics Urge Riley to Reconsider Math Endorsements," *Education Week,* November 24, 1999 (also at *www.edweek.org*), for a discussion of reactions to the letter.

8. Personal communication, January 2000.

9. In 1989 and the early 1990s, the National Council of Teachers of Mathematics published three sets of standards relevant to this story: the *Curriculum and Evaluation Standards for School Mathematics* (Reston, Va.: NCTM, 1989); the *Professional Standards for Teaching Mathematics* (Reston, Va.: NCTM, 1995); and the *Assessment Standards for School Mathematics* (Reston, Va.: NCTM, 1995). The document that drew the most attention was the *Curriculum and Evaluation Standards,* which I will refer to here as the NCTM *1989 Standards.* In 2000, the NCTM published a new standards document, the *Principles and Standards for School Mathematics* (Reston, Va.: NCTM, 2000), which I will refer to as the NCTM *PSSM 2000.*

10. Mark Baldassare, *California in the New Millennium: The Changing Social and Political Landscape* (Berkeley: University of California Press, 2000).

11. Richard White, "Money Changes Everything: What California Taught America," *The New Republic,* December 1, 1997, 38.

CHAPTER 2. "OURS IS NOT TO REASON WHY. JUST INVERT AND MULTIPLY"

Epigraph: Norman Anning, "The Heart of Algebra," in Raleigh Schorling, *The Teaching of Mathematics* (Ann Arbor, Mich.: Ann Arbor Press, 1936), 230.

1. See James Stigler and James Hiebert, *The Teaching Gap: Best Ideas from the World's Teachers for Improving Education in the Classroom* (New York: Free Press, 1999). Paul Cobb and his colleagues call this the "school mathematics tradition," a tradition now widely documented by survey and observational studies. See Paul Cobb, Terry Wood, Erna Yackel, and Betsy McNeal, "Characteristics of Classroom Mathematics Traditions: An Interactional Analysis," *American Educational Research Journal* 29 (Fall 1992): 573–604. See also John A. Dossey, Ina V. S. Mullis, Mary M. Lindquist, and Donald L. Chambers, *The Mathematics Report Card: Are We Measuring Up? Trends and Achievement Based on the 1986 National Assessment,* Report No. 17-M-01 (Princeton, N.J.: National Assessment of Educational Progress, Educational Testing Service, 1988); Susan S. Stodolsky, *The Subject Matters: Classroom Activity in Math and Social Studies* (Chicago: University of Chicago Press, 1988); Susan S. Stodolsky, Scott Salk, and Barbara Glaessner, "Student Views

about Learning Math and Social Studies," *American Educational Research Journal* 28 (Spring 1991): 89–116.

2. See, for example, Walter Secada, "Race, Ethnicity, Social Class, Language, and Achievement in Mathematics," in *Handbook of Research on Mathematics Teaching and Learning,* Doug A. Grouws, ed. (New York: Macmillan, 1992), 623–660; National Center for Educational Statistics, *High School and Beyond: An Analysis of Course-Taking Patterns in Secondary Schools as Related to School Characteristics* (Washington, D.C.: U.S. Department of Education, 1985). National Center for Education Statistics, *Language Characteristics and Academic Achievement: A Look at Asian and Hispanic 8th Graders in NELS:88* (Statistical analysis report NCES 92–479, Washington, D.C.: U.S. Department of Education, Office of Educational Research and Improvement, 1992); Sue A. Maple and Frances K. Stage, "Influences on the Choice of Math/Science Major by Gender and Ethnicity," *American Educational Research Journal* 28 (Spring 1991): 37–60; Frances K. Stage and Sue A. Maple, "Incompatible Goals: Narratives of Graduate Women in the Mathematics Pipeline," *American Educational Research Journal* 33 (Spring 1996): 23–51. While these analyses are based on patterns in the 1980s, not 2002, I cite them here to portray the context in which these California reforms of the 1980s unfolded. These are the statistics and findings that fueled the concerns of educators in the mid- to late-1980s, when this study began.

3. National Research Council, *Moving Beyond Myths: Revitalizing Undergraduate Mathematics* (Washington, D.C.: National Academy Press, 1991).

4. Walter Colburn (paper presented at the Assistant Masters Society, 1830), 22.

5. National Education Association, *Report of the Committee of Ten on Secondary School Studies* (Washington, D.C.: U.S. Government Printing Office, 1893), 233.

6. Eliakim Hastings Moore, "On the Foundations of Mathematics," in *The Teaching of Mathematics: A Source Book and Guide,* Raleigh Schorling, ed. (Ann Arbor, Mich.: Ann Arbor Press, 1936), 45. See also John Ewing, "Mathematics: A Century Ago—A Century from Now," *Notices in the AMS* 43 (June 1996), 663–672, for a discussion of Moore's contributions to teaching mathematics.

7. Alfred North Whitehead, *An Introduction to Mathematics* (Oxford: Oxford University Press, 1911), 8.

8. Mathematical Association of America, "The Reorganization of Mathematics in Secondary Education: A Report by the National Committee on Mathematical Requirements (1923)" in *Teaching of Mathematics,* Schorling, ed. (Ann Arbor, Mich.: Ann Arbor Press, 1936), 6.

9. Frank M. McMurry, "What Is the Matter with Arithmetic?" *Education* 54 (April 1934): 449–451.

10. In Bob Moon, *The 'New Maths' Curriculum Controversy: An International Story* (Philadelphia: Falmer, 1986).

11. Jerome Bruner, *The Process of Education* (Cambridge, Mass.: Harvard University Press, 1960).

12. George E. DeBoer, "What We Have Learned and Where We Are Headed: Lessons from the Sputnik Era" (paper presented at a symposium hosted by the Center for

Science, Mathematics, and Engineering Education, October 1997) (also at *nas.edu/sputnik*).

13. For an analysis of the fate of one such curriculum—Man, a Course of Study (MACOS), see Peter B. Dow, *Schoolhouse Politics: Lessons from the Sputnik Era* (Cambridge, Mass.: Harvard University Press, 1991).

14. Max Beberman, *An Emerging Program of Secondary School Mathematics* (Cambridge, Mass.: Harvard University Press, 1960), 44. Also see Dow, *Schoolhouse Politics*, 20–28.

15. Emphasis added.

16. Sherman K. Stein, *Strength in Numbers: Discovering the Joy and Power of Mathematics in Everyday Life* (New York: Wiley, 1996), 80.

17. Jeremy Kilpatrick, "Five Lessons from the New Math Era" (paper presented at a symposium hosted by the Center for Science, Mathematics, and Engineering Education, October 1997) (also at *www.nas.edu/sputnik*).

18. In Moon, *'New Maths.'* See also Kilpatrick, "Five Lessons."

19. Tom Lehrer, That Was the Year that Was, Reprise Records, 1965 (recording).

20. For a discussion on New Math, see Seymour B. Sarason, *Revisiting "The Culture of the School and the Problem of Change"* (New York: Teachers College Press, 1996).

21. Kilpatrick, "Five Lessons."

22. Peter Dow, "Sputnik Revisited: Historical Perspectives On Science Reform" (paper presented at a symposium hosted by the Center for Science, Mathematics, and Engineering Education, October 1997) (also at *www.nas.edu/sputnik*); John Goodlad et al., *Looking Behind the Classroom Door: A Useful Guide to Observing Schools in Action* (Worthington, Ohio: Charles A. Jones, 1974).

23. See, for example, David Tyack and Larry Cuban, *Tinkering Toward Utopia: A Century of Public School Reform* (Cambridge, Mass.: Harvard University Press, 1995); Larry Cuban, *How Teachers Taught: Constancy and Change in American Classrooms, 1880–1990* (New York: Teachers College Press, 1993).

24. Morris Kline, *Why Johnny Can't Add: The Failure of the New Math* (New York: St. Martin's, 1973).

25. Hans Freudenthal, "New Maths or New Education?" *Prospects* 9: 321.

26. Donald S. Freeman, Therese M. Kuhs, Andrew C. Porter, Robert E. Floden, William H. Schmidt, and John R. Schwille, *Do Textbooks and Tests Define a National Curriculum in Elementary School Mathematics?* (East Lansing, Mich.: Institute for Research on Teaching, Michigan State University, October, 1981), 1.

27. Maureen Dowd, "Liberties: Cuomos vs. Sopranos," *New York Times*, April 22, 2001 (also at *www.nytimes.com*).

28. E. D. Hirsch, *The Schools We Need and Why We Don't Have Them* (New York: Doubleday, 1996), and Diane Ravitch, *Left Back: A Century of Failed School Reforms* (New York: Simon and Schuster, 2000).

29. Deborah Tannen, *The Argument Culture: Moving from Debate to Dialogue* (New York: Random House, 1998), 31.

30. Alfred North Whitehead, *An Introduction to Mathematics* (Oxford: Oxford University Press, 1948), 2.

31. Georg Polya, *How to Solve It: A New Aspect of Mathematical Method* (Princeton, N.J.: Princeton University Press, 1945), vii.

32. G. H. Hardy, *A Mathematician's Apology* (London: Cambridge University Press, 1969), quotations at 80 and 84.

33. Reuben Hersh, *What Is Mathematics Really?* (New York: Oxford University Press, 1997). Emphasis added.

34. Joseph J. Schwab, "Education and the Structure of the Disciplines" in *Science, Curriculum, and Liberal Education: Selected Essays*, Ian Westbury and Neil J. Wilkof, eds. (Chicago: University of Chicago Press, 1978), 242. Emphasis added.

35. Marshall McLuhan, *Understanding Media: The Extensions of Man* (New York: McGraw-Hill, 1964).

36. Aristophanes, *The Clouds*, quoted in Martha C. Nussbaum, *Cultivating Humanity: A Classical Defense of Reform in Liberal Education* (Cambridge, Mass.: Harvard University Press, 1997), 1.

37. See Robert Davis, "Mathematics As a Performing Art," *Journal of Mathematical Behavior* 8 (1987): 143–160; Dossey et al., *Mathematics Report Card*; Alan Schoenfeld, "Explorations of Students' Mathematical Beliefs And Behaviors," *Journal for Research in Mathematics Education* 20 (July 1989): 338–355.

38. Diane Jean Schemo, "Worldwide Survey Finds U.S. Students Are Not Keeping Up," *New York Times*, December 6, 2000; Duke Helfand, "U.S. Math, Science Students Still Trail Top Ranks," *Los Angeles Times*, December 6, 2000; and "World Education League: Who's Top?" *The Economist*, March 29–April 4, 1997.

39. NCTM, *Curriculum and Evaluation Standards for School Mathematics* (Reston, Va.: NCTM, 1989); NCTM, *Professional Standards for Teaching Mathematics* (Reston, Va.: NCTM, 1991); and NCTM, *Assessment Standards for School Mathematics* (Reston, Va.: NCTM, 1995). For an analysis of the development of the NCTM *1989 Standards* and the role of the NCTM in reform, see Douglas B. McLeod, Robert E. Stake, Bonnie Schappelle, Melissa Mellissinos, and Mark J. Gierl, "Setting the Standards: NCTM's Role in the Reform of Mathematics Education" in *Bold Ventures: Case Studies of U.S. Innovations in Mathematics Education*, Senta A. Raizen and Edward D. Britton, eds. (Dordrecht: Kluwer Academic, 1996), as well as Jeremy Kilpatrick and G. M. A. Stanic, "Paths to the Present" in *Seventy-five Years of Progress: Prospects for School Mathematics*, Iris M. Carl, ed. (New York: Macmillan, 1995), 3–17.

40. Throughout this book, I will use the shorthand of NCTM *1989 Standards* to signify the set of standards since they share certain characteristics. To make things even more complicated, while I was writing this book, a new set of standards was issued. To differentiate those from the earlier ones, I will call the later version the *Principles and Standards for School Mathematics (PSSM)* (Reston, Va.: NCTM, 2000).

41. Diane Ravitch, *National Standards in American Education: A Citizen's Guide* (Washington, D.C.: Brookings, 1996).

42. My co-principal investigators on the project were Deborah Loewenberg Ball, David Cohen, and Penelope Peterson. See the methodological appendix, "'This Frightful

Toil'," for a discussion of the study, as well as David K. Cohen and Heather Hill, *Learning Policy: When State Education Works* (New Haven: Yale University Press, 2002).

43. I have, at the same time, aimed to avoid the new age solipsism that characterizes some recent scholarship across many fields.

44. A. S. Byatt, *On Histories and Stories: Selected Essays* (Cambridge, Mass.: Harvard University Press, 2000), 6.

CHAPTER 3. CAPTURING PROFESSIONAL CONSENSUS

Epigraphs: Ron Brandt, "On Curriculum in California: A Conversation with Bill Honig," *Educational Leadership* 47 (November 1989): 10–13, quotation at 11. Honig has been the object of much research. I benefited from reading the work of Donald J. Freeman, *California's Curriculum Reform Guidelines for Elementary Schools: 1983–1988* (East Lansing, Mich.: Center for the Learning and Teaching of Elementary Subjects, Institute for Research on Teaching, College of Education, Michigan State University), and Lisa Carlos and Michael Kirst, *California Curriculum Policy in the 1990s: "We Don't Have to Be in the Front to Lead"* (San Francisco: WestEd and PACE, April 1997); California Education Code, Section 60000.

1. See Norman L. Webb, "Mathematics Education: Reform in California," in *Science and Mathematics Education in the United States: Eight Innovations.* Proceedings of a conference (Paris: Organization for Economic Cooperation and Development, 1993).

2. "Manipulatives" are tools for representing mathematical ideas. Sometimes teachers make their own manipulatives, using ice cream sticks packaged in bundles of ten to teach students ideas about arithmetic, for example. Companies specializing in instructional materials have produced other kinds of manipulatives: clear plastic geometric shapes that teachers can put on an overhead projector to demonstrate geometric principles or "fraction bars" that students can use to work out problems through representations of them before turning to the more abstract, paper-and-pencil representation.

3. All quotations from interviews are verbatim. Most informants remain anonymous, with the exception of Honig, Elizabeth Stage, Joan Akers, Walter Denham, and Judy Mumme, whose identities are impossible to mask. Names listed in public documents or cited in other texts are not anonymous.

4. "Political Maneuvering Begins in California After Honig Convicted," and "Educators Lament Verdict Will Remove Influential Leader from National Scene," *Education Week*, February 10, 1993 (also at *www.edweek.org*).

5. National Commission on Excellence in Education (NCEE), *The Nation at Risk: The Imperative of Educational Reform* (Washington, D.C.: U.S. Government Printing Office, 1983).

6. David Cohen and James Spillane, "Policy and Practice: The Relations Between Governance and Instruction," in Gerald Grant, ed., *Review of Research in Education* 18 (1992): 3–49.

7. See, for example, William H. Clune, "Institutional Choice as a Theoretical Framework for Research on Educational Policy," *Educational Evaluation and Policy Analysis* 9 (1987): 117–132; and William A. Firestone, Susan H. Fuhrman, and Michael W. Kirst, *The Progress of Reform: An Appraisal of State Education Initiatives* (New Brunswick, N.J.: Center for Policy Research in Education, 1989). Other CPRE researchers included Deborah Loewenberg Ball, David K. Cohen, Richard Elmore, Margaret Goertz, Diane Massell, and Allan Odden, among others.

8. Donald S. Freeman, Therese M. Kuhs, Andrew C. Porter, Robert E. Floden, William H. Schmidt, and John R. Schwille, *Do Textbooks and Tests Define a National Curriculum in Elementary School Mathematics?* (East Lansing, Mich.: Institute for Research on Teaching, Michigan State University, October, 1981).

9. Cohen and Spillane, "Policy and Practice," 19–20.

10. Marshall Smith and Jennifer O'Day, "Systemic School Reform," in *The Politics of Curriculum Testing*, Susan Fuhrman and Betty Malen, eds. (Philadelphia: Falmer), 233–267, quotation at 254.

11. Ron Brandt, "On Curriculum in California," 13.

12. Mandated in California State Education Code Sections 60200–60205.

13. Susan H. Fuhrman, William H. Clune, and Richard F. Elmore, "Research on Education Reform: Lessons on the Implementation of Policy," *Teachers College Record* 90 (Winter 1998): 237–257, quotation at 240.

14. California State Department of Education, *Instructional Materials and Framework Adoption: Policies and Procedures* (Sacramento: California State Department of Education, 1988), 5.

15. *Systemic Reform* (CPRE Research Report Series RR-025, New Brunswick, N.J.: Consortium for Policy Research in Education, October 1992), 9.

16. Alfred Manaster ran the Mathematics Diagnostic Test Project (MDTP) out of the University of California, San Diego. The project developed tests that would identify students' strengths and weaknesses in topics shown to be integral to success in later mathematics courses. Tests included the pre-calculus test, the intermediate algebra tests, the elementary algebra test, and an algebra readiness test that was introduced in 1987. Tens of thousands of California high school students took these tests, which were then used to detect problems concerning their knowledge and skill before entering the CSU and UC systems. See Alfred B. Manaster, "Mathematics Diagnostic Testing Project," *The ComMuniCator* 11 (June 1987).

17. Amy Gutmann, *Democratic Education* (Princeton, N.J.: Princeton University Press, 1987).

18. A note here about labels and side taking. During the over ten years of my story, many groups formed. Sides were often taken, and sometimes labels were attached: "traditionalist," "conservative," "reformer," "anti-reformer," "constructivist." At times, increasingly so later in the story, there was polarization and finger pointing. Yet when people sat at tables to talk, they often discovered that they agreed about many things. Largely this was because they did not belong to the black-and-white, easily dichotomized camps that rumors suggested they did. Furthermore, there was considerable variation in beliefs and commitments, with

some people more zealous about an idea—drill and practice or constructivism, say—than others. Throughout this story, I aim neither to overstate the differences nor label groups of individuals unfairly. To differentiate between the educators who pushed these reforms and the individuals who later raised questions, sometimes critical, I use labels like "reformer" and "critic." When those critics then become a new wave of reformers, I label them as such, for reform in this story tilts first toward progressive ideas, then toward something more traditional (but not entirely). I do not use these labels judgmentally, nor do I have a single, clear articulation of the beliefs associated with any group (given the internal variation in those beliefs and ideas). There is no one California, no one new math, and no one unified and monolithic block of reformers or their critics. This is a theme of the story that I return to in the final chapter.

19. The *1985 Framework*, as well as subsequent documents, also had implications for middle and secondary school curricula. For more information concerning those, see, for example, Norman L. Webb, "State of California: Restructuring of Mathematics Education."

20. California State Department of Education, *Mathematics Framework for California Public Schools, K–12* (Sacramento: California State Department of Education, 1985), 1.

21. See Denis C. Phillips, "The Good, the Bad, and the Ugly: The Many Faces of Constructivism," *Educational Researcher* 24 (October 1995): 5–12.

22. Jeremy Kilpatrick. "Five Lessons from the New Math Era" (paper presented at a symposium sponsored by the Center for Science, Mathematics, and Engineering Education, October 1997) (also at *www.nas.edu/sputnik*).

23. Ellen Gilchrist, *Falling Through Space* (New York: Little, Brown, 1987), as well as Madeline L'Engle *Two-Part Invention: The Story of a Marriage* (San Francisco: Harper and Row, 1988).

24. Alba Thompson. "Teachers' Beliefs and Conceptions: A Synthesis of the Research," in *Handbook of Research on Mathematics Teaching and Learning*, Doug Grouws, ed. (New York: Macmillan, 1992), 127–146.

25. Reuben Hersh, *What Is Mathematics, Really?* (New York: Oxford University Press, 1997), 5.

26. California State Department of Education, *Mathematics Framework*, 1.

27. *A Sampler of Mathematics Assessment*, 1991, in materials compiled by Cathy A. Pierce, Vita Unified School District, Mathematics Mentor Project. Quotation taken from a district memo, "Mathematics open-ended questions," written by Cathy Pierce in 1993.

28. Raleigh Schorling, *The Teaching of Mathematics: A Source Book and Guide* (Ann Arbor, Mich.: Ann Arbor Press, 1936), 22.

29. Schorling, *Teaching of Mathematics*, 25.

30. Carl Sandburg, "Arithmetic, *The Complete Poems of Carl Sandburg* (New York: Harcourt Brace Jovanovich, 1970)."

31. See, e.g., Daniel Chazan and Deborah Loewenberg Ball, "Beyond Being Told Not to Tell," *For the Learning of Mathematics* 19 (1999): 2–10.

32. Dan Walters, "Schools Loom as Big Issue," *The Sacramento Bee*, October 24, 1997 (also at *www.sacbee.com*).

33. Peter Schrag, *Paradise Lost: California's Experience, America's Future* (New York: New Press, 1998), p. 13.

34. California State Department of Education, *Mathematics Framework*, vii.

35. Richard P. Feynman, "Judging Books by Their Covers," *"Surely You're Joking, Mr. Feynman!" Adventures of a Curious Character* (New York: Norton, 1985), 288–302.

36. James Thompson, *Organizations in Action: Social Science Bases of Administrative Theory* (New York: McGraw-Hill, 1967).

37. Freeman, *California's Curriculum Reform*, 8.

38. Quoted in Brandt, "On Curriculum in California," 11–12.

39. Walter Denham, "District Selection of Elementary Mathematics Textbooks," *The ComMuniCator* 12 (March 1988): 11.

40. Freeman, *California's Curriculum Reform*, 41.

41. Another, less progressive high school curriculum guide was also published. Here I focus on the one relevant to this story, the *K–8 Curriculum Guide*.

42. California State Department of Education, *K–8 Model Curriculum Guide* (Sacramento: California State Department of Education, 1987), vii.

43. California State Department of Education, "The New CAP," undated.

44. Eva L. Baker, "Researchers and Assessment Policy Development: A Cautionary Tale" *American Journal of Education* 102 (August 1994): 450–473.

45. Grant Wiggins, "Teaching to the (Authentic) Test," *Educational Leadership* 46 (April 1989): 41–47, quotation at 42.

46. California State Department of Education, *A Sampler of Mathematics Assessment* (Sacramento: California State Department of Education, 1991).

CHAPTER 4. EARLIER REFORMS AND THEIR LEGACIES

Epigraph: James G. March, "Education and the Pursuit of Optimism," *Texas Tech Journal of Education* 2 (1975): 5–17, quotation at 9.

1. Joseph Featherstone, "Foreword," in Herbert Kohl, *Growing Minds: On Becoming a Teacher* (New York: Harper and Row, 1984), ix–xviii.

2. Advisory Committee on Mathematics, *The Strands Report* (Sacramento: California State Department of Education, 1962).

3. It might have been a prudent move for the authors of the 1985 *Framework* to offer similar caveats in order to explain why so much time was spent discussing teaching for understanding and so little arguing for the "basics" as well.

4. Advisory Committee on Mathematics, *The Strands Report*, 12–13.

5. Statewide Mathematics Advisory Committee, *Mathematics Program, K–8: 1967–1968 Strands Report, Part 1* (Sacramento: California State Department of Education, 1968).

6. See Statewide Mathematics Advisory Committee, *Mathematics Program, K–8: 1967–1968 Strands Report, Part 2* (Sacramento: California State Department of Education, 1968).

7. See Robert B. Davis, *Discovery in Mathematics: A Text for Teachers Containing Top-*

ics, Techniques, Methods, and Materials for a Supplementary First Course in Introductory Mathematics (Reading, Mass.: Addison-Wesley, 1964) and *Explorations in Mathematics: A Text for Teachers* (Palo Alto, Calif.: Addison-Wesley, 1967).

8. See California State Department of Education, *Mathematics Improvement Programs: Summary Report 1968–1971* (Sacramento: California State Department of Education, 1971); and *Mathematics Improvement Programs: Final Report of the Specialized Teacher Project, 1971–72* (Sacramento: California State Department of Education, 1972).

9. An up-to-date listing of the Math Solutions materials is available at *www.mathsolutions.com.*

10. David Cohen, "What Standards for National Standards?" *Phi Delta Kappan* 76 (June 1995): 751–757, quotation at 755–756. Lee S. Shulman, "Autonomy and Obligation: The Remote Control of Teaching," in Lee S. Shulman and Gary Sykes, eds., *Handbook of Teaching and Policy* (New York: Longman, 1983), 484–504.

11. See Philip A. Cusick, *The Educational System: Its Nature and Logic* (New York: McGraw-Hill, 1992).

CHAPTER 5. NETWORKS AND THEIR LEADERS

Epigraphs: John Seely Brown and Paul Duguid, *The Social Life of Information* (Boston: Harvard Business School, 2000), 140–141; William A. Firestone, "Educational Policy as an Ecology of Games," *Educational Researcher* 18 (October 1989): 18–24, quotation at 23.

1. The widespread distaste for traditional professional development is widely accepted among teachers, although there is little research on what teachers actually learn in such settings. See Mark A. Smylie, "The Enhancement Function of Staff Development: Organizational and Psychological Antecedents to Individual Teacher Change," *American Educational Research Journal* 25 (Spring 1998): 1–30; and Suzanne M. Wilson and Jennifer Berne, "Teacher Learning and the Acquisition of Professional Knowledge: An Examination of Research on Contemporary Professional Development," in A. Iran-Nejad and P. D. Pearson, eds., *Review of Research in Education* 24: 173–209.

2. See *www.lhs.berkeley.edu/equals/equals.html.*

3. See *www.gse.berkeley.edu/outreach/bawp/whatis.html.*

4. The California Science Project was created in 1988. Literature and foreign language became part of the California Subject Matter Project in 1989.

5. Judith Warren Little, W. H. Gerritz, D. S. Stern, et al., *Staff Development in California: Public and Personal Investment, Program Patterns, and Policy Choices* (San Francisco: Far West Laboratory for Educational Research and Development, 1987).

6. Ibid. See also Kathy Medina, Mark St. John, Barbara Hennan, Judy Hirabayashi, Dawn Huntwork, Katherine Landreth, and Laura Stokes, *The Nature of Teacher Leadership: Lessons Learned from the California Subject Matter Projects, Report 13* (Inverness, Calif.: Inverness Research Associates, June 1997).

7. California has a three-tier university system: the California State University system educated most teachers in the state at the time of our study. The University of

California system is more research-oriented, with smaller teacher education programs. The community college tier does not educate teachers; becoming credentialed in California required a fifth year of study during the time of our study.

8. See Mark St. John, *The California Subject Matter Projects: A Summary of Evaluation
Findings, 1993 to 1996* (Inverness, Calif.: Inverness Research Associates, Report 11,
December 1996). See James R. Pennell and William A. Firestone, "Changing
Classroom Practices Through Teacher Networks: Matching Program Characteris-
tics with Teacher Characteristics and Circumstances," *Teachers College Record* 98
(Fall 1996): 46–76, for a brief summary and analysis of the California Subject
Matter Project as well.

9. See *A Report of the Holmes Group: Tomorrow's Teachers* (East Lansing, Mich.: The
Holmes Group, April 1986), 3. See also the report of the Task Force on Teaching
as a Profession, *A Nation Prepared: Teachers for the 21st Century* (New York:
Carnegie Forum on Education and the Economy, 1986).

10. For a summary of research on this topic, see Deborah Loewenberg Ball, Sarah
Theule Lubienski, and Denise Spangler Mewborn, "Research on Teaching Mathe-
matics: The Unsolved Problem of Teachers' Mathematical Knowledge," in Virginia
Richardson, ed., *Handbook of Research on Teaching*, 4th edition (Washington, D.C.:
American Educational Research Association, 2001), 433–456, and Liping Ma,
*Knowing and Teaching Elementary Mathematics: Teachers' Understanding of Funda-
mental Mathematics in China and the United States* (Mahwah, N.J.: Erlbaum, 1999).

11. See Suzanne M. Wilson, Sarah Theule Lubienski, and Steven Mattson, "Where's
the Mathematics?" (paper presented at the annual meeting of the American Educational Research Association, New York City, April 1996).

12. The New Standards Project is a joint project of the National Center on Education
and the Economy and the Learning Research and Development Center at the University of Pittsburgh. It produces curriculum and assessment materials, as well as
extensive professional development. Several central actors in the California mathematics story have participated in the development of New Standards materials,
including Elizabeth Stage and Phil Daro. See *www.ncee.org/OurPrograms/nsPage
.html.*

13. See Gary M. Lichtenstein, Milbrey W. McLaughlin, and Jennifer Knudsen, *Teacher
Empowerment and Professional Knowledge* (New Brunswick, N.J.: Consortium for
Policy Research in Education, 1991), 5.

14. Seymour B. Sarason, *Revisiting "The Culture of the School and the Problem of
Change"* (New York: Teachers College Press, 1996), 352.

15. For a discussion of the challenges facing professional development for mathematics teachers, particularly with reference to the *mathematics* of that professional development, see Hung-Hsi Wu, "The Professional Development of Mathematics
Teachers," *Notices of the AMS* 46 (May 1999): 535–542.

16. See Mark St. John, Judy Hirabayashi, and Kathleen Dickey, *The Work of the CSMP
Teacher Leaders: A Summary of Key Findings from a Statewide Survey*, Report 14 (Inverness, Calif.: Inverness Research Associates, June 1997).

17. See Suzanne M. Wilson and Jo Allen Lesser, "'I Am a Part of All That I Have Met':

Toward a Better Understanding of Teacher Learning" (Alba Thompson Memorial Lecture delivered at the 19th annual meeting of the North American chapter of the International Group for the Psychology of Mathematics Education, Normal, Illinois, October 1997).

18. Henry Moore as quoted in Donald Hall, *Life Work* (Boston: Beacon, 1993), 54.

19. See Jeannie Oakes, "Keeping Track, Part 1: The Policy and Practice of Curriculum Inequality," *Phi Delta Kappan* 62 (September 1986): 12–17, and "Keeping Track, Part 2: Curriculum Inequality and School Reform," *Phi Delta Kappan* 62 (October 1986): 148–154.

20. See Robert Coles, *Doing Documentary Work* (New York: Oxford University Press, 1997); Robert P. Moses, "Remarks on the Struggle for Citizenship and Math/Science Literacy," *Journal of Mathematical Behavior* 13 (March 1994): 107–111; and Robert P. Moses and Charles E. Cobb, Jr., *Radical Equations: Math Literacy and Civil Rights* (Boston: Beacon, 2001).

21. See John I. Goodlad, *A Place Called School: Prospects for the Future* (New York: McGraw-Hill, 1984); Daniel Lortie, *Schoolteacher: A Sociological Study* (Chicago: University of Chicago Press, 1975); Susan Moore Johnson, *Teachers at Work: Achieving Success in Our Schools* (New York: Basic Books, 1990); and Kathleen Casey, *I Answer with My Life: Life Histories of Women Teachers Working for Social Change* (New York: Routledge, 1993).

22. See Philip A. Cusick, *The Educational System: Its Nature and Logic* (New York: McGraw-Hill, 1992).

23. See *www.cmc-math.org*.

24. See Mary Laycock, "Multiplication Strategies," in *The ComMuniCator* 12 (December 1987): 38–39.

25. See *www.marcycookmath.com/index.html*.

26. Lichtenstein, et al., *Teacher Empowerment*. See also Susan H. Fuhrman and Diane Massell, *Issues and Strategies in Systemic Reform* (Consortium for Policy Research in Education Research Report Series RR-025, New Brunswick, N.J., October 1992).

27. Lichtenstein, et. al. *Teacher Empowerment*.

28. Moses, "Remarks on the Struggle for Citizenship," 110.

29. John Seely Brown and Paul Duguid, *The Social Life of Information* (Boston, Mass.: Harvard Business School, 2000), 126. See, as background, Jean Lave, *Cognition in Practice: Mind, Mathematics and Culture in Everyday Life* (New York: Cambridge University Press, 1988), and Jean Lave and Etienne Wenger, *Situated Learning: Legitimate Peripheral Participation* (New York: Cambridge University Press, 1993).

30. See, for example, Ann Lieberman and Maureen Grolnick, "Networks and Reform in American Education," *Teachers College Record* 98 (Fall 1996): 7–45; Ann Lieberman and Milbrey McLaughlin, "Networks for Educational Change: Powerful and Problematic," *Phi Delta Kappan* 73 (May 1992): 673–677; James R. Pennell and William A. Firestone, "Changing Classroom Practices Through Teacher Networks: Matching Program Features with Teacher Characteristics and Circumstances," *Teachers College Record* 98 (Fall 1996): 46–76; and William A. Firestone and James

R. Pennell, "Designing State-Sponsored Teacher Networks: A Comparison of Two Cases," *American Educational Research Journal* 34 (Summer 1997): 237–266.

CHAPTER 6. RIDING THE TIGER

Epigraph: Walter Denham, "California Department of Education Report: The State of Mathematics Education," *The ComMuniCator* 15 (September 1990): 9.

1. Susan H. Fuhrman and Richard F. Elmore, "Understanding Local Control in the Wake of State Education Reform," *Educational Evaluation and Policy Analysis* 12 (Spring 1990): 82–96.

2. Joan L. Hermann, Richard S. Brown, and Eva L. Baker, *Student Assessment and Student Achievement in the California Public School System* (Center for the Study of Evaluation, National Center for Research on Evaluation, Standards, and Student Testing (CRESST), University of California, Los Angeles, 2000, Report 519).

3. See Jeannie Oakes, "What Educational Indicators? The Case for Assessing the School Context," *Educational Evaluation and Policy Analysis* 11 (Summer 1989): 181–200, quotation at 189.

4. Hermann, Brown, and Baker, *Student Assessment*, 2.

5. See Lauren B. Resnick and Daniel P. Resnick, "Assessing the Thinking Curriculum: New Tools for Educational Reform," in *Changing Assessments: Alternative Views of Aptitude, Achievement, and Instruction*, Bernard R. Gifford and Mary Catherine O'Connor, eds. (Boston: Kluwer Academic, 1992), 337–375, quotation at 355.

6. See Lorraine M. McDonnell, *The Politics of State Testing: Implementing New Student Assessments* (CSE Technical Report 424, National Center for Research on Evaluation, Standards, and Student Testing (CRESST), Graduate School of Education and Information Studies, University of California, Los Angeles, 1997).

7. For a cross-case comparison of similar assessment reforms in California, Kentucky, and North Carolina, see McDonnell, *Politics of State Testing*.

8. Jean Kerr Stenmark, *Assessment Alternatives in Mathematics: An Overview of Assessment Techniques that Promote Learning* (Berkeley: Regents, University of California, 1989).

9. Grant Wiggins, *Educative Assessment: Designing Assessments to Inform and Improve Student Performance* (San Francisco: Jossey Bass, 1998); Grant Wiggins, "Practicing What We Preach In Designing Authentic Assessments," *Educational Leadership* 54 (December 1996/January 1997): 18–25; Grant Wiggins, "Creating Tests Worth Taking," *Educational Leadership* 49 (May 1992): 26–33.

10. See National Research Council, *Everybody Counts: A Report to the Nation on the Future of Mathematics Education* (Washington, D.C.: National Academy Press, 1989), 70. See also Grant Wiggins, "A True Test: Toward More Authentic and Equitable Assessment," *Phi Delta Kappan* 70 (May 1989): 703–713; Doug A. Archbald and Fred M. Newmann, *Beyond Standardized Testing: Assessing Authentic Academic Achievement in the Secondary School* (Reston, Va.: National Association of Secondary School Principals, 1988).

11. These problems come from materials collected in one school district outside of Sacramento, California, in 1993.

12. See California Mathematics Council, *Standardized Tests and the California Mathematics Curriculum: Where Do We Stand? A Review of Content Alignment* (Clayton, Calif.: CMC, 1987), 7.

13. Alfred North Whitehead, *An Introduction to Mathematics* (Oxford: Oxford University Press, 1911), 8.

14. Rebecca B. Corwin, Susan Jo Russell, and Cornelia Teirney developed the unit at TERC, with input from Joan Akers, Marilyn Burns, and Mark Ogonowski, *Seeing Fractions: A Unit for the Upper Elementary Grades* (Sacramento: California Department of Education, 1991).

15. See Ann S. Rosebery and Mark S. Ogonowski, *Seeing Fractions Evaluation Report* (Cambridge, Mass.: TERC, June 1991).

16. Kris Acquarelli and Judith Mumme, "A Renaissance in Mathematics Education Reform," *Phi Delta Kappan* 77 (March 1996): 478–482.

17. National Commission on Excellence in Education, *A Nation at Risk: The Imperative for Educational Reform* (Washington, D.C.: U.S. Department of Education, 1983).

18. See William A. Firestone, Susan H. Fuhrman, and Michael W. Kirst, *The Progress of Reform: An Appraisal of State Education Initiatives* (Consortium for Policy Research in Education, Research Report Series RR-014, New Brunswick, N.J., 1989).

19. James R. Pennell and William A Firestone, "Changing Classroom Practices Through Teacher Networks: Matching Program Features with Teacher Characteristics and Circumstances," *Teachers College Record* 98 (Fall 1996): 46–76.

20. See Janet Hageman Chrispeels, "Educational Policy Implementation in a Shifting Political Climate: The California Experience," *American Educational Research Journal* 34 (Fall 1997): 453–481.

21. See California Department of Education, *It's Elementary* (Sacramento: California State Department of Education, 1992), a synthesis of all the reforms aimed at elementary schools; *Caught in the Middle* (Sacramento: California State Department of Education, 1987), a report that summarized the status quo of middle schools and proposed reforms; and *Second to None* (Sacramento: California State Department of Education, 1992), a parallel statement about the state of secondary education in California and future plans for improvement.

22. National Council of Teachers of Mathematics, *An Agenda for Action: Directions for School Mathematics for the 1980s* (Reston, Va.: National Council of Teachers of Mathematics, 1980).

23. National Research Council, *Everybody Counts: A Report to the Nation on the Future of Mathematics Education*, 1–2.

24. Ibid., 81–84.

25. National Research Council, *Moving Beyond Myths: Revitalizing Undergraduate Mathematics* (Washington, D.C.: National Academy Press, 1991); Lynn Steen, ed., *On the Shoulder of Giants: New Approaches to Numeracy* (Washington, D.C.: National Academy Press, 1990); and National Research Council, *Reshaping School Mathematics: A Philosophy and Framework for Curriculum* (Washington, D.C.: National Academy of Sciences, 1990).

26. National Research Council, *Moving Beyond Myths*, 1.

27. Ibid.

28. See Robert B. Davis, "Understanding 'Understanding'," *Journal of Mathematical Behavior* 11 (1992): 225–241.

29. For an overview and analysis of the activities and impact of CAMS, see Patrick M. Shields, Camille Marder, and Choya L. Wilson, *A Case Study of the California Alliance for Mathematics and Science (CAMS) 1992–1993* (Menlo Park, Calif.: SRI International, October 1996).

30. "A Tidal Wave of Innovation One Drop at a Time," *CSINsations* (Fall 1994), 1.

31. California State Department of Education, *1992 Mathematics Framework for California Public Schools (K–12)* (Sacramento: CDE, 1992), vii.

32. California Department of Education, *Mathematics Framework for California Schools, K–12* (Sacramento: CDE, 1985), 1.

33. Ibid., 52–53.

34. Ibid., ix.

CHAPTER 7. THE TIDE TURNS

Epigraph: Richard White, "What California Taught America," *The New Republic*, December 1, 1997; William Kittredge, *Who Owns the West?* (San Francisco: Mercury House, 1996).

1. This sampling strategy is used frequently with assessments that involve items that test more than simple recall. See the NAEP website: *nces.ed.gov/nationsreportcard/pubs/guide/ques20.shtml*.

2. Michael W. Kirst and Christopher Mazzeo, "The Rise, Fall, and Rise of State Assessment in California: 1993–96," *Phi Delta Kappan* 78 (December 1996): 319–323.

3. Lorraine M. McDonnell, *The Politics of State Testing: Implementing New Student Assessments* (CSE Technical Report 424, National Center for Research on Evaluation, Standards, and Student Testing (CRESST), Graduate School of Education and Information Studies, University of California, Los Angeles, 1997).

4. For example, see Nanette Asimov, "School Test Foes Not Satisfied by State Offer: They Will Continue to Sue Districts Over Use of Exam" *San Francisco Chronicle*, May 3, 1994, A15.

5. Adrienne D. Coles, "Suit Argues Essay Questions on Test in Indiana Are 'Psychologically Intrusive,'" *Education Week* November 8, 1995, 16.

6. Mary Lee Smith, Walter Heinecke, and Audrey J. Noble, *The Politics of Assessment: A Case Study of Policy and Political Spectacle* (CSE Technical Report 468, National Center for Research on Evaluation, Standards, and Student Testing (CRESST), Graduate School of Education and Information Studies, University of California, Los Angeles, 1997); and Mary Lee Smith, *The Politics of Assessment: A View from the Political Culture of Arizona* (CSE Technical Report 420, National Center for Research on Evaluation, Standards, and Student Testing (CRESST), Graduate School of Education and Information Studies, University of California, Los Angeles, 1996).

7. As quoted in McDonnell, *Politics of State Testing,* 36.
8. See E. D. Hirsch, *The Schools We Need and Why We Don't Have Them* (New York: Doubleday, 1996); and Diane Ravitch, *Left Back: A Century of Failed School Reforms* (New York: Simon and Schuster, 2000).
9. None of these problems were a surprise to scholars of testing, who had known for some time of the difficulties inherent in building more "authentic" assessments. See, for example, George F. Madaus and Thomas Kellaghan, "The British Experience with 'Authentic Testing,'" *Phi Delta Kappan* 74 (February 1993): 458–469.
10. McDonnell, *Politics of State Testing,* 23.
11. Jodi Wilgoren and Richard O'Reilly, "Test Scoring Far off Mark: CLAS Results Skewed by Small Samples," *San Jose Mercury News,* April 10, 1994.
12. Ann Bancroft, "CLAS Test Quality Control Criticized," *San Francisco Chronicle,* August 3, 1994, A15–A16.
13. National Center for Education Statistics, *NAEP 1994 Reading Report Card for the Nation and the States* (Washington, D.C.: NCES, 1996). See also *nces.ed.gov/ nationsreportcard/* and *nces.ed.gov/nationsreportcard/states/profile.asp?state=CA.*
14. David Tyack and Larry Cuban, *Tinkering Toward Utopia: A Century of Public School Reform* (Cambridge: Harvard University Press, 1995), 82–83. The literature on how teachers shape reforms is vast. See, for examples, Larry Cuban, *How Teachers Taught: Constancy and Change in American Classrooms, 1980–1980* (New York: Longman, 1984), David K. Cohen, *Plus Ça Change* (East Lansing, Mich.: National Center for Research on Teacher Education, Issue Paper No. 88–83, 1988), and Michael W. Kirst and Gail R. Meister, "Turbulence in American Secondary Schools: What Reforms Last?" *Curriculum Inquiry* 15 (Summer 1986): 169–186.
15. Milbrey Wallin McLaughlin, "Learning from Experience: Lessons from Policy Implementation," *Educational Evaluation and Policy Analysis* 9 (Summer 1987): 171–178, quotation at 175.
16. See Iris R. Weiss, "The Status of Science and Mathematics Teaching in the United States: Comparing Teacher Views and Classroom Practice to National Standards," *NISE Brief* 1 (Madison, Wisc.: National Institute for Science Education, June 1997).
17. "Report: $322 Billion Needed to Fix, Build Nation's Schools," *EDCAL* May 15, 2000, 9.
18. See Peter Schrag, *Paradise Lost: California's Experience, America's Future* (New York: New Press, 1998), for an analysis of the factors that led to this decline. Proposition 13 was passed in 1978 in response to California's high property taxes, slashing them by 30 percent and imposing a 1 percent cap on all local tax rates. It also mandated a supermajority, two-thirds vote for any special taxes. Proposition 98, the Classroom Instructional Improvement and Accountability Act, was passed in 1988 and amended by Proposition 111 in 1990.
19. See, for example, Larry V. Hedges, Richard D. Laine, and Rob Greenwald, "Does Money Matter? A Meta-Analysis of Studies of the Effects of Differential School Inputs on Student Outcomes," *Educational Researcher* 23 (April 1994): 5–14; Eric A. Hanushek, "The Impact of Differential Expenditures on School Performance," *Ed-*

ucational Researcher 18 (May 1989): 45–51; and Eric A. Hanushek, "Money Might Matter Somewhere: A Response to Hedges, Laine, and Greenwald," *Educational Researcher* 23 (May 1994): 5–8.

20. In addition, by 1998, California would have 45 percent of our country's immigrant children as residents, and the number of children not proficient in English would exceed the total public school enrollments of thirty-eight other states. See Elaine Woo, "Seeking Causes and Solutions at Seven California Campuses" *Los Angeles Times,* Sunday May 17, 1998 (also at *www.latimes.com*).

21. Schrag, *Paradise Lost,* 121–122.

22. Jamal Abedi, Carol Lord, and Joseph R. Plummer, *Final Report of Language Background as a Variable in NAEP Mathematics Performance* (CSE Technical Reports 429 and 424, National Center for Research on Evaluation, Standards, and Student Testing (CRESST), Graduate School of Education and Information Studies, University of California, Los Angeles, 1997).

23. See Lynelle Jolley, "The Honig Reforms," *California Journal,* June 1996, 28.

24. Nanette Asimov, "Wilson's Plan for Changes in CLAS Test: Proposal Would Drastically Alter Exam," *San Francisco Chronicle,* p. A12, A16.

25. Quoted in McDonnell, *Politics of State Testing,* 55.

26. Susan H. Fuhrman and Diane Massell, *Issues and Strategies in Systemic Reform* (Consortium for Policy Research in Education Research Report Series RR-025, New Brunswick, N.J., October 1992), 9. This difference in public involvement might account, in part, for the very different stories of systemic reform that have unfolded nationwide. For example, Kentucky's reforms included discussions and goal setting several years before framework development.

27. David K. Cohen, "What Standards for National Standards?" *Phi Delta Kappan* 76 (June 1995): 751–757, quotation at 754–755.

28. Michael Apple, "Do the Standards Go Far Enough? Power, Policy, and Practice in Mathematics Education," *Journal for Research in Mathematics Education* 23 (November 1992): 412–440.

29. See *www.mathematicallycorrect.com/allen1.html.*

30. Chester E. Finn, Jr., "What If Those Math Standards Are Wrong?" *Education Week* 12, January 20, 1993 (also at *www.edweek.com*).

31. Saxon Publishers, Inc., Advertisement, "Proposed Math-Testing Standards Damaging to Minorities," *Education Week* October 11, 1995, 8–9.

32. Jack Price, "President's Report: Selling and Buying Reform: If We Build It, Will They Come?" *Journal for Research in Mathematics Education* 26 (November 1995): 487–490, quotation at 489.

33. Nanette Asimov, "Wilson Vetoes Bill to Extend CLAS Test: Without It, There's No Statewide Exam," *San Francisco Chronicle,* September 28, 1994, A13. Innovative statewide assessment programs experienced similar difficulties in other states. The Arizona Student Assessment Program (ASAP) was suspended in 1996 so that it could be replaced by norm-referenced, standardized tests.

34. The logic of multiple methods goes something like this: we teach children many

things, and no one measure is sufficient or adequate for measuring everything we want children to learn. So, rather than trying to develop one assessment that measures everything, it might be more prudent to use multiple methods.

35. McDonnell, *Politics of State Testing.*
36. Quoted in Alex Pham, "California Math Rush: When Houghton Mifflin Texts Won OK, Reformers Cried Foul," *Boston Globe,* November 9, 1994, 66.
37. Ibid., 66.
38. Ibid.
39. The scholarship on textbook writing and production suggests that considerable forces are at play that do not have the needs of children or teachers in mind. This is something the educators knew and the board members did not necessarily know. See Frances Fitzgerald's classic study of history textbooks, *America Revised: History Schoolbooks in the 20th Century* (Boston: Little, Brown, 1979).
40. Debra J. Saunders, "Duck, It's the New New Math," *San Francisco Chronicle,* September 26, 1994, A23 (also at *www.sfgate.com*).
41. Debra J. Saunders, "There Is No One Answer," *San Francisco Chronicle,* February 1, 1995, at *www.sfgate.com*. See also Saunders, "New-New Math Blunders On."
42. Debra J. Saunders, "Crashing the Educrat Oligarchy," *San Francisco Chronicle,* November 19, 1996 (also at *www.sfgate.com*).
43. See California Department of Education, *Improving Mathematics Achievement for All California Students: The Report of the California Mathematics Task Force* (Sacramento, Calif.: CDE, 1995).
44. Debra J. Saunders, "Educrats, New-New Math and Eastin," *San Francisco Chronicle,* August 6, 1996 (also at *www.sfgate.com*).
45. Chester E. Finn and Diane Ravitch, *Education Reform: 1995–1996. A Report from the Educational Excellence Network to Its Education Policy Committee and the American People* (Indianapolis: Hudson Institute, August 1996), 41.
46. See George Lakoff, *Moral Politics: What Conservatives Know That Liberals Don't* (Chicago: University of Chicago Press, 1996), for a discussion of the rigidity of some extreme conservative perspectives, as well as David Berliner, "Educational Psychology Meets the Christian Right: Differing Views of Children, Schooling, Teaching, and Learning," *Teachers College Record* 98 (Spring 1997): 381–416.
47. See Chester E. Finn, Jr., "What If Those Math Standards Are Wrong?" *Education Week* 12, January 20, 1993 (also at *www.edweek.com*).
48. As quoted in John R. Novak, Alexander Chizhik, and Susane Moran, *Final Report on an Evaluation of the California Mathematics Diagnostic Testing Project* (Los Angeles: Center for the Study of Evaluation, UCLA), 149
49. Middle school teachers are commonly not certified to teach mathematics. This is especially true in a state like California, where, in 1993, only 49.8 percent of high school mathematics teachers reported having majored in mathematics. Given this dearth of qualified high school teachers, anyone who has a strong background in mathematics gets quickly pulled into high schools to teach, and good elementary school teachers get promoted to teaching middle school. See Victor Bandeira de Mello and Stephen P. Broughman, *1993–1994 Schools and Staffing Survey: Selected*

Results (Washington, D.C.: U.S.D.E., Office of Educational Research and Improvement, NCES-96–312, 1996), 123.

50. Debra J. Saunders, "New-New Math Blunders On," *San Francisco Chronicle*, December 23, 1994 (also at *www.sfgate.com*).

51. Hung-Hsi Wu, "The Role of Open-Ended Problems in Mathematics Education," *Journal of Mathematical Behavior* 13 (January 1994): 115–128.

52. Ibid., 121.

53. See *www.dehnbase.org/hold/* for information on HOLD.

54. HOLD, "Suggestions and Recommendations for Improvement of the 1989 NCTM Standards," January 15, 1996 (also at *www.dehnbase.org/hold/*).

55. See Elizabeth Darling, "Middle School Math Changes Planned: Parents Don't Want to Lose Traditional Course Offerings," *Palo Alto Weekly*, May 24, 1994.

56. Chris Kenrick, "Tradition and Change," *Palo Alto Weekly*, June 8, 1994.

57. See, for example, Lori Aratani, "Crowd of 200 Divided by Best Way to Teach Math," *San Jose Mercury News*, March 16, 1995; and Elizabeth Darling, "Debate Divides Crowd," *Palo Alto Weekly*, March 17, 1995.

58. For an analysis of the forces at play in this debate, see Lisa Rosen, "Calculating Concerns: The Politics of Representation in California's 'Math Wars'" (Ph.D. diss., University of California, San Diego, 2000).

59. Robert C. Johnson. "California District Has Had It with Rude Parents," *Education Week* 27, April 22, 1998 (also at *www.edweek.com*).

60. Paul Clopton. Originally printed in *University City Light/La Jolla Light*, January 4, 1996.

61. See Henry L. Alder, "Presentation to the State Board of Education," December 7, 1995 (also at *ourworld.compuserve.com/homepages/mathman/index.html*).

62. See *ourworld.compuserve.com/homepages/mathman/index.html*.

63. E. D. Hirsch, "Mathematically Correct," speech to the California State Board of Education, April 10, 1997 (also at *mathematicallycorrect.com/edh2cal.html*). For thoughtful analyses of the problems of education research see, for example, Mary M. Kennedy, "The Problem of Evidence in Teacher Education," in *The Role of the University in the Preparation of Teachers*, R. Roth, ed. (Pennsylvania: Falmer Press, Taylor and Francis, 1999), 87–107; Ellen Condliffe Lagemann, *An Elusive Science: The Troubling History of Education Research* (Chicago: University of Chicago Press, 2000); and Ellen Condliffe Lagemann and Lee S. Shulman, eds., *Issues in Education Research: Problems and Possibilities* (San Francisco: Jossey Bass and the National Academy of Education, 1999).

64. See, for example, Liping Ma, *Knowing and Teaching Elementary Mathematics: Teachers' Understanding of Fundamental Mathematics in China and the United States* (Mahwah, N.J.: Erlbaum, 1999); and James W. Stigler and James Hiebert, *The Teaching Gap: Best Ideas from the World's Teachers for Improving Education in the Classroom* (New York: Free Press, 1999).

65. Judie Panneton, "Math Framework: Adding up to Trouble?" *EDCAL* August 19, 1996, 1, 4.

66. Schrag, *Paradise Lost*, 19.

67. State Superintendent of Instruction, California State Board of Education, and California Commission on Teacher Credentialing, *Mathematics Program Advisory*, adopted September 12, 1996, 2–3.

68. Philip A. Cusick and Jennifer Borman, "Reform of and by the System: A Case Study of a State's Effort at Curricular and Systemic Reform," *Teachers College Record* 104 (2002).

69. Richard Hofstader, *Anti-intellectualism in American Life* (New York: Knopf, 1963).

70. David Labaree, "Public Goods, Private Goods: The American Struggle Over Educational Goals," *American Educational Research Journal* 34 (Spring 1997): 39–81.

71. Russell Baker, "Mr. Right," *New York Review of Books*, May 17, 2001, 4–6, 8; quotation at 8.

72. Joan Didion, "Reply," *New York Review of Books*, October 8, 1998, 58.

CHAPTER 8. DUELING STANDARDS

1. See Lisa Carlos and Michael Kirst, *California Curriculum Policy in the 1990s: "We Don't Have to Be in Front to Lead"* (San Francisco: WestEd and PACE, 1997).

2. Although all districts used standardized tests, some were norm-referenced, others criterion-referenced. A few districts used tests that included performance-oriented items. The tests had to meet standards for technical quality, but they did not allow for cross-district comparisons. See Joan L. Hermann, Richard S. Brown, and Eva L. Baker, *Student Assessment and Student Achievement in the California Public School System* (Center for the Study of Evaluation, National Center for Research on Evaluation, Standards, and Student Testing (CRESST), University of California, Los Angeles, 2000, Report 519).

3. Michael W. Kirst and Christopher Mazzeo, "The Rise, Fall, and Rise of State Assessment in California: 1993–96," *Phi Delta Kappan* 78 (December 1996): 319–323.

4. See California State Department of Education, *Mathematics Program Advisory* (Sacramento: California State Department of Education, California State Board of Education, California Commission on Teacher Credentialing, September 12, 1996).

5. Debra J. Saunders, "Four Star Math Follies," *San Francisco Chronicle*, August 5, 1997 (also at *www.sfgate.com*).

6. See Tom Romberg, "Mediocre Is Not Good Enough," *New York Times*, August 11, 1997; Bernard F. Erlwanger, "The Building Blocks," *New York Times*, August 17, 1997; Edmond David, "A Question of Choice," *New York Times*, August 17, 1997; and Suzanne Sutton, "Don't Deny Math's Rigor," *New York Times*, August 17, 1997 (also at *www.nytimes.com*).

7. Lynne Cheney, "Once Again, Basic Skills Fall Prey to a Fad," *New York Times*, August 11, 1997, A13.

8. The number of countries participating in TIMSS varies according to the dimension of the analysis. Forty-eight countries were involved in the curriculum analysis; 41 participated in the eighth-grade achievement testing (Pop. 2); only 26 participated in Pop. 1 (fourth-grade) achievement testing. This explains the variations in the sample size.

9. See James W. Stigler and James Hiebert, *The Teaching Gap: Best Ideas from the World's Teachers for Improving Education in the Classroom* (New York: Free Press, 1999).

10. William H. Schmidt, C. C. McKnight, and Senta A. Raizen, *A Splintered Vision: An Investigation of U.S. Science and Mathematics Education* (Boston: Kluwer, 1996). See also *timss.bc.edu* and *ustimss.msu.edu*.

11. Stigler and Hiebert, *The Teaching Gap*. These results resonate with and complement the curricular analyses offered in Schmidt, McKnight, and Raizen, *A Splintered Vision*.

12. *The Economist*, March 29–April 4, 1997.

13. See President Clinton's remarks, "Clinton Convenes Top Leaders: Challenges Nation to Improve Math and Science Education," March 16, 1998, Springbrook High School, Silver Spring, Maryland. See *www.ed.gov/americacounts/*.

14. The California Education Round Table is a coalition of businesses, higher education institutions, and K–12 schools. Its membership includes representatives from the California Postsecondary Education Commission, the University of California, the Association of Independent California Colleges and Universities, the California Community Colleges, the California State University system, as well as Delaine Eastin, state superintendent of instruction. The task forces include schoolteachers, administrators, parents, state department staff, and representatives from industry. See California Education Round Table, "Content Standards in English and Mathematics for High School Graduates" (Sacramento, Calif.: California Education Round Table, September 1996). See also Drew Lindsey, "K–12, Higher Ed Official Join to Rebuild California Standards," *Education Week*, November 8, 1995 (also at *www.edweek.com*).

15. The actual report was written collaboratively by Robert C. Dixon, Douglas W. Carnine, Dae-sik Lee, Joshua Walling, and David Chard, "Report to the California State Board of Education and Addendum to Principal Report Review of High Quality Experimental Mathematics Research" (Eugene, Ore.: National Center to Improve the Tools of Educators, March 1998).

16. Ibid., 2.

17. Ibid., 13.

18. Ibid., 7.

19. Compiled by Bill Jacob, "Collected Notes on a 'Review of High Quality Experimental Mathematics Research,' by Douglas Carnine et al.," draft version May 3, 1998.

20. Jerry P. Becker and Bill Jacob, "The Politics of California School Mathematics: The Anti-Reform of 1997–99," *Phi Delta Kappan* 81 (March 2000): 529–537.

21. Douglas Carnine, "Why Education Experts Resist Effective Practices (And What It Would Take to Make Education More Like Medicine" (also at *www.edexcellence.net/library/carnine.html*).

22. See, for example, Romel Hernandez, "UO Professor Advises Bush on Education," *The Oregonian*, November 9, 1999 (also at *www.oregonlive.com/communities/education/99/11/sc110901.html*).

23. One of the challenges with imposing order on this chaotic system was that efforts

worked in parallel, and their chronology was confusing. For example, while the rewriting of the *1999 Framework* took several years (with the final document issued in 1999), the commission's work, started around the same time, but within a much shorter timeframe, ended in early 1998. This might lead a reader to worry about the out-of-sequence presentation of these efforts. I err on the side of reporting by activity (framework development, commission standards development, etc.) rather than hold to a strict chronological accounting.

24. Lorraine M. McDonnell and M. Stephen Weatherford, *State Standards-Setting and Public Deliberation: The Case of California* (CSE Technical Report 506, National Center for Research on Evaluation, Standards, and Student Testing (CRESST), University of California, Los Angeles, September 1999), 34.

25. Bill Evers, "Keep the Academic Bar High," *New York Times,* September 23, 1997 (also at *www.nytimes.com*).

26. See Richard Colvin, "State Board May Return Math Classes to the Basics Education: Standards Commission, Schools Chief Criticize Proposal as Encouraging Less Thinking, More Memorization," *Los Angeles Times,* December 1, 1997 (also at *www.latimes.com*).

27. My thanks to Richard Askey, Hyman Bass, and Hung-Hsi Wu for their advice on this example. For other insights into the process, see Hung-Hsi Wu, "The 1997 Mathematics Standards Wars," in *What Is at Stake in the K–12 Standards Wars: A Primer for Educational Policy Makers,* Sandra Stotsky, ed. (New York: Peter Lang Publishers, 2000), 3–31.

28. California State Board of Education, *Mathematics Content Standards for California Public Schools: Kindergarten Through Grade 12* (Sacramento: CDE, December 1997), quotation at p. 20.

29. Jacques Steinberg, "In Math Standards, California Stresses Skills Over Analysis," *New York Times,* December 14, 1997; and "Clashing Over Education's One True Faith," *New York Times,* Sunday, December 14, 1997 (also at *www.nytimes.com*).

30. "Board of Education OK's Revised Math Standards," *EdCal* 27, December 22, 1997, 1, 9.

31. Ralph A. Raimi and Lawrence S. Braden, *State Mathematics Standards: An Appraisal of Math Standards in 46 States, the District of Columbia, and Japan* (Thomas B. Fordham Foundation, Fordham Report Volume 2, Number 3, March 1998), 25.

32. See June Kronholz, "Numbers Racket: 'Standards' Math Is Creating a Big Division in Education Circles," *Wall Street Journal,* November 5, 1997, A1, A6.

33. See, for example, Marie Cocco, "Confessions of the World's Worst Math Thinker," *Newsday,* reprinted in the *NCTM News Bulletin,* December 1997, 9–10.

34. Dan Walters, "Another Jolt on Education," *Sacramento Bee,* February 28, 1997, A3.

35. National Public Radio, Morning Edition, December 2, 1997. See also Steinberg, "Clashing Over Education's One True Faith," and "In Math Standards, California Stresses"; and Richard Lee Colvin, "State Endorses Back-to-Basics Math Standards," *Los Angeles Times,* December 2, 1997, A18, A20, A21.

36. See Lee S. Shulman, "Professing the Liberal Arts," in *Education and Democracy:*

Re-Imagining Liberal Learning in America, Robert Orrill, ed. (New York: College Entrance Examination Board, 1997), 151–171.

37. See Deborah Anderluh "Bitter Debate on Math Shift: State Education Board Set to Adopt New Standards," *Sacramento Bee*, December 7, 1997 (also at *www.sacbee.com*).

38. Dan Walters, "Eastin, School Board Face Off," *Sacramento Bee*, January 26, 1998 (also at *www.sacbee.com*).

39. See Dan Walters, "Basic Backers Win on Math," *Sacramento Bee*, December 2, 1997 (also at *www.sacbee.com*).

40. Performance standards were also supposed to be set, but the commission was terminated prior to their development.

41. See James Ridgway and Alan Schoenfeld, "Balanced Assessment: Designing Assessment Schemes to Promote Desirable Change in Mathematics Education" (core paper for the email conference on assessment, European Association for Research in Learning and Instruction, 1994); and James Ridgway, "From Barrier to Lever: Revising Roles for Assessment in Mathematics Education," *NISE Brief* 2 (Madison, Wisc.: National Center for Improving Science Education, January 1998) (also at *www.educ.msu.edu/mars/personnel/ba.html*).

42. "California State Board Overwhelmingly Selects Stanford 9 Test," company press release, Monday, November 17, 11:45 EST. Chestnut Hill, Mass. (business wire).

43. "Experts Report Flaws," *Substance*, September 2000, 53.

44. Dan Walters, "Testing Vital, But This One?," *Sacramento Bee*, October 9, 1997 (also at *www.sacbee.com*).

45. Hermann, Brown, and Baker, *Student Assessment and Student Achievement*, 12.

46. Ibid.

47. Ibid.

48. "Riley Urges Students to Take Tougher Courses: Challenges Schools and States to Raise Academic, Testing and Teaching Standards in Math and Science," February 1998. Press release, available at *www.ed.gov*.

49. Hyman Bass, "Mathematicians and the National Eighth Grade Test," *Notices of the AMS* 45 (May 1998): 589–593.

50. "Letter to President Clinton," August 26, 1997 (see *mathematicallycorrect.com/letter.htm*).

51. Richard W. Riley, "The State of Mathematics Education: Building a Strong Foundation for the 21st Century," *Notices of the AMS* 45 (April 1998): 487–491, quotation at 487–488.

52. Debra Viadero, "Academics Urge Riley to Reconsider Math Endorsements," *Education Week* November 24, 1999 (see *www.edweek.org*).

53. "An Open Letter to United States Secretary of Education, Richard Riley," advertisement in the *Washington Post*, November 18, 1999, A5.

54. Several critics have posted their papers and analyses on the Internet. See, e.g., *www.nscl.msu.edu/~Etsang/CMP/cmp.html* (Tsang's website) and *www.math.berkeley.edu/~Ewu/* (Wu's website).

55. "An Open Letter," *Washington Post*.

56. Debra J. Saunders, "Where's the Math?" *San Francisco Chronicle*, October 17, 1999 (see *www.sfgate.com*).

57. As quoted in Rick Green, "Division in the Math Ranks," *Hartford Courant*, November 28, 1999 (also at *www.ctnow.com*).

58. As quoted in Rick Green, "Division in the Math Ranks."

59. Personal communication.

60. See *hoover.stanford.edu/research/conferences/22497.html*.

61. For other examples, see Hung-Hsi Wu, "What Is So Difficult About the Preparation of Mathematics Teachers" (Berkeley: University of California, Berkeley, 2002). Other papers by Professor Wu are available on his website, *math.berkeley.edu/~Ewu/*.

62. For a description of the process, see Roger Howe, "The AMS and Mathematics Education: The Revision of the 'NCTM Standards,'" *Notes of the AMS* 45 (February 1998): 243–247.

63. Coordinating Review Committee, "Final Report of the Coordinating Review Committee for the National Council of Teachers of Mathematics: Principles and Standards for School Mathematics" (Washington, D.C.: Center for Science, Mathematics, and Engineering Education, Center for Education, National Research Council, 2000). For a summary of the review process, see Joan Ferrini-Mundy and W. Gary Martin, "Developing *Principles and Standards for School Mathematics:* The Role of Feedback and Advice," unpublished manuscript, 2001.

64. Lisa Black, "'New New' Math Causes Some Division," *Chicago Tribune*, April 13, 2000.

65. Anemona Hartocollis, "Math Teachers Back Return of Education to Basic Skills," *New York Times*, April 13, 2000

66. Bill Evers and Jim Milgram, "The New Consensus in Math: Skills Matter," *Education Week* 19, May 24, 2000, 56, 44.

67. Deborah Loewenberg Ball, "Implementing the NCTM Standards: Hopes and Hurdles"(paper presented at a conference on Telecommunications as a Tool for Educational Reform: Implementing the NCTM Standards, Aspen Institute, Queenstown, Maryland, December 2–3, 1991).

68. Debra J. Saunders, "Crashing the Educrat Oligarchy," *San Francisco Chronicle*, November 19, 1996 (see *www.sfgate.com*).

69. As quoted in Debra Viadero, "Academics Urge Riley to Reconsider."

70. Ze'ev Wurman, "Letter to the Editor," *Education Week*, December 8, 1999 (also at *www.edweek.org*).

71. David Labaree, " Public Goods, Private Goods: The American Struggle Over Educational Goals," *American Educational Research Journal* 34, (Spring 1997): 39–81, quotation at 41.

72. Jerome Bruner, "Postscript: Some Reflections on Education Research," in *Issues in Education Research: Problems and Possibilities,* Ellen Condliffe Lagemann and Lee S. Shulman, eds. (San Francisco: Jossey Bass, 1999), 399–409, quotations at 402.

73. Ibid., 402–403.

74. See, for example, Donna E. Muncey and Patrick J. McQuillan, *Reform and Resistance in Schools and Classrooms: An Ethnographic View of the Coalition of Essential Schools* (New Haven: Yale University Press, 1996).
75. Lee S. Shulman, "Those Who Understand: Knowledge Growth in Teaching," *Educational Researcher* 14 (February 1986): 4–14.
76. Simon Singh, *Fermat's Enigma: The Epic Quest to Solve the World's Greatest Mathematical Problem* (New York: Anchor Books, 1997), 26–27.
77. Ibid., p. x.
78. Deborah Loewenberg Ball and Hyman Bass, "Crossing Boundaries for a Scholarship of Teaching," paper presented at the Multiple Discourses of a Scholarship of Teaching Conference, Center for the Scholarship of Teaching, College of Education, Michigan State University, East Lansing, October 2000.
79. Clifford Geertz, "Thick Description: Toward an Interpretive Theory of Culture," in *The Interpretation of Cultures: Selected Essays* (New York: Basic Books, 1973), 3–30.
80. Marjorie Coeyman, "Changing America's Path to Reform," *Christian Science Monitor*, May 30, 2000.

CHAPTER 9. PARSNIPS AND ORCHIDS SIDE BY SIDE

Epigraph: Susan Ohanian, *Garbage Pizza, Patchwork Quilts, and Math Magic: Stories about Teachers Who Love to Teach and Children Who Love to Learn* (New York: Freeman, 1992), 94.

1. John Derbyshire, "The Hardest 'R'," *National Review* 52, June 5, 2000, 27–29.
2. David B. Tyack and William Tobin, "The 'Grammar' of Schooling: Why Has It Been So Hard to Change?" *American Educational Research Journal* 31 (Fall 1994): 453–479. See also Milbrey Wallin McLaughlin, "Implementation as Mutual Adaptation: Change in Classroom Organization," *Teachers College Record* 77 (1976): 339–351.
3. Susan H. Fuhrman and Richard F. Elmore, "Understanding Local Control in the Wake of State Education Reform," *Educational Evaluation and Policy Analysis* 12 (Spring 1990): 82–96.
4. See Andrew Porter, Robert Floden, Donald Freeman, William Schmidt, and John Schwille, "Content Determinants in Elementary School Mathematics," in *Effective Mathematics Teaching*, Douglas A. Grouws, Thomas J. Cooney, and D. Jones, eds. (Reston, Va.: National Council of Teachers of Mathematics, 1988), 96–113.
5. William H. Schmidt, Doris Jorde, Leland S. Cogan, Emilie Barrier, Ignacio Gonzalo, Urs Moser, Katsuhiko, Toshio Sawada, Gilbert A. Valverde, Curtis McKnight, Richard S. Prawat, David E. Wiley, Senta A. Raizen, Edward D. Britton, and Richard G. Wolfe, *Characterizing Pedagogical Flow: An Investigation of Mathematics and Science Teaching in Six Countries* (Dordrecht: Kluwer, 1996), 131.
6. James W. Stigler and James Hiebert, *The Teaching Gap: Best Ideas from the World's Teachers for Improving Education in the Classroom* (New York: Free Press, 1999).
7. See, for example, William A. Firestone, Sheila Rosenblum, Beth D. Bader, and

Diane Massell, *Education Reform from 1983 to 1990: State Action and District Responses* (CPRE Research Report Series RR-021, New Brunswick, N.J.: Consortium for Policy Research in Education, December 1991); and Janet Hagemann Chrispeels, "Educational Policy Implementation in a Shifting Political Climate," *American Educational Research Journal* 34 (Fall 1997): 453–481.

8. Suzanne M. Wilson and Robert E. Floden, "Hedging Bets: Standards-Based Reform in the Classroom," in *From the Capitol to the Classroom: Standards-Based Reform in the States,* Susan H. Fuhrman, ed. (100th Yearbook of the National Society for the Study of Education, Part II, Chicago: University of Chicago Press, 2001), 193–217.

9. A full listing of all the researchers involved can be found in my acknowledgments, which appear at the front of the book.

10. Nine descriptions of teachers' responses to the reforms were published in two special issues of education journals: *Educational Evaluation and Policy Analysis* (vol. 12, Fall 1990), and *The Elementary School Journal* (vol. 93, November 1992). Thick descriptions of practice and teachers' responses to the reforms also appear in dissertations based on the study. The full list of publications is available on my website.

11. See the methodological appendix at the back of this book, "This Frightful Toil," as well as David K. Cohen and Heather Hill, *Learning Policy: When State Education Works* (New Haven: Yale University Press, 2002).

12. I am grateful to Heather C. Hill for her generous work on the survey data and willingness to help us all understand and use the results. These tables come from her analyses with David Cohen.

13. Wilson and Floden, "Hedging Bets."

14. Larry Cuban, *How Teachers Taught: Constancy and Change in American Classrooms 1890–1980* (New York: Longman, 1984).

15. William A. Firestone, David Mayrowetz, and Janet Fairman, "Performance-Based Assessment and Instructional Change: The Effects of Testing in Maine and Maryland," *Educational Evaluation and Policy Analysis* 20 (Summer 1998): 95–113, quotation at 111.

16. Linda Darling-Hammond and Arthur E. Wise, "Beyond Standardization: State Standards and School Improvement," *Elementary School Journal* 85 (January 1985): 315–336, quotation at 316.

17. Denise Cantlon, Sharon Rushcamp, and Donald Freeman, "The Interplay Between State and District Guidelines for Curriculum Reform in Elementary Schools," in *The Politics of Curriculum and Testing: The 1990 Yearbook of the Politics of Education Association,* Susan Fuhrman and Betty Malen, eds. (London: Falmer, 1991), 63–80.

18. David K. Cohen, "Policy and Practice: The Classroom Impact of State and Federal Education Policy" (East Lansing: College of Education, Michigan State University, unpublished manuscript), quotations at 19–20.

19. Cantlon, Rushcamp, and Freeman, "Interplay Between State and District," 76.

20. David K. Cohen and Deborah Loewenberg Ball, "Relations Between Policy and

Practice: A Commentary," *Educational Evaluation and Policy Analysis* 12 (Fall 1990): 249–256.

21. See Suzanne M. Wilson, Robert Floden, and Joan Ferrini-Mundy for an analysis of this literature in *Teacher Preparation Research: Current Knowledge, Recommendations, and Priorities for the Future* (Seattle: Center for the Study of Teaching Policy, University of Washington, March 2001). Also see Liping Ma, *Knowing and Teaching Elementary Mathematics: Teachers' Understanding of Fundamental Mathematics in China and the United States* (Mahwah, N.J.: Erlbaum, 1999). Among the studies that demonstrate this lack of knowledge among elementary and secondary school teachers and prospective teachers in the United States is the seminal work of Deborah Loewenberg Ball, "Prospective Elementary and Secondary Teachers' Understanding of Division," *Journal of Research in Mathematics Education* 21 (March 1990): 132–144; Deborah Loewenberg Ball, "The Mathematical Understandings that Prospective Teachers Bring to Teacher Education," *Elementary School Journal* 90 (March 1990): 449–466.

22. David K. Cohen, "A Revolution in One Classroom: The Case of Mrs. Oublier," *Educational Evaluation and Policy Analysis* 12 (Fall 1990): 311–330.

23. Derbyshire, "The Hardest 'R," quotation at 27–29.

24. Diane Ravitch, *Left Back: A Century of Failed School Reforms* (New York: Simon and Schuster, 2000).

25. Linda McNeil, *Contradictions of Control* (Boston: Routledge, 1986); Michael Sedlak, Christopher Wheeler, Diana Pullin, and Philip Cusick, *Selling Students Short: Classroom Bargains and Academic Reform in the American High School* (New York: Teachers College Press, 1986); and Theodore R. Sizer, *Horace's Compromise: The Dilemma of the American High School* (Boston: Houghton Mifflin, 1984).

26. See, for example, Andrew J. Coulson, *Market Education: The Unknown History* (New Brunswick, N.J.: Transaction Publishers, 1999); and Thomas Sowell, *Inside American Education: The Decline, the Deception, the Dogmas* (New York: Free Press, 1993).

27. H. G. Bissinger, *Friday Night Lights* (New York: Addison-Wesley, 1990); Reba Page, "The Uncertain Value of School Knowledge: Biology at Westridge High," *Teachers College Record* 100 (Spring 1999): 554–601.

CHAPTER 10. TOWARD A CIVIL, CONSTRUCTIVE DISCOURSE

Epigraph: Clifford Geertz, "The State of the Art," *Available Light: Anthropological Reflections on Philosophical Topics* (Princeton, N.J.: Princeton University Press, 2000), 89–142, quotation at 107.

1. William Schmidt, "Learning from TIMSS" (presentation at Planning the Future: A Summer Institute for Superintendents, Bellaire, Michigan, June 26, 2001).

2. Deborah Loewenberg Ball, "Prospective Elementary and Secondary Teachers' Understanding of Division," *Journal of Research in Mathematics Education* 21 (March 1990): 132–144; Deborah Loewenberg Ball, "The Mathematical Understandings that Prospective Teachers Bring to Teacher Education," *Elementary School Journal* 90 (March 1990): 449–466; and Liping Ma, *Knowing and Teaching Elementary*

Mathematics: Teachers' Understanding of Fundamental Mathematics in China and the United States (Mahwah, N.J.: Erlbaum, 1999).

3. David K. Cohen and Deborah Loewenberg Ball, "Relations Between Policy and Practice: A Commentary," *Educational Evaluation and Policy Analysis* 12 (Fall 1990): 331–338.

4. See Michael W. Kirst, Bari Anhalt, and Robert Marine, "Politics of Science Education Standards," *Elementary School Journal* 97 (March 1997): 315–328, for an analysis of the inner and outer circles of participants and interest groups in standards development and education reform.

5. Michael W. Kirst and Gail Meister, "Turbulence in American Secondary Schools: What Reforms Last?" *Curriculum Inquiry* 15 (Summer 1985): 169–186, quotation at 183–184.

6. David N. Plank and William L. Boyd, "Antipolitics, Education, and Institutional Choice: The Flight from Democracy," *American Educational Research Journal* 31 (Summer 1994): 263–281, quotation at 276.

7. I am indebted to David Cohen for helping me articulate these issues.

8. I am grateful to Mark St. John for pointing out this distinction.

9. Murray Edelman, *Constructing the Political Spectacle* (Chicago: University of Chicago Press, 1988), 15.

10. David K. Cohen, "Policy and Practice: The Classroom Impact of State and Federal Education Policy" (College of Education, Michigan State University, East Lansing, unpublished manuscript, 1989–1990), quotation at 14.

11. Robert D. Putnam, *Bowling Alone: The Collapse and Revival of American Community* (New York: Simon and Schuster, 2000), 399. See also, for example, Robert Axelrod, *The Evolution of Cooperation* (New York: Basic Books, 1984); Amy Gutmann and Dennis Thompson, *Democracy and Disagreement* (Cambridge, Mass.: Belknap Press of Harvard University, 1996); Robert Putnam, *Making Democracy Work: Civic Traditions in Modern Italy* (Princeton, N.J.: Princeton University Press, 1993); and John Rawls, *A Theory of Justice* (Cambridge, Mass.: Harvard University Press).

12. Lorraine M. McDonnell and M. Stephen Weatherford, *State Standards-Setting and Public Deliberation: The Case of California* (CSE Technical Report 506, National Center for Research on Evaluation, Standards, and Student Testing (CRESST), University of California, Los Angeles, September 1999), 9.

13. Putnam, *Bowling Alone*, 18–19.

14. Putnam, *Bowling Alone*, 306. See also the work of Anthony S. Bryk, Valerie E. Lee, and Peter B. Holland, *Catholic Schools and the Common Good* (Cambridge, Mass.: Harvard University Press, 1993); and James P. Comer, *School Power: Implications of an Intervention Project* (New York: Free Press, 1980). This observation presents a particular problem in California, a state—according to Putnam's analysis—with middling social capital. The test score drop in the 1980s might have been due to a drop in social capital. Similarly, if the scores rise in the future, it might have more to do with the networks and the increased social capital than with any curricular or pedagogical decisions or policies.

15. Ibid., 28.

16. I am, of course, not so naïve as to think that *everyone* was being completely forthcoming when they claimed to be concerned foremost with the children or American democracy. But most people, I would claim, were.

17. James Madison, *The Federalist Papers*, 10, as cited in Putnam, *Bowling Alone*, 337.

18. Putnam, *Bowling Alone*, 361.

19. Ibid., 338.

20. Ibid., 23.

21. Ibid., 23.

22. Mathematics Learning Study Committee, *Adding It Up: Helping Children Learn Mathematics* (Washington, D.C.: National Academy Press, 2001).

23. See Francis Fukuyama, *Trust: The Social Virtues and the Creation of Prosperity* (New York: Free Press, 1995), for a sweeping analysis of the role of trust in healthy societies.

24. David B. Tyack and William Tobin, "The 'Grammar' of Schooling: Why Has It Been So Hard to Change?" *American Educational Research Journal* 31 (Fall 1994): 453–479, quotation at 478–479.

METHODOLOGICAL APPENDIX

Epigraphs: Janet Malcolm, *The Silent Woman: Sylvia Plath and Ted Hughes* (New York: Vintage Books, 1993), 204–205; T. S. Eliot, "The Function of Criticism," in *Selected Essays 1917–1932* (New York: Harcourt Brace, 1932), 18.

1. Frederick Erickson, "Qualitative Methods in Research on Teaching," in *Handbook of Research on Teaching*, 3d edition, Merlin C. Wittrock, ed. (New York: Collier Macmillan, 1986), 119–160.

2. John Dewey, "The Nature of Method," in *John Dewey on Education: Selected Writings*, R. D. Archambault, ed. (Chicago: University of Chicago Press), 387–403, quotation at 393–394.

3. For example, Donald J. Freeman, *California's Curriculum Reform Guidelines for Elementary Schools: 1983–1988* (Center for the Learning and Teaching of Elementary Subjects, Institute for Research on Teaching, College of Education, Michigan State University, East Lansing).

4. Multiple grants supported the work of each study. A complete list is provided in my acknowledgments.

5. See Matthew B. Miles and A. Michael Huberman, *Qualitative Data Analysis: A Sourcebook of New Methods* (Beverly Hills, Calif.: Sage Publications, 1984), for an explication of multimethod, multisite designs.

6. During our tenure together, the principal investigators collaboratively wrote multiple explanations of our research method. These most often were crafted for research proposals. I take this description from a methodological memo I wrote in 1990. However, the writing on our project was almost always collaborative, and so this next section is best understood as the collective work of Deborah Ball, David Cohen, Penelope Peterson and myself, with helpful suggestions from Ralph Putnam and others.

7. See, for examples, Sharon Feiman-Nemser, "Learning to Teach," in *Handbook of Teaching and Policy*, Lee S. Shulman and Gary Sykes, eds. (New York: Longman, 1983), 150–170; Virginia K. Richardson, "Significant and Worthwhile Change in Teaching Practice," *Educational Researcher* 19 (October 1990): 10–18.

8. Because the studies varied, the number of case studies varied as well, ranging between 30 and 100. Numbers also varied because teachers changed assignments, schools, districts, and grade levels, which challenged our ability to keep track of the relevant nested contexts rationally laid out in the study's design. On average, we gathered sufficient data on approximately 75 teachers over multiple years.

9. Mary M. Kennedy, Deborah Loewenberg Ball, G. Williamson McDiarmid, and William Schmidt, *A Study Package for Tracking Teacher Learning* (Technical Report 91–1, East Lansing: Michigan State University, National Center for Research on Learning, 1991).

10. *Educational Evaluation and Policy Analysis* 12 (Fall 1990) and *Elementary School Journal* 93 (November 1992). Another special section of the *Journal for Educational Policy* 11 (1996) also included case study material. Several dissertations focused on the experiences of individual teachers in the midst of these reforms, including Nancy E. Jennings, *Interpreting Policy in Real Classrooms: Case Studies of State Reform and Teacher Practice* (New York: Teachers College Press, 1996); and S. G. Grant, *Reforming Reading, Writing, and Mathematics: Teachers' Responses and the Prospects for Systemic Reform* (Mahwah, N.J.: Erlbaum, 1998).

11. See David Tyack, "Ways of Seeing: An Essay on the History of Compulsory Education," *Harvard Educational Review* 46 (August 1976): 355–389.

12. Andrea Lash, Rebecca R. Perry, and Joan E. Talbert, "Survey Of Elementary Mathematics Education in California: Technical Report and User's Guide to SAS Data Files" (Stanford, Calif.: Center for Research on the Context of Teaching, June 1996); Andrea Lash and Joan E. Talbert, "Survey of Elementary Mathematics Education in California: Technical Report, Interview Survey" (Stanford, Calif.: Center for Research on the Context of Teaching, June 1996); and David K. Cohen and Heather Hill, *Learning Policy: When State Education Works* (New Haven: Yale University Press, 2002).

13. Deborah Loewenberg Ball and David K. Cohen, "Developing Practice, Developing Practitioners: Toward a Practice-Based Theory of Professional Education," in *Teaching as the Learning Profession: Handbook of Policy and Practice*, Linda Darling-Hammond & Gary Sykes, eds. (San Francisco: Jossey Bass, 1999).

14. Suzanne M. Wilson and Jennifer Berne, "Teacher Learning and the Acquisition of Professional Knowledge: An Examination of Research on Contemporary Professional Development," in A. Iran-Nejad and P. David Pearson, eds., *Review of Research in Education* 24 (1999): 173–209.

15. See Richard F. Elmore, "Backward Mapping," *Political Science Quarterly* 94 (1979): 601–616; and Richard F. Elmore and Milbrey W. McLaughlin, *Steady Work: Policy, Practice, and the Reform of American Education* (Santa Monica, Calif.: RAND, 1988).

16. See, for example, Pamela K. Geist, *Reforming Mathematics Teaching: Examining The*

Relationship Between Instructional Policy and a Teacher's Opportunities to Learn (Ph.D. diss., Michigan State University, 1998).

17. See, for example, Suzanne M. Wilson, Penelope L. Peterson, Deborah Loewenberg Ball, and David K. Cohen, "Learning by All," *Phi Delta Kappan* 77 (March 1996): 468–476, as well as other articles in *Phi Delta Kappan* 77 (March 1996).

18. See, for example, Jere E. Brophy, "The De Facto National Curriculum in U.S. Elementary Social Studies: Critique of a Representative Example," *Journal of Curriculum Studies* 24 (September/October 1992): 401–447.

19. See, for example, Janine T. Remillard, *Changing Texts, Teachers, and Teaching: The Role of Curriculum Materials in Mathematics Education Reform* (Ph.D. diss., Michigan State University, 1996).

20. See, for examples, Carol A. Barnes, *Understanding the Standards Reform: Conflict and Capacity* (New York: Teachers College Press, forthcoming 2002); Sue Poppink, *National Programs and Local Responses: Enacting the New Title I* (Ph.D. diss., Michigan State University, 2000); James P. Spillane, "School Districts Matter: Local Educational Authorities and State Instructional Policy," *Educational Policy* 10 (1996): 63–87; and James P. Spillane, "State Policy and the Non-Monolithic Nature of the Local School District: Organizational and Professional Considerations," *American Educational Research Journal* 35 (Spring 1998): 33–63.

21. Simultaneously, we were working in a College of Education where others were investigating similar issues, including Philip A. Cusick and Jennifer Borman, James Spillane and Charles Thompson, James Spillane and John Zeuli. In addition, we frequently sought advice from colleagues, including Gary Sykes and Susan Florio Ruane.

22. Data collection in other states was led by Tammi Chun, Catherine Clark, Carolyn Harrington, Janie Clark Lindle, and Joe Petrosko.

23. The states included California, Colorado, Florida, Kentucky, Maryland, Michigan, Minnesota, and Texas.

24. Again, this was a collaborative project and any description of the method is best understood as jointly authored by Robert Floden, Margaret Goertz, Diane Massell, and myself.

25. See, for example, chapters by Margaret Goertz, Diane Massell, Suzanne Wilson, and Robert Floden in *From the Capitol to the Classroom: Standards-Based Reform in the States*, Susan Fuhrman ed. (100th Yearbook of the National Society for the Study of Education, Part II, Chicago: University of Chicago Press, 2001).

26. See, for example, Allyn Jackson, "The Math Wars: California Battles It Out Over Mathematics Education Reform, Part I," *Notices of the AMS* 44 (June/July 1997): 695–702; and "The Math Wars: California Battles It Out Over Mathematics Education Reform, Part II," *Notices of the AMS* 44 (August 1997): 817–823.

27. Barney G. Glaser and Anselm L. Strauss, *The Discovery of Grounded Theory: Strategies for Qualitative Research* (Chicago: Aldine, 1967).

28. Janet Malcolm, *The Silent Woman*, 204–205.

29. Edward R. Tufte, *The Visual Display of Quantitative Information* (Cheshire, Conn.: Graphics, 1983), 191.

30. See Annie Dillard, *The Writing Life* (New York: Harper & Row, 1989); Natalie Goldberg, *Wild Mind: Living the Writer's Life* (London: Riter, 1991); Stephen King, *On Writing: A Memoir of a Craft* (New York: Scribner's, 2000); Ann Lamott, *Bird by Bird: Some Instructions on Writing and Life* (New York: Pantheon, 1994); William K. Zinsser, *On Writing Well: An Informal Guide to Nonfiction* (New York: Harper-Perennial, 1994).

31. Wayne Booth, Gregory G. Colomb, and J. M. Williams, *The Craft of Research* (Chicago: University of Chicago Press, 1995);Howard S. Becker, *Tricks of the Trade: How to Think about Your Research While Doing It* (Chicago: University of Chicago Press, 1998); and Matthew B. Miles and A. Michael Huberman, *Qualitative Data Analysis: A Sourcebook of New Methods* (Beverly Hills, Calif.: Sage Publications, 1984).

32. See, for example, William Foote Whyte, *Participant Observer: An Autobiography* (Ithaca, N.Y.: ILR Press, 1994); *Street Corner Society: The Social Structure of an Italian Slum* (Chicago: University of Chicago Press, 1955); Annette Lareau, *Home Advantage: Social Class and Parental Intervention in Elementary Education* (New York: Falmer Press, 1989).

33. See, for example, Ruth Behar, *The Vulnerable Observer: Anthropology That Breaks Your Heart* (Boston: Beacon, 1996); and Clifford Geertz, *After the Fact: Two Countries, Four Decades, One Anthropologist* (Cambridge, Mass.: Harvard University Press, 1995); and Clifford Geertz, *Available Light: Anthropological Reflections on Philosophical Topics* (Princeton, N.J.: Princeton University, 2000).

34. As a doctoral student, I also got an M.S. in statistics. It seemed, at the time, a good thing to do, for it provided a welcome break from writing papers and allowed me to exercise the more numerical aspects of my mind. Even though I only sporadically use the specific statistical tools I acquired at Stanford, the principles I gleaned from those classes are touchstones for all my research and help me enormously as a teacher of research.

35. Edward R. Tufte, *The Visual Display of Quantitative Information* (Cheshire, Conn.: Graphics, 1983); *Envisioning Information* (Cheshire, Conn.: Graphics Press, 1990); and *Visual Explanations: Images and Quantities, Evidence and Narrative* (Cheshire, Conn.: Graphics, 1997). Tufte, too, had the good fortune of knowing Lincoln Moses, one of the teachers to whom he dedicates his third book.

36. Robert D. Putnam, *Bowling Alone: The Collapse and Revival of American Community* (New York: Simon and Schuster, 2000); and Robert D. Putnam, Robert Leonardi, and Raffaella Y. Nanetti, *Making Democracy Work: Civic Traditions in Modern Italy* (Princeton: Princeton University Press, 1993).

37. Philip A. Cusick, *The Educational System: Its Nature and Logic* (New York: McGraw-Hill, 1992), 13.

38. Todd Gitlin, *The Twilight of Common Dreams: Why America Is Wracked by Culture Wars* (New York: Henry Holt, 1995); Robert Hughes, *Culture of Complaint: A Passionate Look into the Ailing Heart of America* (New York: Warner Books, 1993).

39. Diane Ravitch, "50 States, 50 Standards: The Continuing Need for National Voluntary Standards in Education," *Brookings Review* 14 (Summer 1996): 6–9. For de-

scriptions of the "history wars," see Catherine Cornbleth and Dexter Waugh, *The Great Speckled Bird: Multicultural Politics and Education Policymaking* (New York: St. Martin's, 1995), and Gary B. Nash, Charlotte A. Crabtree, and Ross E. Dunn, *History on Trial: Culture Wars and the Teaching of the Past* (New York: Knopf, 1997).

40. Robert Darnton, "Extraordinary Commonplaces," *New York Review of Books*, December 21, 2000, 82–87, quotation on 82.

41. Ibid., p. 87.

42. Karl R. Popper, *The Logic of Scientific Discovery* (New York: Harper & Row, 1968).

43. Robert Coles, *Doing Documentary Work* (New York: Oxford University Press, 1997).

44. Malcolm, *The Silent Woman.*

45. Coles, *Doing Documentary Work.*

46. Susan Addington and Judith Roitman, "Who Is Dick Askey and Why Is He So Upset about the Standards?" *Mathematics Teacher* 89 (November 1996), 626–627.

47. Diane Ravitch, *Left Back: A Century of Failed School Reforms* (New York: Simon and Schuster, 2000).

48. Coles, *Doing Documentary Work.*

49. George Orwell, *The Road to Wigan Pier* (London: Secker & Warburg, 1959); Bill Buford, *Among the Thugs* (New York: Norton, 1992).

50. Helen Garner, *The First Stone: Some Questions about Sex and Power* (Sydney, Australia: Picador, 1995).

Index